CHIC
HAROLD WA
R00222

D0569699

R00222 47034

DATE			

POPULAR LIBRARY

THE FRUSTRATION OF POLITICS

THE FRUSTRATION OF POLITICS

Truman, Congress, and the Loyalty Issue 1945-1953

Francis H. Thompson

Rutherford • Madison • Teaneck
Fairleigh Dickinson University Press

London: Asssociated University Presses

Associated University Presses, Inc.
Cranbury, New Jersey 08512

Associated University Presses
Magdalen House
136-148 Tooley Street
London SE1 2TT, England

Library of Congress Cataloging in Publication Data

Thompson, Francis H 1930–
The frustration of politics.

Bibliography: p.
Includes index.
1. Loyalty-security program, 1947-
2. United States—Politics and government—
1945-1953. 3. Truman, Harry S., Pres. U.S.,
1884-1972. I. Title.
JK734.T56 353.001'3242 77-74399
ISBN 0-8386-2132-5

For Julia, Amy, Jo, and Delia

and my mother, Mrs. Pauline Thompson

PRINTED IN THE UNITED STATES OF AMERICA

CONTENTS

INTRODUCTION

The Truman years—1945-1953—might be appropriately termed the turbulent years. The problems that Harry Truman faced as president of the United States were numerous and complex; none, however, was more persistent than the one which emanated from charges made in and out of Congress that the Communists had successfully infiltrated the government bureaucracy. The resulting controversy raged throughout the Truman presidency and gained particular intensity with the sudden rise to prominence of Senator Joseph R. McCarthy in February 1950.

Truman's most conspicuous answer to the insidious pressure concerning anti-Communism was the inauguration, by his March 1947 Executive Order, of a far-reaching loyalty probe of all government employees. The administration's loyalty-security program drew immediate criticism from all sides of the political spectrum. Many conservatives contended that it did not go far enough; most liberals felt it went much too far.

The liberatarian critique of the loyalty program was presented in several excellent contemporary studies,[1] but a liberal consensus developed that was not unfavorable to the president. Broad support was expressed for his hard-line policy toward the Soviet Union, accompanied by reluctant acknowledgment that the increased fear of internal subversion, in part generated by such a confrontation, necessitated some response from the administration. The loyalty-security program, though it remained a point of contention, was nevertheless considered preferable to the alternatives offered by the

Red hunters in Congress and elsewhere. Truman was generally praised for his devotion to civil liberties as is evidenced by, among other things, his refusal to release loyalty files to various congressional investigating committees and his veto of the restrictive McCarran Internal Security Act.

The liberal view was voiced by Cabell Phillips in his book *The Truman Presidency*, published in 1966 and still the best overall account of the Truman administration. Phillips considered the loyalty program as a regrettable but necessary response to the political pressures of the time.[2] Alan Harper, in his more specific study, *The Politics of Loyalty*, generally concurred. Though not uncritical, Harper stressed the president's concern for individual rights and attributed the rise of Senator McCarthy to a myriad of factors beyond the president's power to control.[3]

Before the end of the 1960s, a few writers had already begun to challenge the traditional interpretation. According to Michael Parenti, "It seems never to have occurred to liberals that . . . their advocacy of a wholesale cold-war effort abroad exacerbated the very public anxieties which bred witchhunting at home."[4] The opinions expressed by Parenti and others paved the way for the major new-left works that appeared early in the next decade. Truman emerged from such studies as less the victim than the villain—the perpetrator of fear and suspicion.[5]

The new-left point of departure from the older thesis rested in the collective view that the administration's hard-line policy toward the Soviet Union was a serious mistake, and that the inflamatory rhetoric used to gain public acceptance of such a wrongheaded policy led directly to the rise of Senator McCarthy. According to Richard Freeland, the emotions so skillfully stirred by McCarthy "were aroused and their patterns of belief developed . . . as the result of a deliberate and highly organized effort by the Truman administration in 1947-1948 to mobilize support for the program of economic assistance to Europe. . . ."[6] Still another revisionist, Athan Theoharis, concluded that the administration's "anti-Communist rhetoric, the thrust of its appeals, both before and after McCarthy's Wheeling speech, did not differ substantively from that of McCarthy and his conservative Congressional supporters."[7]

Theoharis, whose work set the tone for the new-left critique, greately exaggerated Truman's power to sway public opinion by his rhetoric. There have indeed been a few leaders throughout history who possessed the gift of mass persuasion; Truman, however, was not one of them. There can be no doubt that he talked in tough, crisis tones about the threat posed by international communism. But he was just as vocal, both publicly and privately, in his denial that the nation was in any danger from internal subversion. In consideration of such a disclaimer, it is difficult to imagine how anyone could find Truman's appeals comparable to those of Senator McCarthy.

In addition, the revisionist thesis seems to presume, most tenuously, that if Truman and his advisors had refrained from a hard-line policy, the Soviet Union would have reacted in kind. As a result, the old wartime comradeship would have continued and the cold-war confrontation been averted. Hence, there would have been no domestic Red scare. Such assumptions are specious and unrealistic. Can it be stated with any degree of certainty, even from a vantage point of three decades, that the Soviet Union did not intend to fill the power vacuum created by the defeat of the Axis powers? Certainly many learned observers at the time warned the president that Russia would move in just such an aggressive manner. It seems more logical to assume that any American policy, short of complete acquiescence, would have been suspect in the eyes of Premier Stalin. Perhaps the origins of the cold war would be better understood if more attention were focused on the deep-seated suspicions held by the leaders of both sides.

In the eyes of the revisionists, one of the more villainous acts of the Truman administration, was the establishment of the loyalty program. Instituting such a program, only days after the enunciation of the Truman Doctrine, was seen as an important part of the package to "sell" the new hard line toward Russia. And it would have been difficult indeed to convince anyone of the necessity to take a firm stand against the Soviet Union's supposed expansionist ambitions without some attemp to deal with the incessant charges that Communists were everywhere in our own government service. But the evidence does not show that Truman was, from the outset, intent on the establishment of "absolute security."[8] On the contrary, there is every indication that the president never seriously entertained any such illusion and, in fact, always had serious doubts about the wisdom of his own loyalty program.

The Truman loyalty-security program was hastily drawn up and contained serious and quite obvious flaws. Those who have so strenuously denounced it, however, seem to have contented themselves with the notion that if Truman had simply ignored the whole issue of internal security it would have somehow disappeared, and McCarthy would have remained an obscure and frustrated senator from Wisconsin. Such an incredibly naive view overlooks a number of important facts, notably the long-time preoccupation by Congress with the problem of internal Communist subversion. It had sharpened in 1938 with the establishment of the House Un-American Activities Committee, had abated to some extent in the war years, then increased again noticeably in the immediate postwar period. The president's loyalty program, in fact, only narrowly headed off a vigorous attempt by Congress to legislate its own purge of the government bureaus. There was apparently to be some form of loyalty investigation and it is difficult to conceive of any program dominated by Congress that would have been preferable to the one initiated by Truman.

The new-left interpretation is certainly provocative and contains a measure of plausibility when viewed in an extremely narrow context. It loses credibility, however, when examined in a broader, less simplistic framework. The revisionists have concentrated too much on Truman's supposed sins to the exclusion of the many complex realities of the post-World War II period. In truth, the whole thesis seems to have developed from the disillusionment born of the Vietnam disaster.

An effort has been made throughout the course of this study to judge Truman within the context of his own time—to examine, with the available evidence, his administration's efforts in the area of loyalty and security. To do less, to render judgment on the Truman administration by a later set of circumstances, is to write nonhistory. It must be remembered that Harry Truman did not conjure up the Red scare; it was an inherited problem from the first. The right-wing extremists, both Democrats and Republicans, had initiated their compaign long before Truman assumed the duties of the presidency.

Yet, in another sense, all presidents, regardless of their intentions, must be held accountable for their actions—and for what might have been possible at a given time in history. With that thought in mind, I have attempted to evaluate the Truman administration's reaction to the fears and pressures engendered by the congressional search for subversives.

NOTES

1. The definitive study of the loyalty program is Eleanor Bontecou, *The Federal Loyalty-Security Program* (Ithaca, N.Y.: Cornell University Press, 1953). Two excellent contemporary critiques are Alan Barth, *The Loyalty of Free Men* (New York: Viking Press, 1951): and Francis Biddle, *The Fear of Freedom* (Garden City, N.Y.: Doubleday, 1952).

2. Cabell Phillips, *The Truman Presidency: The History of a Triumphant Succession* (New York: Macmillan Co., 1966).

3. Alan Harper, *The Politics of Loyalty: The White House and The Communist Issue* (Westport, Conn.: Greenwood Publishing Co., 1969).

4 Michael Parenti, *The Anti-Communist Impulse* (New York: Random House, 1969), p. 96.

5. The two most influential of the revisionist works are Richard M. Freeland, *The Truman Doctrine and the Origins of McCarthyism: Foreign Policy, Domestic Politics, and Internal Security, 1946-1948* (New York: Alfred A. Knopf, 1972): and Athan

Theoharis, *Seeds of Repression: Harry S. Truman and the Origins of McCarthyism* (Chicago: Quadrangle Books, 1971). A less distinguished revisionist account is Bert Cochran, *Harry Truman and the Crisis Presidency*, (New York: Funk and Wagnalls, 1973).

6. Freeland, *The Truman Doctrine*, p. 5.
7. Theoharis, *Seeds of Repression*, p. 31.
8. Ibid., p. 102.

ACKNOWLEDGMENTS

There are many people who have helped me in the preparation of this book, and a number of them I would like to thank in particular. A special note of appreciation goes to several of my professors from ages past—Dr. Timothy P. Donovan, Dr. James V. Reese, and Dr. Jacquelin Collins, whose constructive criticism and direction were a constant help in the early stages of the manuscript.

Several of my colleagues at Western Kentucky University have taken their valuable time to read all or part of this work at some stage of its development: Dr. Lowell Harrison, Dr. Marion Lucas, Dr. Crawford Crowe, and Dr. Drew Harrington. A particular note of gratitude is given to Dr. Harrison, who not only provided helpful suggestions and needed encouragement, but who also set a worthy example with his own research and writing. Two graduate students at Western Kentucky University, Nelda Wyatt and Denise Walker, have performed yeoman service in typing drafts, in proofreading, and in running down specific information. They always responded with enthusiasm and a smile. Thanks also to the many other students who, through the years, expressed interest in my work at one time or another. Such concern helped sustain me at critical moments.

A number of archivists and librarians have provided me with valuable assistance. In particular, I cannot say enough for the tremendous help provided by the staff at the Harry S Truman Library. It was their assistance in locating the primary source material that made this study possible. Each and every member of the library staff was most courteous and obliging during each of my several visits there, and I am most grateful. The Truman Library is a nice place to work.

To a large degree, much of the research for this book, especially the last two visits to Independence, was made possible by grants from the Western Kentucky University Faculty Research Committee. Thanks are due that group not only for its contributions to my project, but for the many other research activities they have encouraged through the years.

And finally, a sincere thanks to my family who simply put up with me during my more mercurial moments while this book was in preparation.

F. H. Thompson

November 20, 1978

1
THE GENESIS OF THE TRUMAN LOYALTY PROGRAM

I have little patience with people who take the Bill of Rights for granted.

On April 13, 1945, one day after he assumed the duties of the presidency, Harry S. Truman spoke to a group of reporters and made the following plea:

> If you ever pray, pray for me now. I don't know whether you fellows ever had a load of hay fall on you, but when they told me yesterday what had happened, I felt like the moon, the stars, and all the planets had fallen on me.[1]

The feeling expressed by the president was understandable. Few men have entered that high office at a more critical time in the nation's history. Indeed, the problems which faced Truman "are not likely to be overestimated and to overstate them would be next to impossible."[2]

One of the most difficult of those problems, and one that would haunt the Truman administration from first to last, resulted from the persistent charge made by certain members of Congress and others that Communists had successfully infiltrated high positions in the government of the United States. The problem, which evolved into an almost continuous eight-year struggle between Truman and Congress, had been in the process of development for many years.

To find the origins of the "paranoid style in American politics," as Professor Richard Hofstadter defined the phenomenon, it would be necessary to go back at least to the first Alien and Sedition Acts of 1798. At various times since, the nation has been preoccupied by fear of for instance Irish Catholics, immigrants in general, and other groups of every stripe and shade. Communists were elevated to a select position on the list after the Bolshevik revolution of 1917 and the subsequent withdrawal of Russia from the war.

The wave of violent strikes that swept the country in 1919 were attributed by many to the work of Communist agents in the United States. The fear thus generated gave rise to the first period of Red hysteria which was led on the national level by Attorney General A. Mitchell Palmer. The intensity of the scare was on the wane by 1920 but the xenophobia aroused by Palmer and his associates continued throughout the decade of the 1920s. In addition, the United States government maintained a firm policy of nonrecognition of the new Soviet regime.[3]

The onslaught of the Great Depression escalated fears of Communist infiltration and prompted a number of congressional investigations. One of the first was chaired, and dominated, by conservative Republican Representative Hamilton Fish from New York. The Fish Committee, after six months of hearings in 1930, concluded that the Communist party in the United States was revolutionary, as it openly proclaimed itself to be, that it owed allegiance to the Communist International, and that its further activities should be outlawed in the United States. One committee member, Representative John Edward Nelson of Maine, dissented from the majority opinion. He conceded the potential danger from internal Communist subversion but warned against an obsession with such dangers to the exclusion of the even graver threat posed by international communism.

Additional hearings were conducted in 1934-1935 by a select committee headed jointly by Representatives John McCormick of Massachusetts and Samuel Dickstein of New York. The McCormick-Dickstein Committee, later praised for the judicious manner in which it directed the hearings, devoted the major portion of its time to Fascist activity; the Communist problem, however, received adequate attention. Earl Browder, executive secretary of the Central Committee, in his testimony, estimated Communist party membership at 24,000 in 1934, with many thousands of other supporters who sympathized with the party's goals.

In the mid 1930s, the Communist party U.S.A. suddenly disavowed its previous revolutionary character and adopted a more moderate, reform-oriented position. As a result, party membership had increased significantly by 1938. From that point, the number of active members fluctuated according to what particular theme the party supported at a given time.[4] Whatever the exact number of Communists, and the figures vary with the source consulted, the fear of communism persisted throughout the entire depression decade.

In April 1937, Representative Dickstein proposed the establishment of a permanent committee to keep check on all un-American activities; his subsequent resolution to that effect was denied. The events in Europe in the next thirteen months changed the outlook dramatically. In May 1938, a resolution similar to Dickstein's was passed under the authorship of conservative Democratic Representative Martin Dies of Texas.[5] Although it was assumed by many that the committee would look into the scope of all so-called un-American activities, it was apparent from the outset that the chairman's interest was more confined.

Representative Dies soon turned the newly formed House Committee on Un-American Activities into a forum to attack government employees suspected of Communist sympathies, and to seek legislation to prevent the employment of such disloyal persons in the future.[6] Witch-hunters in general,

George Seldes noted, "never took a step without proclaiming that it was necessary to save their respective nations from 'Bolshevism.' It is all old stuff—fabricated in Italy, finished in Germany and now being peddled in Washington."[7]

The activities of the Dies committee represented "Red baiting" at its most articulate level. Although Dies was at first considered little short of a fool, he soon made his point, especially with those who could see the political advantages of such raucous activity.[8] Truman later concluded that the Dies committee set the precedent "which has plagued the Congress ever since."[9] Certainly it cannot be said with any degree of accuracy that the charges made by the House committee were completely groundless. There is ample evidence that the Communists did successfully penetrate the federal bureaucracy in the 1930s.[10] There is still significant disagreement as to the extent of such penetration but, though exaggerated, it was not insignificant. That fact alone, however, should in no way excuse the irresponsibility displayed by Representative Dies and the other members of his committee.

On August 2, 1939, Congress, in part as a response to the increased anti-Communist pressure engendered by the Dies committee, passed the Hatch Act, which was designed "to prevent pernicious political activity."[11] Section 9A of that Act forbade employment in the federal bureaucracy of any person who belonged to a political party or any other organization which advocated the overthrow by force of the United States government. That section represented an "explicit recognition by Congress of the necessity for barring from government employment those whose interests were directed to the destruction of the traditional American way of life."[12] The Hatch Act was significant because it marked a historic break with regard to the judgment of fitness for government employment. Heretofore, eligibility for such employment had been judged on the basis of qualifications and character, and any inquiry into religious or political affiliation was expressly forbidden by Civil Service Rule I, adopted in 1884.[13]

The Seventy-sixth and Seventy-seventh Congresses further demonstrated their intention to root out any subversive elements in government when they enacted Public Laws 671 and 808, which granted summary dismissal powers to the War and Navy Departments. The secretaries of those respective departments were given the power to remove any employee in the interests of national security, other laws with regard to employment or dismissal notwithstanding.[14]

Congress continued in 1941 to press for action, when riders were attached to all appropriations bills which expressly forbade payment of federal money to any person who belonged to an organization which advocated the overthrow by force of the United States government.[15] In that same year, Congress appropriated $100,000 to finance an investigation by the Federal Bureau of Investigation of all employees alleged to be members of subversive organizations. Once the investigation was completed, the necessary reports were to be submitted, without recommendations, to the various department heads for whatever appropriate action they might see fit to take. Many of the department heads, in turn, asked for advice from the Justice Department. In 1942, Attorney General Francis Biddle created an interdepartmental committee of four members for the purpose of advisement.[16]

Part of the assistance rendered by the attorney general was the distribution to all government agencies of a descriptive memorandum which listed so-called subversive organizations. The list, specified for the use of various officials in the government, was not made available for public consumption. A basic area of conflict between the executive and legislative branches of the government was clearly discernible at that point, as Attorney General Biddle insisted that activity rather than membership in the listed organizations was to be stressed; others, such as Martin Dies, felt that membership alone was sufficient to warrant dismissal.[17]

On February 5, 1943, President Roosevelt issued Executive Order 9300 which replaced the attorney general's committee with an "Interdepartmental Committee on Employee Investigations." The new committee concerned itself with permanent employees only and stayed within the confines of those Acts already passed by Congress. Hence, a person would be subject to removal if, (1) he belonged to an organization which advocated the overthrow of the United States government by force or, (2) he personally advocated violence as a means of effecting political change.[18] The new interdepartmental committee remained only an advisory body; authority for removal of any suspected employee continued to rest with the department head. Standards varied widely throughout the departments, and few of those responsible displayed any real enthusiasm for a purge. From July 1, 1940 to March 31, 1947, only 1,313 persons were ruled ineligible for government employment for reasons of disloyalty. Congress remained restive and continually voiced concern over the lack of will or of uniformity in the administration of the loyalty program.[19]

That was the general situation with regard to employee loyalty when Harry Truman assumed the duties of the presidency in April 1945. However, events had already taken place some two weeks before the death of President Roosevelt that would serve to revive the Communist issue—an issue that would plague the new president throughout his years in the White House.

On February 28, 1945, the security officer for the Office of Strategic Services accidentally discovered that a classified document from that office had been published in *Amerasia* magazine. A subsequent raid on the New York offices of the magazine turned up dozens of other supposedly classified government documents. The FBI entered the case on March 11 and immediately implicated Phillip Jaffe and Kate Mitchell, the editors of *Amerasia*. A recording, inadmissable as evidence, also implicated John Stewart Service of the Department of State.[20] On June 22, under orders from President Truman, the FBI arrested those persons involved in the

Amerasia incident. The Justice Department, however, showed little inclination to push the prosecution. James M. McInerney, a special prosecutor for the department, indicated that the stolen documents contained little information of value, and none that would endanger national security. Although a charge of espionage was never proven, the presence of that many government documents in the files of a magazine whose editors were thought by many to be sympathetic toward communism certainly suggested the possibility of organized espionage.[21]

The *Amerasia* disclosure was only a starter. In February 1946, the director of the FBI, J. Edgar Hoover, presented to Truman a report on the statements of two confessed Communist spies, Elizabeth Bentley and Whittaker Chambers. The confessions implicated, among others, Harry Dexter White, assistant secretary of the Treasury, whom Truman had just nominated for the position of United States Director of the International Monetary Fund.[22]

Truman's later statements in regard to White indicated that the president was unsure what course of action to follow. In any case, after consultation with Tom Clark, who was now Attorney General, and Secretary of the Treasury Fred Vinson, the president steadfastly refused to withdraw White's nomination.[23] It is to the president's credit that he evidently decided there was simply not sufficient proof of White's guilt to warrant what would amount to a denunciation of his nominee. Had Truman been "more prudent than brave, he could have eased White out at almost any time in the spring or summer of 1946 and rid himself of a possible future embarrassment. But he liked to think that a man was innocent until proven guilty."[24] This was an early indication that Harry Truman had much more than a superficial feeling for individual rights.

Perhaps the most alarming evidence of Communist intrigue resulted from the report of the Canadian Royal Commission in June 1946, which revealed the existence in Canada of a large and well-organized espionage ring. Igor Gouzenko, the member of the ring who informed on his fellow conspirators, also indicated that a similar group was active in the United States. The part of the commission's report that caused the most dismay concerned the tactics employed by the Communists on those "in critical positions, with a 'susceptibility to Communist ideology.' "[25] Congress reacted sharply to the report, and the search for Communists began in earnest. The new president would soon feel the heat as the nation appeared on the brink of another witch-hunt of the 1920 variety.

Harry Truman had entered the White House under the most difficult of circumstances; the people knew this and so did the Congress. It was therefore no surprise that the president received a rather generous display of support from the Seventy-ninth Congress in his first few months in office.[26] By January 1946, however, the honeymoon was over and the press began to take note of Truman's increased troubles with the legislative branch. The president expressed his hope to improve these relations through a direct appeal to the people.[27] He found it an almost impossible task. The problems that always beset a postwar administration—price controls, labor unrest, and a host of others—had already piled up. Certainly not the least of those problems was the menace of communism.

The House Committee on Un-American Activities continued its relentless search for subversives. Some members of Congress, however, felt greater concern over the influence and power of the house committee—"a power so vast that it would take a committee of Holmeses and Brandeises to use that power and still preserve the constitutional liberties guaranteed every American citizen."[28]

Various figures were cited in Congress to describe the actual strength of the Communist party. In May 1946, there was talk of some 70,000 actual Communists, 500,000 fellow travelers, and 150,000 underground workers—figures that, if taken literally, were enough to cause considerable uneasiness.[29] On

May 17, 1946, Representative John Rankin of Mississippi called for a purge of the federal payrolls.[30] Rankin's colleague from Mississippi, Representative Dan R. McGehee, went a step further in June when he contended that "the. . .dogmas of the Communist Party are absolutely contrary to America, and its further activity should be outlawed in this country."[31]

The increased concern over possible Communist infiltration had previously led the House Committee on the Civil Service to appoint a subcommittee composed of J. M. Combs (chairman), George H. Fallon, and Edward H. Rees "to make such investigation as it may deem proper with respect to employee loyalty and employment policies and practices in the Government of the United States."[32] The report of this subcommittee was submitted to Congress on July 20, 1946, and to President Truman on July 25.[33] The committee traced the historical background of loyalty investigations since 1939, and drew special attention to the lack of uniformity. The interdepartmental committee created in 1943 still used personal advocacy of violent change, or membership in an organization that advocated violent overthrow of the government, as the standard for removal. The civil service, on the other hand, used the concept of "reasonable doubt" as its guide for dismissal. In addition it was noted that some departments were hesitant to act at all, because they regarded loyalty investigations as criminal trials. Others acted on mere rumor and suspicion. The subcommittee therefore recommended that. . .

> a commission be established. . .and that this committee make a thorough study of existing laws and the adequacy of existing legislation. . .and to present to the Congress. . . a complete and unified program that will give adequate protection to our government against individuals whose primary loyalty is to governments other than our own.[34]

Included in the Combs report was a supplementary or minority report submitted by Edward Rees, which indicated that he did not feel the majority report had emphasized the urgency required. Rees was highly critical of the Civil Service Commission, which he felt had been lax in discharging questionable employees, and he recommended that "Congress, through the House Civil Service Committee, should take action and should do it soon."[35]

There was indication of considerable executive activity in that area, in the form of staff discussions, over two weeks before the Combs report was submitted.[36] A note attached to the report revealed that there was some talk at the time about the preparation of an executive order to create the commission requested by the subcommittee.[37] The president's decision not to act at that particular time remains a mystery. It may simply have been a case of procrastination, or perhaps Truman recognized the issue for what it really was—a hoax—and was therefore reluctant to follow up on the committee's request. Still, in a political sense, this would have been the time to act if there was to be any action at all. The president, in view of later events, would doubtless come to regret that moment of indecision.

One month after the Combs report had been submitted to the president, *Time* magazine drew attention to the obvious lack of activity on the part of the executive branch with regard to the loyalty question. That widely read periodical pointed out that if Communists were, in fact, in policy positions, as many members of Congress claimed, they were very apt to remain there.[38]

If the executive branch was silent in midsummer 1946, certain members of Congress certainly were not. Representative Daniel A. Reed reflected the attitude of many of his colleagues when he declared, on July 15, 1946, that "our government departments are harboring communists in key positions where they can best carry on their subversive activities."[39] Still another member of the House, Walter C. Ploeser of Missouri, insisted that "this year's Congressional elections must have as their basic issue the question of Communism in

America. . . .Their stooges in the Congress and in the executive branch of the Federal government are the most effective tools to power. . . .This is a year of decision."[40]

It would be difficult to prove that communism was the main issue in the November elections of 1946, but it certainly was a major one. Marquis Childs reported in his *Washington Post* column, December 2, 1946, that the Communist issue was the thing that swept the Republicans to victory in November.[41] There were undoubtedly many fears and anxieties about the country that year and the Republicans played skillfully to each of them.

One of the more important factors that contributed to the Republican landslide was a general, overall dissatisfaction with presidential leadership. Truman made no public statements and indeed took no active part in the campaign. Democrats were quite happy to have him remain in Independence, and party leaders attempted to revive the New Deal spirit with recordings of FDR's speeches. It did not work. The people, upset by consumer shortages and many other problems, were ready for a change. In his attempts to deal with such problems, Truman had alienated all sides of the political spectrum. His tough approach toward the unions in the spring 1946 rail dispute had upset liberals in general. His fight with the Seventy-ninth Congress over the restrictive Case labor bill, and his narrowly successful veto of that piece of legislation, had seriously alienated the conservatives but at the same time failed to win back any substantial support from labor.[42] Truman found himself damned by one group or another regardless of his actions.

The 1946 elections constituted a disastrous setback for the Democratic party and it lost control of Congress for the first time since 1930. Although the Truman leadership had faltered at times, it was naive and unfair to assume, as many liberals did, that a stronger, more eloquent president could have satisfactorily led the rebellious Seventy-ninth Congress.

"Liberals who were disillusioned with Truman's inability to lead seemed to forget that Roosevelt had lost control of Congress long before his death. What the progressives missed was the power of FDR's *style*, not necessarily his ability to achieve liberal goals."[43]

The Republican sweep in November 1946 was quite impressive. When the votes were tabulated they held a 51 to 45 edge in the Senate, 246 to 188 in the House, and controlled 25 governorships to 23 for the Democrats.[44] Democratic Representative William Fulbright of Arkansas suggested that Truman, since he had been repudiated by the electorate, should appoint Republican Senator Arthur Vandenberg as secretary of state and then resign. Vandenberg would then assume the duties of the presidency in the absence of a vice president.[45] A rather "sharp" reply from Truman ended any suggestions along that line. The president took the defeat in a subdued manner and pledged to continue to do, "without regard to political considerations, what seems to me to be for the welfare of all our people."[46] He did not, however, overlook the significance of the Republican victory, especially as it applied to the Communists-in-government issue.

Two weeks after the election, the president finally moved to take the initiative in the fight against communism when he issued Executive Order 9806, which established the President's Temporary Commission on Employee Loyalty to "inquire into the standards, procedures, and organizational provisions for (a) the investigation of persons who are employed by the United States Government or are applicants for such employment, (b) the removal or disqualification from employment of any disloyal or subversive person."[47] The editor of the *Washington Post*, on November 27, 1946, struck a responsive chord when he voiced approval of the temporary commission, but noted that the delay "affords another melancholy instance of the lateness and littleness that seem to dog every act of the Truman administration."[48] The order obviously should have come shortly after release of the Combs report in July of 1946. As a result of the badly timed appointment, Truman could hardly escape the charge that he had been forced to yield to persuasive congressional pressure.

Perhaps the most important factor in Truman's decision to appoint the temporary commission was his concern over the congressional trend toward the introduction of more and more restrictive legislation in the loyalty field. The election of a Republican Congress had increased this concern.[49] As 1946 drew to a close, Truman's fears appeared to be well founded, as the GOP pledged greater efforts against the "Reds" in the year to follow.[50]

There is some evidence that Truman, although certainly aware of the past revelations of subversive activity, was not overly fearful of the dangers of internal communism. In his State of the Union Message in January 1947, he made no mention of the temporary commission. He did note the areas of disagreement between the Congress and himself, but he called for a spirit of cooperation to work together for the common good. "We shall be risking the nation's safety. . .if we do not. . . ." Security, Truman contended, "rests. . .on civil liberties and human freedoms. . . ."[51] Another indication of the president's personal ideas about the problem of communism in the United States was contained in a February 28, 1947, letter to Governor George H. Earle of Pennsylvania. The president stated that "People are very much wrought up about the Communist 'bugaboo' but I am of the opinion that the country is perfectly safe so far as Communism is concerned—we have too many sane people."[52]

Truman's apparent lack of any deep concern over the menace of internal communism was not shared by others in his administration. Attorney General Clark, in a memorandum to the chairman of the temporary commission, A. Devitt Vanech, stressed the urgency of the situation and proclaimed the very "serious threat which even one disloyal person constitutes to the security of the Government of the United States."[53] Although Truman was soon to voice the same opinion, it is doubtful that he ever felt the Communists were as serious a threat to the internal security of the United States as some would have had the nation believe.

The Communist hunters in Congress, however, continued to keep the issue alive. That fact was clearly illustrated in the Senate hearings to determine the fitness of Truman's nominee, David Lilienthal, to head the Atomic Energy Commission. Lilienthal, under constant attack for many weeks, was accused of everything from being a supporter of leftist causes to knowingly harboring Communists on the government payroll. An old foe of Lilienthal from TVA days, Senator Kenneth McKellar of Tennessee, went so far as to intimate that the nominee could not be trusted because "his parents were born in Czechoslovakia."[54] In his own defense, Lilienthal stated, "I will be very glad to be lynched if in the process of that lynching this lesson about what our history means is learned. . .in terms of protection of the individual citizen against irresponsible charges of 'witch hunters.' "[55]

No one would question the right of the Senate to probe any nominee's fitness for such a vital post, but the harangue against David Lilienthal bordered on partisan irresponsibility. As the *New York Times* reported, "It is difficult to avoid suspicion that the battle over Mr. Lilienthal's appointment was as good as ended last week until some Republicans thought they saw in the slow-motion tactics of Mr. McKellar an opportunity to make political capital at the expense of the administration."[56]

At various times during the Lilienthal hearings, charges of "Communist" and "New Dealer" were used almost interchangeably. The use of the latter epithet gave credence to the contention that much of the Communist "bugaboo" that infected the Congress at that time could be traced in part to a deep-seated conservative frustration after twelve years of liberal Democratic government.[57] In the final analysis, it was the actions taken by responsible senators from both parties, such as Democrat Tom Connally from Texas and Republican Arthur Vandenberg from Michigan, who secured Lilienthal's nomination. Vandenberg characterized as "fantastic fabrication" the charge that Lilienthal was sympathetic to Communist causes.[58]

As the acrimonious hearings of the Senate Atomic Energy Commission progressed through the first months of 1947, other groups also, in and out of Congress, rallied the nation to a defense against the Red menace. The United States Chamber of Commerce estimated that 400 Communists held high government positions and demanded a congressional investigation.[59] Doubtless Congress did not need much prodding. As one Republican noted, the Eightieth "Congress opened daily with a prayer and ended with a probe."[60]

In March, the House Committee on Un-American Activities opened hearings on a bill to outlaw the Communist party in the United States. William Bullitt, United States minister to France at the outbreak of World War II, warned of an aggressive Soviet Union, but he opposed any law that would outlaw the party in this country.[61] William Green of the AFL, in his testimony, voiced a similar opposition. Such an act, Green contended, would be "tantamount to a declaration of voluntary bankruptcy of the ideas and ideals of American democracy."[62] He also contended that a suppression of the Communist party would only serve to drive the members underground. A similar view was expressed by the director of the FBI, J. Edgar Hoover, who warned, at the same time, that the goal of the Communist party "is the overthrow of our government."[63] Hoover further stated that the Communist fifth column was a definite menace, that it was better organized than the Nazi fifth column of World War II, and that its members should certainly be barred from government service.[64] At the time of Hoover's appearance before the House Committee on Un-American Activities in March of 1947, no less than six different bills designed either to limit or to destroy the Communist party in the United States had already been introduced in the first session of the Eightieth Congress.[65] The Communist problem in fact was receiving more than its share of attention.

At the height of this superheated campaign of anti-Bolshevism, communist guerrilla activity against the British supported Greek government signaled what many American policy makers interpreted as the first move in a Soviet master plan of aggression. On March 9, 1947, the *New York Times* reported that President Truman had determined to take a tough line against the Soviet Union's expansionist ambitions and was prepared to widen America's role in world affairs.[66]

The *Times'* prediction was prophetic as Truman, before a joint session of Congress on March 12, 1947, proposed a dramatic departure from America's traditional role in world affairs. The Truman Doctrine requested aid for those nations, specifically Greece, who sought assistance to maintain their independence. The opening sentence of the president's address set the tone—"The gravity of the situation which confronts the world today necessitates my appearance before a joint session of the Congress. The foreign policy and the national security of this country are involved."[67] Such a crisis tone "indicated that officials felt that the American people needed a jolt to arouse them to support so revolutionary a departure."[68]

It appeared from the beginning of his presidency that "Truman, like so many Americans, held contradictory attitudes toward the Soviet Union, was puzzled by its behavior, and was uncertain of its intentions."[69] Although the evidence strongly suggests that the president sincerely hoped to maintain friendly relations with the Soviets, he soon concluded that there was no reciprocal feeling evident among their leaders. In the spring of 1946, Truman received a synthesis of reports from various governmental agencies—the CIA, the State Department, and others—all of which warned of aggressive Soviet intentions. The administration, at that point committed itself fully to a hard-line policy toward the Soviet Union.[70]

Recent revisionist studies suggest that American policy makers seriously misinterpreted Soviet postwar aims and thereby precipitated an uneasy confrontation. Although the arguments are persuasive, there is not really sufficient evidence to warrant such a drastic conclusion. There were, to be sure, serious misinterpretations on both sides but the United States appears to have had fewer alternatives than the revisionists assume. Perhaps a clearer vision of the origins of the cold war will emerge when efforts are directed less at identifying scapegoats and more toward a reexamination of all policy options during the period 1945-1947.

The Truman Doctrine was generally well received in the press and Truman was praised for his courage. Felix Belair, Jr., in an article entitled "Truman Assumes Lead in Fight on Communism," declared that:

> Having been repudiated in the Congressional elections as leader of the party of supposed Communist sympathies, Mr. Truman would now lead the free peoples of the world in the fight against Communist inspired totalitarianism. And in the process. . .he has stolen a lot of Republican thunder. . .[71]

With the announcement of the Doctrine, Truman had taken the initiative in the struggle against international communism. At the same time, the president evidently realized the need to do something about supposed Communist subversives at work on the home front. On March 2, 1947, Truman received the report of his Temporary Commission on Employee Loyalty, appointed in November 1946. The commission, after a review of past loyalty procedures, concluded that "while the Commission believes that the employment of disloyal or subversive persons represents more than a speculative threat to our system of government, it is unable. . .to state with any degree of certainty how far-reaching that threat is."[72] The commission warned, however, against a preoccupation with employee loyalty, apart from counterespionage which the president's commission felt was important to protect the nation against subversive activity.

The report concluded with the commission's recommendations to unify and improve the government's loyalty program.[73] The standard for removal from employment was to be that "on all evidence, reasonable grounds exist for believing that the person involved is disloyal to the Government of the United States."[74] Those areas to be considered in making such a judgment were:

1. Sabotage, espionage, or attempts or preparation therefor, or knowingly associating with spies or saboteurs;
2. Treason or sedition or advocacy thereof;
3. Advocacy of revolution or force or violence to alter our constitutional form of government;
4. Intentional, unauthorized disclosure. . .of documents or information of a confidential or nonpublic character. . .;
5. Performing or attempting to perform his duties, or otherwise acting, so as to serve the interests of another government. . .;
6. Membership in, affiliation with, or sympathetic association with any foreign or domestic organization. . . designated by the Attorney General as totalitarian, fascist, communist. . . .[75]

The president's temporary commission felt it had struck a proper balance between the maintenance of security and the protection of the rights of the individual employee. The president evidently felt likewise, for he adopted the report of his commission with few important alterations.[76] On March 21, 1947, Truman issued Executive Order 9835, "Prescribing Procedures for the Administration of an Employees Loyalty Program in the Executive Branch of the Government." The program, as outlined in the president's executive order, required at least a nominal check for over two million government employees with a full yield investigation if evidence indicated possible disloyalty.[77]

Executive Order 9835 was, noted Cabell Phillips, "a milestone in the life of the United States—a wretched one that sanctioned government prying into the privacy of its citizens' minds and consciences. But it was an inevitable one in the context of the time. . . ."[78] The president was aware of the possibilities of Communist infiltration and consequently saw the need to tighten security precautions. Truman was, however, far more concerned with Soviet expansionist ambitions abroad, as he clearly revealed in his announcement of the Truman Doctrine on March 12. The loyalty program simply "imparted an essential element of consistency to his Greco-Turkish Program."[79] It would have seemed foolish and inconsistent to pledge the United States to stand against Communist expansion abroad and ignore the supposed threat from Communist subversion at home. The latter was particularly true in light of the persistent congressional charges over the previous ten years.

The president, sensitive to such charges, was also fearful of the kind of restrictive legislation in the field of loyalty and security then under consideration in Congress. At the moment when Truman issued the loyalty order, the House Committee on Un-American Activities was preparing to open its hearings on the bill to outlaw the Communist party in the United States.[80] The president felt that he must seize the initiative and did so with the announcement of Executive Order 9835.

The initial reaction to the loyalty order of March 21 was varied. The Americans for Democratic Action endorsed the aims of the program but warned that the procedure did not assure a fair trial.[81] The *New Republic* asserted that the "already existing demoralization of liberal-minded government workers. . .was now verging on hysteria."[82] These specific reactions will be examined in more detail in the next chapter, but the general accusation, that the loyalty order constituted a direct attack on federal employees, was simply untenable. The question really centered not on whether the nation would have a loyalty program but who should plan, initiate, and operate such a program. As James Wechsler noted, "If liberals cannot face the reality of communist intrigue. . .the Congressional cops will run the show; if liberals cannot offer an affirmative, clearly defined plan of democratic self-defense the witch hunt may be truly upon us."[83]

On the whole, Congress did not respond unfavorably to the president's program, although a certain pettiness was detectable in some remarks of its members. Robert Rich of Pennsylvania stated that the president had recognized that his administration was infested with "Reds" only after he had decided to stop the Communist advance overseas.[84] Representative Everett M. Dirkson of Illinois pointed out that the Democratic administrations had always been rather soft on communism and he wondered at the sudden show of force.[85] Karl Mundt pronounced the Truman loyalty program as "precisely that which the House Committee on Un-American Activities has been advocating for at least four years."[86]

What Representative Mundt said was true, but the evidence indicates that Truman had much more regard for individual liberties than did certain members of the House committee. From the beginning, the president pledged that there would be no witch-hunt.[87] In a letter to Philip Murray, who had expressed alarm over possible violations of individual rights, Truman declared that "the order was most carefully drawn with the idea in view that the Civil Rights of no one would be infringed upon. . . ."[88] Tom Clark indicated that Truman was deeply concerned with individual rights, had expressed that concern on numerous occasions, and was more disturbed by the possible harm that might come from the loyalty order than hopeful of any good it might accomplish.[89] Regard for civil liberties was clearly revealed in discussions among members of the administration over what part the Federal Bureau of Investigation should play in the loyalty investigations.

In a memorandum from J. Edgar Hoover to the attorney general, dated March 28, 1947, the bureau's director voiced the opinion that the FBI should be given more investigative power. Hoover did not feel that department heads should be given the responsibility of discharging subversives. He contended that those same gentlemen had possessed such power in the past and had been most reluctant to use it.[90] Three days later, March 31, 1947, in another memorandum to the attorney general, Hoover objected strenuously to a statement by Harry Mitchell, president of the Civil Service Commission, which supposedly questioned the right of the FBI to investigate persons covered by the Hatch Act. Hoover, in an obvious show of temper, suggested that the "Civil Service Commission be given the full, complete, entire and conclusive responsibility for conducting all investigations of Government employees about whose loyalty there is any questions whatsoever."[91]

The civil service had, in fact, voiced strenuous objections, in the form of a written statement by Harry Mitchell and Frances Perkins, also on the Civil Service Commission, to an increased investigative role for the bureau. They contended that the civil service should be allowed to conclude the investigation of an applicant for employment, and that the commission should not be required to turn over the loyalty aspects of a case to the FBI.[92]

A penciled note from Clark Clifford, an influential member of the White House staff, reveals clearly where the president stood in the matter: "President feels very strongly anti-FBI and sides positively with Mitchell and Perkins—wants to be sure and hold FBI down, afraid of 'Gestapo.' "[93] George Elsey, another member of the White House Staff, did not believe the president's fears of the FBI were justified.[94] In fact, from discussions among various staff members, it is evident that most of them favored an increased role for the bureau at the same time conceding the possible danger of the overextension of such an obviously independent police force.[95]

The staff recommendations were persuasively drawn up and called for more activity on the part of the FBI. They were submitted to Truman in a memorandum from Clifford on May 6, 1947. It was recommended that the bureau be allowed to fingerprint all present employees. If derogatory information was revealed, the FBI would conduct a full field investigation. New applicants would also be checked by the bureau against their files, and by the civil service against other relevant sources of information. Again, if derogatory information was revealed, the FBI would conduct an investigation. Clifford concluded:

> I am fully cognizant of the dangers to our civil rights which we face in the matter of loyalty investigations, and I share your feelings of concern. It is precisely because of the dangers involved that I believe that the FBI is a better agency than the Civil Service to conduct loyalty investigations for new employment—the more highly trained and administrated an agency is, the higher should be its standards. . . .[96]

On May 9, 1947, a revision of those recommendations provided that in case of new employees the civil service would no longer be required to turn over loyalty cases to the FBI, but "may" request more information from the bureau if they desire.[97]

On that same day the president submitted a request for $24,900,000, to administer the loyalty program through June 30, 1948. Of that sum, $16,160,000 would be set aside for the Civil Service Commission and $8,740,000 for the FBI.[98] Although the largest share of money was alloted to the civil service, the figures represented an increase for the Federal Bureau of Investigation. On May 10, the *Washington Post* noted that the FBI was to be given a more prominent role.[99]

It has been suggested that the president's apprehension over the investigative role of the FBI was foolish—that he should have been more concerned with the dangers posed by such an extensive loyalty probe. There is an element of truth in the suggestion. It appears quite likely that Truman did seriously underestimate the potential threat to individual liberties.[100] Still, the president's objections to an increased role for the FBI should not be lightly dismissed. He did so, it would seem, because he recognized the inherent danger when any police force as large and well organized as the Federal Bureau of Investigation is granted such extensive power—in the case of the FBI it was virtually unchecked power. Truman was also aware that the bureau's reports contained much unsubstantiated information that might, if leaked, severely damage innocent persons. Recent revelations of the abuse of power by investigative agencies do indeed make the president's concern in 1947 seem far from trivial.

Although it was hoped that appropriations to implement the loyalty program would be approved without delay, such was not the case. Congress immediately made known its determination to control the purse. Also, as previously noted, certain members felt the FBI should be given an even greater role. Clifford, in a May 23 memorandum to the president, noted that a special assistant to the attorney general, E. Devitt Vanech, had expressed some concern over possible political difficulties in connection with the appropriation hearings on the president's budget estimates, because the FBI had not been given full responsibility for all investigations. Clifford did not concur, insisting that the program was sound, and concluding that Vanech was simply "making mountains out of molehills."[101] The president penciled a short reply: "Clark: you have properly diagnosed the case. But J. Edgar will in all probability get this backward-looking Congress to give him what he wants. Its [*sic*] dangerous. HST."[102]

There was an additional delay in the implementation of Executive Order 9835 because of several attempts by Representative Rees to push a bill through Congress as a substitute for the president's program. Rees insisted that the solution to the problem of loyalty "lies with the Congress in providing adequate legislation under which the executive branch can discharge employees, since it is clear that the executive branch is reluctant to assume this responsibility on its own initiative."[103] Rees introduced, on April 10, 1947, H. R. 3023, "Providing for a Federal Employees Loyalty Act of 1947."[104] The bill was subsequently referred to the House Committee on the Post Office but was never reported.[105] The author did not despair, however, and continued to push for a congressional substitute.

On June 12, 1947, Congressman Rees introduced H. R. 3813, "a bill to provide for removal from, and the prevention of appointment to, offices or positions in the executive branch of the Government of persons who are found to be disloyal to the United States."[106] The bill was similar to the president's executive order in many respects, but it placed the authority for dismissal with an independent loyalty board, separate and apart from the civil service; the latter, Rees charged, had been lax in its purge of disloyal employees.[107]

H. R. 3813 was subsequently reported out of the House Post Office Committee and vigorously debated. Representative Adolph J. Sabath of Illinois, who spoke in opposition, contended that the president's order was well conceived, had suitable provisions to protect individual rights, and would prove adequate to locate and remove disloyal employees. The Rees bill, Sabath stated, represented "a belated effort of the Republicans to get back in the groove of their redbaiting campaign. . . ."[108] Helen Gahagan Douglas of California charged that H. R. 3813 was simply the culmination of a fourteen-year Republican effort to "get," not Communists, but New Deal Democrats.[109] Despite the exhortations of Sabath and Douglas, the Rees bill, with several amendments attached, passed the House of

Representatives July 15, 1947, by a vote of 319 to 61.[110] It was then referred to the Senate Committee on the Civil Service, but never reported out of that committee.[111]

As the Rees bill languished in the Senate committee, the Congress finally, on July 31, 1947, voted the appropriations necessary for the implementation of the president's loyalty program. The $11,000,000 appropriated was, however, far less than the amount requested by the president. Also, the division of funds was substantially altered with $7,400,000 marked for the FBI and only $3,000,000 for the Civil Service Commission.[112] As the president had predicted, Hoover did, in fact, "get what he wanted."

The twenty-three-man Loyalty Review Board, with a prominent Republican, Seth Richardson, as the chairman, was appointed by President Truman in November 1947. Although there was general praise for those selected to serve on the board, many people warned of the inherent dangers to civil liberties in such investigative procedures.[113] In his statement to the new Loyalty Board on November 14, Truman attempted to allay such fears, as he reiterated his promise to avoid anything that remotely resembled a witch-hunt. "The government, as the largest employer in the United States, must be the model of a fair employer."[114]

NOTES

1. Harry S. Truman, *Memoirs, Year of Decision* vol. 1, (Garden City, N.Y.: Doubleday, 1955), p. 19.

2. Louis W. Koenig, *The Truman Administration: Its Principles and Practices* (New York: New York University Press, 1956), p. 1.

3. Alan Harper, *The Politics of Loyalty: The White House and the Communist Issue, 1946-1952* (Westport, Conn.: Greenwood Publishing Corporation, 1969), pp. 9-11.

4. Earl Latham, *The Communist Controversy in Washington: From the New Deal to McCarthy* (New York: Atheneum, 1969), pp. 33-62.

5. Harper, *The Politics of Loyalty*, pp. 13-14.

6. Eleanor Bontecou, *The Federal Loyalty-Security Program* (Ithaca, N.Y.: Cornell University Press, 1953), p. 8.

7. George Seldes, *Witch Hunt: The Techniques and Profits of Red Baiting* (New York: Modern Age Books, 1940), p. 280.

8. Ibid., p. 274.

9. Harry S. Truman, *Memoirs*, vol. 2, *Years of Trial and Hope* (Garden City, N.Y.: Doubleday, 1956), p. 275.

10. Barton J. Bernstein and Allen J. Matusow, *The Truman Administration: A Documentary History* (New York: Harper and Row, 1966), p. 356.

11. Report of the President's Temporary Commission on Employees Loyalty, OF 2521, Truman Papers, Truman Library, Independence, Mo.

12. Ibid.

13. Ibid.

14. Ibid.

15. John W. Caughey, *In Clear and Present Danger: The Crucial State of Our Freedoms* (Chicago: University of Chicago Press, 1958), p. 103.

16. Roger S. Abbott, "Federal Loyalty Program: Background and Problems," *American Political Science Review* 42 (June 1948):487.

17. Ibid., pp. 486-87.

18. Report of the President's Temporary Commission, OF 2521.

19. Abbott, "Federal Loyalty Program," p. 490.

20. Earl Latham, *The Communist Controversy in Washington*, pp. 204-8.

21. Ibid., pp. 210-16.

22. Cabell Phillips, *The Truman Presidency: The History of a Triumphant Succession* (New York: Macmillan Co., 1966), p. 359.

23. Ibid., p. 360.

24. Ibid.

25. Bontecou, *The Federal Loyalty-Security Program*, p. 22.

26. *New York Times*, July 15, 1945.

27. *Newsweek*, January 7, 1946, p. 19.

28. U.S., *Congressional Record*, 79th Congress, 2d sess., 1946, 92, pt. 2, p. 1724. Taken from a speech by Helen G. Douglas of California, February 27, 1946.

29. U.S., *Congressional Record*, 79th Congress, 2d sess., 1946, 92, pt. 4, p. 5209.

30. Ibid.

31. U.S., *Congressional Record*, 79th Congress, 2d sess., 1946, pt. 11, pp. A3124-25.

32. Jennings Randolph to the President, July 25, 1946, OF 252, Truman Papers, Truman Library.

33. U.S., *Congressional Record*, 79th Congress, 2d sess., 1946, 92, pt. 8, pp. 9603-4.

34. Report, Civil Service subcommittee, OF 252, Truman Papers, Truman Library.

35. Supplemental Report, Civil Service subcommittee, OF 252, Truman Papers, Truman Library.

36. *Newsweek*, July 8, 1946, p. 22.

37. Note, George Elsey to Clark Clifford, attached to Civil Service Subcommittee Report, OF 252, Truman Papers, Truman Library.

38. *Time*, August 26, 1946, p. 16.

39. U.S. *Congressional Record*, 79th Congress, 2d sess., 1946, 92, pt. 12, p. A4116.

40. Ibid., p. A4359.

41. *Washington Post*, December 2, 1946.

42. Susan M. Hartmann, *Truman and the 80th Congress* (Columbia: University of Missouri Press, 1971), pp. 3-9.

43. Alonzo L. Hamby, *Beyond The New Deal: Harry S. Truman and American Liberalism* (New York: Columbia University Press, 1973), pp. 135-41.

44. *Time*, November 18, 1946, p. 21.

45. Hartmann, *Truman and The 80th Congress*, p. 18.

46. *Time*, November 18, 1946, p. 21.

47. U.S., National Archives and Records Service, Federal Register Division, *Code of Federal Regulations*, 1943-48 compilation, Executive Orders, p. 589.

48. *Washington Post*, November 27, 1946.

49. Phillips, *The Truman Presidency*, p. 360.

50. *Washington Post*, December 30, 1946.

51. *New York Times*, January 7, 1947.

52. President to Governor George H. Earle of Pennsylvania, February 14, 1947, OF 263, Truman Papers, Truman Library.

53. Memorandum, For A. Devitt Vanech from Tom Clark, February 14, 1947, OF 252, Truman Papers, Truman Library.

54. *Newsweek*, February 17, 1947, p. 32.

55. *New York Times*, February 5, 1947.

56. Ibid., February 2, 1947.

57. Ibid., February 16, 1947.

58. Hartmann, *Truman and The 80th Congress*, p. 33.

59. *New York Times*, February 19, 1947.

60. Quoted in Alfred Steinberg, *The Man From Missouri: The Life and Times of Harry S. Truman* (New York: G. P. Putnam's Sons, 1962), p. 289.

61. *New York Times*, March 25, 1947.

62. Ibid., March 26, 1947.

63. Ibid., March 27, 1947.

64. *Washington Post*, March 22, 1947.

65. *Newsweek*, March 24, 1947, p. 28.

66. *New York Times*, March 9, 1947.

67. Ibid., March 13, 1947.

68. William G. Carleton, *The Revolution in American Foreign Policy; Its Global Range*, 2d ed. (New York: Random House, 1967), p. 162.

69. Alonzo Hamby, *Beyond the New Deal*, p. 116.

70. Ibid., pp. 114-18.

71. *New York Times*, March 16, 1947.

72. Report, President's Temporary Commission on Employee Loyalty, OF 2521, Truman Papers, Truman Library.

73. See Appendix A.
74. Ibid.
75. Ibid.
76. Bontecou, *The Federal Loyalty-Security Program*, p. 76.
77. See Appendix B.
78. Phillips, *The Truman Presidency*, p. 361.
79. *Business Week*, March 29, 1947, p. 108.
80. *New York Times*, March 23, 1947.
81. Ibid., March 31, 1947.
82. *New Republic*, March 31, 1947, p. 10.
83. James Wechsler, "How to Rid the Government of Communists," *Harper's Magazine* 195 (November 1947):490.
84. U.S., *Congressional Record*, 80th Congress, 1st sess., 1947, 93, pt. 2, p. 2540.
85. Ibid., p. 2545.
86. *New York Times*, March 23, 1947.
87. Ibid., May 16, 1947.
88. Truman to Philip Murray, April 15, 1947, OF 252K, Truman Papers, Truman Library.
89. Interview with Justice Thomas C. Clark, Washington, D.C., August 22, 1969.
90. Memorandum, J. Edgar Hoover to Devitt Vanech, March 28, 1947, Loyalty Folder, Vanech Papers, Truman Library.
91. Ibid., March 31, 1947.
92. Summary, Mr. Mitchell's and Miss Perkin's contentions regarding an increased investigative role for FBI, May 5, 1947, Internal Security Folder, Elsey Papers, Truman Library.
93. Note, Clark Clifford, May 2, 1947, Internal Security Folder, Elsey Papers, Truman Library.
94. Notes, George Elsey, May 2, 1947, Internal Security Folder, Elsey Papers, Truman Library.
95. Notes, Staff discussions, Elsey's summary, May 5, 1947, Internal Security Folder, Elsey Papers, Truman Library.
96. Memorandum, For the President from Clifford, on appropriation estimates to carry out provisions of Executive Order 9835, May 6, 1947, Internal Security Folder, Elsey Papers, Truman Library.
97. Memorandum, For the President from Clifford, revised estimates, May 9, 1947, Internal Security Folder, Elsey Papers, Truman Library.
98. Budget Report, on appropriations to carry out provisions of Executive Order 9835, May 9, OF 2, Truman Papers, Truman Library.
99. *Washington Post*, May 10, 1947.
100. Alonzo Hamby, *Beyond the New Deal*, p. 171.
101. Memorandum, For the President from Clark Clifford, May 23, 1947, Internal Security Folder, Elsey Papers, Truman Library.
102. Ibid.
103. U.S., *Congressional Record*, 80th Congress, 1st sess., 1947, 93, pt. 3, p. 3305.
104. Ibid., p. 3318.

105. U.S., *Congressional Record*, 80th Congress, 1st sess., 1947, 93, pt. 14, p. 790.
106. U.S., *Congressional Record*, 80th Congress, 1st sess., 1947, 93, pt. 6, p. 6922.
107. U.S., *Congressional Record*, 80th Congress, 1st sess., 1947, 93, pt. 7, p. 8951.
108. Ibid., p. 8949.
109. Ibid.
110. Ibid., pp. 8979-80.
111. U.S., *Congressional Record*, 80th Congress, 1st sess., 1947, 93, pt. 14, p. 812.
112. Bontecou, *Federal Loyalty-Security Program*, p. 33.
113. *New York Times*, November 9, 1947.
114. Ibid., November 15, 1947.

2
THE OPERATION OF THE LOYALTY-SECURITY PROGRAM: ITS PROBLEMS AND ITS CRITICS

I was very anxious that no injustice be done to any individual. . . .

One of the first steps taken to implement the president's Loyalty-Security program involved the establishment of departmental loyalty boards, and the preparation of rules to govern loyalty procedures in those departments. The rules adopted by the Treasury Department are representative of those prepared throughout the various nonsensitive governmental agencies. It was noted at the outset that those rules would govern the possible removal of any civilian officer of the Treasury Department, "irrespective of tenure, or of manner, method, or nature of appointment."[1] The newly created board would be composed of the administrative assistant to the secretary of the Treasury, who would serve as chairman, the assistant general counsel, and one other member to be chosen by the secretary. The standards to be used to determine an employee's loyalty would be the same as those outlined in Executive Order 9835.[2]

The head of each bureau would be required to report any derogatory information pertaining to an employee to the administrative assistant who would then turn such information over to the general counsel. If the latter determined that there was enough information to warrant charges, a statement would be prepared and delivered to the employee by registered mail. It was specified that the statement should be in sufficient detail, and "as complete as security considerations permit," in order to allow the employee to prepare his defense. The accused would be expected to reply within the time specified in the statement, but in no case in less than fifteen days. It was noted that any charge left unanswered "shall be deemed to be admitted."[3]

The employee would have the right to a hearing if he so requested. The chairman of the loyalty board would be responsible for fixing the time for such an inquiry and would set the date sufficiently far in advance, again no less than fifteen days, in order to allow the employee time to prepare his case. If the employee chose not to request a hearing, the board might, at its own discretion, choose to have one anyway. In that case, the board could require the employee to appear and "answer any questions which the Board deems relevant."[4] The failure to appear upon request would, it was stated, constitute grounds for removal.

The employee under suspicion would have the right to appear, with or without counsel, at the inquiry which was closed to the public. If the suspect requested an appointed attorney, the general counsel, who was required to present the charges, might appoint such a counsel at his own discretion. It was also stated that the employee had the right to introduce witnesses in his own defense, and would be allowed to cross-examine the board's witnesses. All testimony given at the hearing would be under oath, and a written record of the proceedings was required.

When the hearing was completed, the board, after deliberation, was to prepare written recommendations stating whether "reasonable grounds" for a belief that the employee in question was disloyal existed. If the board recommended removal, the employee would be notified, and given seven days to file an appeal and present a written argument in his own behalf. After the time for appeal had lapsed, the general counsel would transmit the record to the secretary with his recommendations.

If the secretary confirmed the decision for removal, the employee was to be immediately suspended without pay, pending an appeal before the Loyalty Review Board. If the employee did not request an appeal, he was then permanently removed from the federal payroll. If an appeal was made before the Loyalty Review Board, the secretary would consider its recommendations and subsequently direct either permanent removal or reinstatement.[5]

Some 800,000 government workers, employed in areas considered sensitive, received different treatment with regard to loyalty investigations. The Department of the Army, the Atomic Energy Commission, and the Voice of America agency treated disloyalty cases as security risks, and did not allow appeal beyond the agency head. Other agencies designated as sensitive followed the procedures outlined by the Loyalty Review Board in any case that involved the question of "loyalty." An employee considered a security risk, however, could not appeal beyond the head of his respective agency.[6]

A casual examination of the procedures involved in loyalty investigations clearly reveals a definite element of concern for the rights of the individual. A closer study, however, exposes just as plainly a number of conspicuous deficiencies. The closed hearing, the forced testimony, and other features stongly suggest a seventeenth century Star Chamber proceeding. There was an immediate protest on the part of many in government service who objected to any perusal of their record for evidence of disloyalty. Colston E. Warne, Professor of Economics at Amherst College and on the staff of the President's Council of Economic Advisors, refused to fill out the loyalty test questionnaire and angrily denied the right of either the executive or Congress to set standards of loyalty. "I am indeed shocked that for the first time in American history heresy hunting has received sanction of the President of the United States."[7]

Truman continued to insist that "the presence within the government of any disloyal or subversive person constituted a threat to our democratic processes."[8] The president, despite such exhortations, was apparently motivated less by a fear of potential subversion than by a desire to silence that vocal minority within the Congress which to him represented a graver threat. In his quasi-appeasement of that minority, Truman did, certainly unwittingly, appear to sanction the "heresy hunting" of which Professor Warne spoke.

Twelve years after he left the presidency, Harry Truman would voice a rather simplistic view in reference to the loyalty question in his administration. He professed never to have understood what had caused all the clamor. After all, he noted, a person was either "loyal or disloyal."[9] Unfortunately, he may have felt much the same back in 1947. Truman's unschematic, populist mind apparently led him, at first, to oversimplify a very complex problem. Certainly no clear-cut distinction could be made between loyalty and disloyalty and he should have recognized that fact. Loyalty, as a state of mind and emotions, obviously meant more than devotion to flag day and most assuredly could not be measured by the standards outlined in the president's loyalty order. Although Truman's motives appeared sincere, his wisdom in the inauguration of such a broad program must remain open to question.

There were some groups, the Sons of the American Revolution, the American Legion, and others, who wholeheartedly endorsed the loyalty program.[10] For the most part, however, it was subjected from the start to a rather divergent and often abusive attack from both the right and the left. Republican Congressman William J. Miller of Connecticut went so far as to suggest that the loyalty program might well be a "witch-hunt" designed to eliminate conservatives who opposed the New Deal and to secure the latter's "totalitarian hold upon the nation. . . ."[11] The American Anti-Communist Association, Inc. evidently felt that the program did not go far enough when they requested that the order be amended to prevent the use of government property by such "subversives" as Henry A. Wallace.[12]

The liberal sentiment was expressed in a radio debate between Representative J. M. Combs of Texas, who spoke in defense of the president's loyalty program, and Arthur Garfield Hays, national director of the American Civil Liberties Union, who branded the loyalty order as "the most outrageous, undemocratic measure that could possibly be conceived."[13] Although Hays was somewhat overzealous, his feelings were not far removed from those expressed by members of many other liberal groups. A number of Yale University professors characterized the loyalty program as a part of a pattern of suppression that would inevitably lead to another 1920s witch-hunt.[14] The National Lawyers Guild viewed the program as one that followed the pattern of the Alien and Sedition Laws of 1798.[15] Clifford J. Durr, a member of the Federal Communications Commission, also assailed the loyalty program, insisting that the possible evils involved far outweighed any good that might be accomplished.[16]

The administration was not without its defenders. Justice Department officials, in a memorandum entitled "Does the President's Loyalty Order Violate Civil Rights?" firmly asserted that the order did not infringe on the individual's rights. This assumption was based on the premise that the loyalty procedures were in accord with the requirements of administrative due process, i.e., notice, hearing, opportunity for rebuttal, and the like. The Justice officials based their argument, however, on their belief in the validity of two basic propositions: (1) that no government employee had a vested right to a place on the public payroll, and (2) that employment by the government was a privilege and not a constitutional right. It was further stated, in that connection, that "the government employee, like Caesar's wife, should be above suspicion."[17]

For that particular line of defense, administration officials drew heavily on Justice Oliver Wendell Holmes' affirmation in the case of *McCuliffe v. City of New Bedford, Massachusetts* in 1892. The case arose when McCuliffe, a New Bedford policeman, was dismissed from the force when he solicited money for a political campaign. Holmes, in his oft-repeated dictum, stated that McCuliffe "may have a constitutional right to talk politics, but he has no constitutional right to be a policeman."[18] In the same way no one had a vested right to be a government employee. Seth Richardson, chairman of the Loyalty Review Board, went one step further when he asserted that the government could legally fire an employee without any inquiry whatsoever.[19]

The proposed threat to the government—the danger the nation was to be protected from—had never been clearly defined. If the main threat was posed only by those who pilfered classified documents, loyalty investigations might well have been restricted to sensitive areas. Instead, it was clear that not only deeds but certain words were considered dangerous.[20] The courts had earlier sanctioned such thinking. The United States Court of Appeals, when it upheld a previous decision against Leon Josephson, who had refused to testify before the House Committee on Un-American Activities, went so far as to state that "Congress could and should curtail freedom of speech where 'there is a clear and present danger'. . . ."[21] Again, they relied on Justice Holmes, who ruled in the case of *Schenck v. United States* in 1919, that the First Amendment did not protect an individual from punishment for "uttering words that may have all the effect of force."[22]

The United States government, therefore, involved itself in a most difficult task when it attempted to determine if and when certain words represented a "clear and present danger." The courts had continually recognized the right to free and open political discussions but also recognized the existence of certain limits to such discussions.[23] The question, then, concerned those limits: at what point did the speaker pass from normal, acceptable political discussion into areas dangerous to the government? The answer often depended not so much on the words as on the intent of the speaker. In a dissenting opinion to the Supreme Court's affirmation in the case of *Dennis v. United States* in 1951, an affirmation based on a modified version of Holmes's "clear and present danger" decision, Justice William O. Douglas stated:

> The crime then depends not on what is taught but on who the teacher is. That is to make freedom of speech turn not on what *is said*, but on the *intent* with which it is said. Once we start down that road we enter territory dangerous to the liberties of every citizen. . . .[24]

Unquestionably, an overreliance on the concept of "dangerous words" opened the way to activities not consistent with a democratic society. Whoever wished to suppress any debate which that particular person considered dangerous could turn to the idea of a "clear and present danger" to justify such suppression.[25] The National Lawyers Guild, in its report on the constitutionality of the loyalty program, noted the tendency to judge "intent" rather than action. The lawyers concluded that "the charges of deceit belong in heresy trials, not in political procedures. The test is action, not the dubious ground of belief about motives."[26]

The whole basic assumption that government employment was a privilege and not a right, that the employee could legally be fired for reasons that seemed justifiable only to the government, undermined procedural safeguards from the beginning. To grant a hearing amounted to an act of mercy on the part of the government rather than the employee's right.[27] Such assumptions were based on specious reasoning, and displayed a serious, if not intentional, disregard for the rights of federal employees.[28] It was that kind of logic which led to the many and often-repeated charges against the loyalty program.

One such charge was based on the belief that the imputation of disloyalty, whether justified or not, would result in permanent damage to the employee. The problem was discussed in a *Washington Post* article of December 18, 1947. The need for some kind of loyalty program was recognized but such a program must be conducted with utmost caution. The government should, it was claimed, find some procedure that would reconcile the need for security with the rights of the individual.[29]

No more serious charge could be made against a government employee than to say, in effect, that he or she had been disloyal to the country. By the charge alone, the employee was most certainly punished.[30] The Holmes dictum that no one had the right to employment simply did not apply in loyalty investigations. The New Bedford policeman, undoubtedly hurt by his dismissal, could nevertheless find another job. The government employee, dismissed on a charge of disloyalty, faced a much more difficult readjustment.[31]

Even if a suspended employee were reinstated, the shock of the investigation, the suspicious glances of his fellow employees, and the possible loss of friends and acquaintances, all might haunt the accused for many years to come.[32] By keeping the proceedings secret it had been hoped to avoid such an outcome. Inevitably, however, leaks occurred, especially from the Loyalty Review Board, to the Congress, the press, and others outside the government.[33] It has even been suggested, and perhaps not unreasonably so, that an employee, if he found himself tainted by suspicions of disloyalty, might turn to the Communists as a last resort.[34]

Once cleared, the employee was not only forced to live with the stigma of having once been investigated for possible disloyalty, but was also required to live with the additional fear that his files might be reopened at any time for review. Such procedure could be considered little short of "cruel and unusual punishment." Truman made note of this in his *Memoirs*:

> Every time a cleared employee moved from one job to another, his file was reviewed again, so that he was forced to answer the same charges over and over again. . . .This is not in the tradition of American fair play and justice.[35]

Another formidable charge brought against the loyalty program concerned its refusal, in a large number of cases, to allow the accused to confront his accusers. A prominent lawyer, later Associate Justice of the Supreme Court Abe Fortas, questioned "whether it is proper for a great governmental department to publish the most damaging statement which can be made about an American citizen today, to wit, that he is disloyal to his country. . . .without giving him a chance to be confronted with witnesses against him."[36] Fortas later claimed that the loyalty board's decision not to allow accused employees to examine FBI reports was a violation of the Bill of Rights.[37]

In the rules of procedure for the conduct of loyalty investigations, as adopted by the Treasury Department, and reviewed earlier in the chapter, it was noted that the employee in question would have the right to cross-examine the board's witnesses. A discrepancy arose when the FBI demanded that its confidential informants not be exposed to such cross-examination. The loyalty boards therefore had either to yield to the FBI's demands or give up the investigation, as the bureau's reports and witnesses more often than not constituted the heart of the board's case.[38] In the final analysis, the loyalty boards chose to acquiesce, falling back on the assumption that the government could, after all, legally dismiss an employee "without extending to such employee any hearing whatsoever."[39] As a result, the full burden of proof fell on the accused, against "persons whom he did not know, whom he could not confront, and whose credibility he could not challenge."[40]

Certain members of the administration also voiced concern over this matter of confidential witnesses. Assistant Secretary of the Interior, C. Girard Davidson, in a letter to Clark Clifford, indicated his belief that an accused should always have the right to confront his accuser. The assistant secretary further indicated his belief that the department should be allowed to conduct its own investigation, if the FBI refused to allow confrontation. He pointed out, however, that the attorney general's directive of October 7, 1947, had expressly forbidden the departments to make such an independent investigation. In conclusion, Davidson observed that many subversives might be retained, due to the reluctance of some boards to act on hearsay evidence.[41]

The continued protest against the rule of no-confrontation led in the fall of 1948 to a slight change in the procedure. Beginning November 1 of that year, the FBI was required to furnish the names of its informants. The bureau's agents might also be required to appear before a loyalty board and testify to the credibility of their confidential witnesses. Their identity, and the opportunity to cross-examine them, continued to be denied to the accused.[42]

Loyalty boards, in defense of their position, continually pleaded for the same rights as private employers.[43] That presumably meant the right not to retain the services of an incompetent employee, not an unreasonable request. But, as President Truman had pointed out, "the government. . .must be the model of a fair employer."[44] To fire an employee for incompetence was one thing, but to charge him with the heinous crime of disloyalty and then deny him less than due process in his defense was something quite different.[45] A private employer would never be allowed such disregard for his employee's rights.

Perhaps the most vehement denunciation of the loyalty program arose over the publication of the attorney general's list of subversive organizations. There were immediate charges that the administration, by the publication of such a list had given sanction to the principle of guilt by association. Of the six categories set forth in Executive Order 9835 to determine whether there were "reasonable grounds" for the belief that a person was disloyal, the sixth, "Association with an organization designated as subversive," unfortunately became the most important.[46]

The first such list of suspect organizations dates back to the passage of the Deportation and Exclusion Laws between the years 1917 and 1919. The provisions of those laws forbade an alien to belong to any group that advocated the overthrow by force of the United States government. Twelve such organizations were listed, under the direction of Attorney General A. Mitchell Palmer who insisted that the burden of proof rested with the alien.[47]

The excesses of Attorney General Palmer aroused such protest that the designation of organizations fell into virtual disuse until the birth of the House Committee on Un-American Activities in 1938, and the subsequent passage of the Hatch Act in 1939. Forty-seven organizations were listed by Attorney General Francis Biddle under the provisions of that Act. The list remained unpublished until released in December of 1947, with a number of additions, under the Truman Loyalty Order.[48]

The general criteria to determine subversive organizations, as developed by officials of the Justice Department, included the following:

1. The actual principles. . .may be deemed to be hostile to American form of government. . .;
2. The aims, purposes, policies and programs of such organizations promote the ideals. . .of any foreign government or of any foreign political party;
3. Such organization is more concerned with the success or failure of foreign political and economic experiments. . .which would result in the destruction. . . of the Republican form of government. . .;

4. The actual principles, methods and mode of operation . . .indicate lack of bona-fide allegiance to the government of the United States;
5. Such organization may be fairly deemed to advocate. . . political or economic changes by radical or revolutionary methods. . .;
6. Such organization is committed to an actual policy and program which sanctions the use of the technique of conspiracy, force. . .and other similar devices to undermine confidence in the government of the United States . . .;
7. Such organization is committed to an actual policy. . . which sanctions the use of techniques enumerated. . . above to deprive any person of rights guaranteed by the the Constitution, or to suppress civil liberties. . .[49]

Attorney General Tom Clark ventured to assure liberals that they had no reason to fear—that the examination of federal employees about to be undertaken by the government would, in effect, stop the smear of all government employees. The attorney general continually vowed there would be no witch hunt but noted that "we are going to separate the chaff from the wheat."[50]

In April of 1947, the Justice Department had some 300 organizations under consideration. Seven months later the number had been reduced to 108. Attorney General Clark, still apparently not completely satisfied, reduced the list to a final eighty-nine organizations, including the forty-seven which had previously been designated by Attorney General Biddle. When the list was released for publication in December 1947, Clark noted that membership in one of the listed organizations should be counted as only one small piece of evidence.[51] "Guilt by association has never been one of the principles of our American Independence. We must be satisfied that reasonable grounds exist."[52]

Earlier, the board of directors of the American Civil Liberties Union had urged that little weight be given to membership in an organization. Activities, stated the board, should be the main criteria. It also voiced the hope that past membership in a listed organization should not be regarded as evidence of disloyalty.[53] Unfortunately such advice was not always heeded.

Before the list was published, there was general criticism that the authority to list subversive groups placed too much power in the hands of the attorney general—by making him alone able to determine who was loyal and who was not loyal.[54] The Justice Department took note of this criticism but denied its validity on the grounds that the attorney general had possessed such power for some time and had always used it "circumspectly." It was also pointed out that such designations were left to the attorney general because he had the best investigative facility in the executive branch, and was subject to the control of the president, should he attempt to use his power in any arbitrary manner.[55]

The attorney general was also charged with arbitrarily listing the eighty-nine organizations without giving them an opportunity to defend themselves. Eleanor Bontecou, in her definitive study of the Truman Loyalty-Security Program, concurs with this allegation.[56] Another contemporary author, Walter Gelhorn, also concludes that "neither the listed organization nor the employee who has had sympathetic association with it enjoys the privilege of trying to show that the attorney general is mistaken."[57]

The first actual test of the legality of the list, the case of *Joint Anti-Fascist Refugee Committee v. McGrath*, came shortly after publication and resulted from the charge that this particular organization had not been granted a fair hearing. Although the decision was inconclusive, it was clear that the court felt the organization had not been given a chance to defend itself, and that its designation as subversive had been made without the presentation of adequate evidence.[58]

Tom Clark pointed out that part of the list had been

in existence since 1943, and that he had felt at the time that it should be published. Relative to the list released in December 1947, Clark stated that the organizations had been contacted, that FBI reports had been considered, and that he personally had made the final determination. He firmly asserted that the organizations that appeared on the final list had, in fact, been given fair hearings. The *Joint Anti-Fascist Committee* case, Clark contended, simply left the false impression that such proceedings had not been conducted. He qualified his remarks, however, when he declared that he had been present personally at only two of the hearings but had "understood" that other officials in the Justice Department had conducted the others. He recalled that after one such inquiry, it had been decided not to name the organization in question. Clark affirmed, however, that he really did not feel that any hearing was necessary—that such a hearing served only as a yardstick.[59] It seemed evident from the start that Clark preferred to judge an organization on the basis of secret, classified data and not on information gathered from an open hearing.[60]

Regardless of the method of designation, the attorney general's "Black List" became the heart of the loyalty program. Henceforth, an employee's acquaintance with the "wrong people," no matter how far in the past or what circumstances accompanied such acquaintances, became prima facie evidence of guilt, and guilt by association became the rule rather than the exception.[61]

A. L. Pomerantz, former senior trial counsel in the Nazi industrialist cases at Nuremburg, denounced the loyalty order in general and the attorney general's list in particular. He contended that the highest ranking Nazis received a more equitable hearing than United States government employees did under the provisions of the president's loyalty order. Although the criminality of certain Fascist organizations was never doubted, it remained necessary to prove that a person had both joined or continued in a particular organization "knowing of its nefarious activities." A government employee, Pomerantz asserted, could be dismissed for nothing more than membership in an organization designated as subversive.[62]

More time should have been taken to examine the character of the various organizations. It was quite possible that a particular group might have been taken over by a Communist group after an employee had joined it, and perhaps without his knowledge.[63] In the course of the investigations, a young psychologist, employed by the Veterans Administration, found himself in considerable difficulty because he had been a member of the American Labor Party of New York in 1938-1939, although that organization had not significantly been influenced by the Communists until much later.[64] For the government to consider membership in that particular organization as suspect was unjustified.

It was also impossible to state with finality that the American Communists had invariably followed the dictates of the Kremlin leaders. It is not beyond reason to suggest that a person might have joined or remained in an organization with full knowledge of its Communist background but without any evil or disloyal intent.[65] Professor Henry Steele Commager presented an interesting observation in that regard.

> If the presence of 'subversives' in an organization is enough to persuade us to drop our membership, all the Communists need to do to destroy our society—say the Republican Party or the American Legion or the Methodist Church—is to join it.[66]

Shortly after publication of the list, Seth Richardson, chairman of the Loyalty Review Board, assured government employees that they should feel free to join any organization, "liberal or conservative, which is not disloyal."[67] Such a statement represented a gross oversimplification of the problem and demonstrated a fundamental weakness of the whole loyalty program. How was an individual to distinguish, precisely, between what was liberal, conservative, or disloyal? It was impossible to make concise, clear-cut distinctions. What one individual might see as a liberal cause, another might view as flagrant disloyalty. As an example, in the late 1920s the American Medical Association branded as Communistic an attempt to extend medical care to veterans for nonservice-related illnesses.[68]

In spite of the criticisms, the organizational lists continued to grow, accompanied by increased fear and anxiety among government employees who searched their minds for past acquaintances who might incriminate them. The total effect was an unhealthy trend toward conformity, which all too often came to be associated with loyalty. To be different, to voice different opinions, indeed, to be creative, might well mark one as suspect. The situation was comparable, as Professor Commager pointed out, to Benjamin Franklin's story of the two Quaker sisters: "I know not how it is, sister, but the older I get the more I find that no one is right but me and thee, and sometimes I am troubled about thee."[69]

The one lesson that should have been learned from the loyalty program was that total security was simply not possible unless the government resorted to the kind of police-state tactics from which the nation was supposed to be protected. Loyalty investigations could and should have been limited to sensitive areas. Instead, under the provisions of Executive Order 9835, the government found itself engaged in the investigation of thousands of people who would never see nor have any access to a classified document.

> The inconspicuous ichthyologist of the Fish and Wildlife service knows many secrets. . .but they are the secrets of the speckled trout rather than the secrets of national defense. . . .Yet the political views and the associations of all these men. . .have been a matter of government scrutiny almost as though they were entrusted with the latest development in chemical warfare. . . .[70]

Such all-inclusive investigation left many wounds, and, in the end, exposed few real subversives.[71] A view of some of the investigations conducted under the loyalty order demonstrated that situation rather clearly.

Far too often, the decision rendered in a loyalty case depended on how the members of a particular board felt about loyalty. Socialism was often confused with communism, and on one occasion an employee was declared a suspect because he had been "in sympathy with the underprivileged."[72] An individual considered too liberal might also be under suspicion. The author of a letter published in the *New York Times,* July 21, 1947, voiced concern over such a possibility. He received a phone call from someone in the State Department requesting information about an acquaintance who was thought to be "pretty liberal in his thinking."[73] Again, in one hearing, a witness for the defense was asked if the defendant had ever expressed himself on Russian composers.[74] To say the least, such inane questions amounted, over a period of time, to a tremendous waste of time and human resources.

Doubtless the Federal Bureau of Investigation, an organization highly trained to prevent subversive activities, wasted a great deal of time compiling page after page of material that added up to little more than rumor and gossip. This is best illustrated by the seventy-two witnesses interviewed by the bureau to determine if a Negro man was acceptable for a position as a part-time postman, in light of the revelation that his wife, some fifteen years before, had contributed money to an organization on the attorney general's list.[75]

A more serious consequence of the loyalty program was the tendency on the part of many to brand as disloyal those who spoke out on racial matters. The increased demand for civil rights no doubt contributed to such fantasy. Abraham Flaxer, president of the United Public Workers of America, brought this to Truman's attention in a letter dated November 24, 1948.[76] Two days later, Truman received a letter from Walter

White, secretary of the National Association for the Advancement of Colored People, who also noted the "increasing tendency on the part of government agencies to associate activity on interracial matters with disloyalty."[77] Walter Gellhorn confirmed this charge when he revealed the following statement made to him one day by the chairman of a departmental loyalty board.

> Of course, the fact that a person believes in racial equality doesn't *prove* that he's a Communist, but it certainly makes you look twice, doesn't it? You can't get away from the fact that racial equality is part of the Communist line.[78]

There were other instances reported of such confused thought. During more than one proceeding, the defendants were asked to give their thoughts on interracial marriage.[79] In one particular hearing, the employee was asked how she felt about the mixture of white and Negro blood in a Red Cross blood bank.[80] Such absurd questions were perhaps exceptions, but they appeared too frequently to be overlooked, and represented an unwarranted intrusion into the personal beliefs of federal employees.

Perhaps the most blatant example of disregard for the rights of government employees occurred in the dismissal of Dorothy Bailey in March of 1948. Miss Bailey, forty-one years of age with fourteen years of government service, was fired from her job as a clerk in the United States Employment Service. Throughout the proceedings, she was never allowed to confront the witnesses who furnished the critical evidence against her. Bailey denied their charges and appealed to the Loyalty Review Board which subsequently upheld the earlier decision against her. In answer to the charge that the witnesses against Dorothy Bailey had offered little more than gossip, Seth Richardson replied that the confidential informants had been "certified to us by the FBI as experienced and entirely reliable."[81]

Bailey felt she had been denied a fair hearing and carried her appeal to the courts. On April 30, 1951, the Supreme Court, unable to reach a majority decision, allowed the judgment of the United States Circuit Court of Appeals, which had earlier upheld the Bailey dismissal, to stand.[82] Justice Henry W. Edgerton of the circuit court, in a dissenting opinion, asserted that her "dismissal violates both the Constitution and the loyalty order. . . ."[83] Associate Supreme Court Justice Douglas, in his dissenting opinion in the Bailey case, stated that:

> She was on trial for her reputation, her job, her professional standing. A disloyalty trial is the most crucial event in the life of a civil servant. If condemned, he is branded for life as a person unworthy of trust. . . .To make that condemnation without meticulous regard for the decencies of a fair trial is abhorrent to fundamental justice.[84]

It was apparent that "meticulous regard for. . .a fair trial" was absent in the hearings afforded Dorothy Bailey. She was not allowed to confront her accusers, and was not made completely cognizant of the basis of the charges against her before the first hearing.[85] The Circuit Court of Appeals frankly admitted that Bailey had not been afforded a fair trial in the true sense of the word, but concluded that the interests of the government must prevail.[86] It would seem, however, as Justice Hugo Black concluded, that the interests of the government were not best served in the kind of proceedings conducted against Dorothy Bailey, as it would have been in a vigorous defense of individual rights as outlined in the First Amendment of the United States Constitution.[87]

As of March 1, 1948, it was reported that 420,000 federal employees had been examined under the Truman Loyalty Order. Of that number, 399 cases had warranted further investigation, 66 had been cleared, and 25 people had resigned before the investigation was completed. Evidence of disloyalty, it was reported, had been found in only eight cases.[88] Such figures indicate clearly (1) that the hysteria over Communist influence in government was without any basis in fact, and (2) that there was no apparent need for such a widespread investigation of government employees. The latter situation became even more apparent with the report issued in December of 1949, which indicated that not one subversive had been uncovered in the investigation of over two million employees.[89] With regard to individual liberties, Tom Clark asserted in September 1948 that the vigorous proceedings against "subversive" elements did "not in the slightest degree infringe upon personal liberties so precious to every true American."[90]

Clark doubtless hoped that such was the case, but a considerable body of evidence indicates that it was not. There were constant infringements upon personal rights—not intended in all cases but infringements nevertheless. The figures show few actual dismissals, but the serious impact upon the thousands of individuals who suffered through investigations, who were ultimately cleared, and who were then forced to live with the idea that their files could be reopened repeatedly for any future investigation, can never be measured.

If the attorney general voiced a bit of overoptimism in his assertion that the rights of the individual had been fully protected, those who cried "witch-hunt" were just as mistaken. There is no reason to doubt Truman's sincerity when he expressed his desire for the individual to be protected. For the most part, the loyalty program was administered with moderation. That point has been overlooked by a number of historians, who collectively contended that the administration somehow created the post-World War II Red hysteria. Such a thesis, as Alonzo Hamby has succinctly noted, "rests upon a naive theory of causation, assuming that the Truman administration caused the cold war and that it could have prevented the McCarthy upsurge by refraining from anti-

Communist policies and rhetoric. It seems far more likely that an administration. . .clinging tenaciously to Popular-Frontism would have suffered lethal right-wing assaults long before 1949."[91]

The Truman Loyalty Program was an honest and sincere attempt not only to reconcile security and individual freedom, but just as surely to quiet the fears engendered by extremists, and to head off more drastic measures already proposed by Congress. The program was, in that respect, considered a necessary evil. Perhaps Truman should have taken heed of President Andrew Jackson's view on such a matter, who stated in his veto of the Bank Bill in 1832, that "there are no necessary evils in government."[92]

Before Truman is judged too harshly, in fact, some distinction must be made between the wishes of the president and the wishes of those in Congress who had been demanding action for some time. Certainly the revelations of past espionage activities and the very temper of the times required some positive response. It was infinitely better that the president, who had demonstrated more than a superficial concern for individual rights, should be the one to take the initiative. In the final analysis, however, the president's program was too broad and depended far "too much for comfort upon the restraint and wisdom of individuals." The results left much to be desired.[93]

By the fall of 1948, there was already talk among administration officials of a possible "overdosage" of internal security, and suggestions for improvement of the loyalty-security program were under discussion.[94] The president's troubles with Congress over this issue had mounted rapidly, and an earlier prediction that the Congress would devote considerable attention to the Communist problem in 1948 had undoubtedly come to pass.[95]

NOTES

1. Rules to govern loyalty procedures in Treasury Department, Loyalty Folder, Vanech Papers, Truman Library.

2. *See* Appendix B.

3. Rules to govern loyalty procedures in Treasury Department Loyalty Folder, Vanech Papers, Truman Library.

4. Ibid.

5. Ibid.

6. Harold W. Chase, *Security and Liberty: The Problem of Native Communism, 1947-55* (Garden City, N.Y.: Doubleday, 1955), pp. 43-44.

7. Newspaper article pertaining to Professor Colston Warne's refusal to fill out loyalty questionnaire, OF 252K, Truman Papers, Truman Library.

8. Statement, Truman on Loyalty Program, OF 252K, Truman Papers, Truman Library.

9. Alan Harper, "The Free Speech Issue in Post-World War II Reconstruction" (Paper read before the American Historical Association, Pacific Coast Branch, Los Angeles, California, August 27, 1964).

10. Resolution, National Society of Sons of the American Revolution, OF 252K, Truman Papers, Truman Library.

11. U.S., *Congressional Record*, 80th Congress, 1st sess., 1947, 93, pt. 2, p. 2461.

12. Memorandum to White House from "W. J. H.," June 13, 1947, OF 252K, Truman Papers, Truman Library.

13. *New York Times*, May 14, 1947.

14. Yale University professors to the President, November 26, 1947, OF 252K, Truman Papers, Truman Library.

15. National Lawyers Guild to the President, June 12, 1947, Loyalty File, Vanech Papers, Truman Library.

16. *New York Times*, April 15, 1947.

17. Statement, Does The President's Loyalty Order Violate Civil Rights?, Loyalty File, Vanech Papers, Truman Library.

18. Zechariah Chafee, *The Blessings of Liberty* (New York: J. B. Lippincott, 1952), p. 34.

19. *New York Times*, December 31, 1947.

20. Francis Biddle, *The Fear of Freedom* (Garden City, N. Y.: Doubleday, 1952), pp. 205-7.

21. *New York Times*, December 6, 1947.

22. Henry S. Commager, ed., *Documents of American History*, vol. 2, *Since 1898*, 8th ed. (New York: Appleton-Century-Crofts, 1968), p. 147.

23. David Fellman, *The Limits of Freedom* (New Brunswick, N. J.: Rutgers University Press, 1959), pp. 106-7.

24. Barton J. Bernstein and Allen J. Matusow, eds., *The Truman Administration: A Documentary History* (New York: Harper & Row, 1966), p. 398.

25. *New York Times*, July 18, 1948.

26. Report, National Lawyers Guild: Analysis of Executive Order 9835, Loyalty File, Vanech Papers, Truman Library.

27. Biddle, *Fear of Freedom*, p. 212.

28. David M. Levitan, "The Responsibility of Administrative Officials in a Democratic Society," *Political Science Quarterly* 61 (December 1946):588.

29. *Washington Post*, December 18, 1947.

30. Biddle, *Fear of Freedom*, p. 215.

31. Chafee, *Blessings of Liberty*, p. 94.

32. Eleanor Bontecou, *The Federal Loyalty-Security Program* (Ithaca, N. Y.: Cornell University Press, 1953), p. 151.

33. Ibid., p. 64.

34. Ibid., p. 31.

35. Harry S. Truman, *Memoirs*, vol. 2., *Years of Trial and Hope* (Garden City, N. Y.: Doubleday, 1956), p. 281.

36. *New York Times*, November 4, 1947.

37. Ibid., December 29, 1947.

38. Ibid., December 28, 1947.

39. Ibid.

40. Cabell Phillips, *The Truman Presidency: The History of a Triumphant Succession* (New York: Macmillan Co., 1966), p. 362.

41. C. Girard Davidson to Clark Clifford, December 29, 1947, Loyalty Folder, Murphy Files, Truman Library.

42. Bontecou, *Federal Loyalty-Security Program*, pp. 60-61.

43. *New York Times*, December 28, 1947.

44. Ibid., November 9, 1947.

45. Ralph S. Brown, Jr., *Loyalty and Security: Employment Tests in The United States* (New Haven, Conn.: Yale University Press, 1958), p. 588.

46. Phillips, *The Truman Presidency*, pp. 361-62.

47. Bontecou, *Federal Loyalty-Security Program*, pp. 159-60.

48. Ibid., pp. 160-67.

49. *See* Appendix C for specific criteria for designating organizations.

50. Draft, Message from the Attorney General, April 14, 1947, Loyalty Folder, Vanech Papers, Truman Library.

51. *Newsweek*, December 15, 1947, p. 23.

52. *New York Times*, December 5, 1947.

53. Statement, Comments by American Civil Liberties Union on Loyalty tests for Government Employees, April 7, 1947, Loyalty Folder, Vanech Papers, Truman Library.

54. *New Republic*, April 14, 1947, p. 13.

55. Note, To Gus Vanech from Joseph Duggan, Loyalty Folder, Vanech Papers, Truman Library.

56. Bontecou, *Federal Loyalty-Security Program*, p. 168.

57. Walter Gellhorn, *Security, Loyalty, and Science* (Ithaca, N. Y.: Cornell University Press, 1950), p. 134.

58. Leo Pfeffer, *The Liberties of an American: The Supreme Court Speaks*, 2d ed. (Boston: Beacon Press, 1963), p. 123. The court found that the listing of organizations

without prior notice was unconstitutional. However, there was a quite evident difference of opinion; there were five concurring opinions delivered, none of which would rank as the opinion of the court.

59. Interview with Justice Thomas C. Clark, Washington, D.C., August 22, 1969.

60. Bontecou, *The Federal Loyalty-Security Program*, p. 168.

61. Ibid., p. 174.

62. *New York Times*, May 4, 1947.

63. Norman Thomas, *The Test of Freedom* (New York: W. W. Norton, 1954), pp. 156-57.

64. Gellhorn, *Security, Loyalty, and Science*, p. 147.

65. *New York Times*, April 29, 1947.

66. Henry S. Commager, *Freedom, Loyalty, and Dissent* (New York: Oxford University Press, 1954), p. 104.

67. *New York Times*, December 28, 1947.

68. Gellhorn, *Security, Loyalty, and Science*, p. 135.

69. Commager, *Freedom, Loyalty, and Dissent*, p. 96.

70. Gellhorn, *Security, Loyalty, and Science*, p. 129.

71. Ibid., p. 171.

72. Biddle, *Fear of Freedom*, p. 221.

73. *New York Times*, July 21, 1947.

74. Bontecou, *The Federal Loyalty-Security Program*, p. 142.

75. Biddle, *Fear of Freedom*, p. 241.

76. Abraham Flaxer to the President, November 24, 1948, OF 252K, Truman Papers, Truman Library.

77. Walter White to the President, November 26, 1948, OF 252K, Truman Papers, Truman Library.

78. Gellhorn, *Security, Loyalty, and Science*, p. 152.

79. Biddle, *Fear of Freedom*, p. 222.

80. Bontecou, *The Federal Loyalty-Security Program*, p. 138.

81. Quoted in Phillips, *The Truman Presidency*, pp. 351-52.

82. Bontecou, *The Federal Loyalty-Security Program*, p. 231.

83. Quoted in Carey McWilliams, *Witch Hunt: The Revival of Heresy* (Boston: Little Brown, 1950), p. 18.

84. Herman C. Pritchett, *Civil Liberties and the Vinson Court* (Chicago: University of Chicago Press, 1954), p. 97.

85. Bontecou, *The Federal Loyalty-Security Program*, pp. 118-19.

86. Ibid., p. 229.

87. Ibid., p. 221.

88. *Time*, March 1, 1948, p. 13.

89. McWilliams, *Witch Hunt*, p. 16.

90. Speech, Tom Clark to Des Moines Trades and Labor Assembly, September 6, 1948, White House Assignment, Spingarn Papers, Truman Library.

91. Alonzo L. Hamby, *Beyond The New Deal: Harry S. Truman and American Liberalism* (New York: Columbia University Press, 1973), p. 401.

92. Richard H. Current and John A. Garraty, eds., *Words That Made American History: Colonial Times to the 1870's* 2d ed. (Boston: Little Brown, 1965), p. 75.

93. *New York Times*, November 2, 1947. From an article by Arthur Schlesinger, Jr., entitled "What is Loyalty?" A Difficult Question."

94. Memorandum, For the President from Stephen Spingarn, October 15, 1948, White House Assignment, Spingarn Papers, Truman Library.

95. *Newsweek*, January 5, 1948, p. 9.

3
TRUMAN VERSUS THE EIGHTIETH CONGRESS: 1948

It is one of the tragedies of our time that the security program of the United States has been wickedly used by demagogues. . . .

Senator Alben W. Barkley of Kentucky, quoted in a *New York Times* article in June 1948, stressed the urgent need for cooperation between the executive and legislative branches of government, especially in regard to all important matters. The relationship, noted the senator, should consist of the president *and* Congress—not the president *versus* Congress. He further maintained that a president who actively sought such a friendly relationship would find it less difficult to secure passage of his legislative program.[1]

The senator's views, though honorable, must be considered naive in the context of the time. It is obvious that no such friendly relationship ever existed between Harry Truman and the Eightieth Republican Congress. There were numerous areas of conflict but none more spectacular than the one precipitated by the various attempts on the part of Congress to force the president to share the administration of the Loyalty-Security program. From the beginning, a powerful faction within the Congress had insisted that the Truman program did not go far enough, that it had not been conducted in good faith, and that subversives were still allowed to operate with impunity.[2] The prominent Red hunters in Congress set about to correct the situation with stronger restrictive legislation and through a series of long and spectacular investigations, all of which resulted in serious encroachments on the power of the executive.

A certain amount of struggle between the president and Congress is a natural and not an unhealthy part of the American political system. But on occasion, the legislative branch has exerted itself beyond those natural limits. The Eightieth Congress assuredly passed those limits in the latter part of 1947 and throughout 1948. When such legislative encroachments occur, as Truman later noted, "It is the duty of the President to say firmly and flatly 'no.' "[3] That was his response at the time and a necessary one, although its consequences proved unfortunate for the president, for the efficiency of the system, and for the nation as a whole.

The investigative power of Congress may be employed in many useful ways, not the least of which is a check on the executive branch. Truman was aware of that fact, since his own senatorial committee had performed such a function in the period 1942-1945 with its perusal of wartime expenditures. The job was accomplished without fanfare or unnecessary publicity, and without embarrassment to the administration. On the other hand, such committees as the House Committee on Un-American Activities served only to frustrate the executive.[4] The committee performed that function with expertise, as no one could have better testified than Harry Truman.

In October 1947, the house committee, under the chairmanship of J. Parnell Thomas, opened its well-publicized hearings into possible Communist influence in the film industry. Of the forty-one witnesses subpoenaed, nineteen assumed an openly defiant attitude from the start. The "unfriendly nineteen," a self-imposed title, were mostly Hollywood writers and the committee's primary targets. The first group of witnesses to testify, however, were of the more friendly variety.[5]

Such well-known film producers as Jack Warner and Louis B. Mayer admitted there had been Communist activity in Hollywood but said it had been checked.[6] Adolph Menjou, in his testimony on October 22, disliked the use of the phrase "Communist propaganda" but had, he said, "seen things that I thought were against. . .good Americanism. . . ." He heartily endorsed the committee's suggestion that the film industry should produce more anti-Communist pictures.[7]

The proceedings warmed considerably as the committee entered the second phase of its investigation, with the appearance of the less cooperative witnesses. The testimony of writer John Howard Lawson set the tone. Lawson was denied the right to read an opening statement and the hearing went downhill from that point, as the committee pressed the witness for answers and the witness lectured the committee on the substance of true Americanism. In the end, Lawson was forceably removed from the room amidst a chorus of boos and cheers from the galleries.[8]

The Hollywood hearings reached a dramatic climax when the House of Representatives, on November 24, 1947, voted overwhelmingly to issue contempt citations against ten of the "unfriendly nineteen." On that same day, Hollywood executives issued a joint statement from New York, which deplored the actions of the writers and declared that "we will not reemploy any of the ten until such time as he is acquitted, or has purged himself of contempt, and declares under oath that he is not a Communist." The action against the "Hollywood Ten" marked the beginning of a blacklist that, with its expansion, would disastrously affect the lives of many people in the next few years.[9]

There were numerous protests against the Hollywood investigation, especially against the methods employed by certain members of the house committee. Eric Johnson, president of the Motion Picture Association, voiced his disapproval of the intimidating questions asked by committee members. "It seems to me that it is getting dangerously easy to call a man a Communist without proof or reasonable suspicion."[10]

Certain individuals in and out of Congress were quick to rush to the defense of the committee. The national commander of the American Legion, James F. O'Neill, stated that "those who attempted to vilify the committee. . .were trying to inject a phony issue—the Bill of Rights—into the dispute." Speaker of the House of Representatives Joseph W. Martin, Jr., defended the Hollywood investigation as necessary and proper. Martin emphasized the seriousness of the Communist threat and suggested that the nation should "give Edgar [Hoover] the green signal. . . ."[11] Such an extreme statement testifies to the mind and mood of the Eightieth Republican Congress in late 1947.

Before the year was out the president would get a preview of the struggle that was to follow with the House Committee on Un-American Activities—a struggle that was to consume the whole of 1948. In October Representative Claire Hoffman of Michigan, chairman of the House Expenditures Committee, had requested and been refused certain confidential files in possession of the Civil Service Commission. He then appealed to the president, but to no avail.[12] Truman indicated that he had found nothing in Hoffman's request to indicate that the Civil Service Commission had not been altogether correct when it classified the various reports as confidential. On that basis the president refused to interfere with the commission's decision not to release such reports.[13]

In January and February of 1948 the House Appropriations Committee conducted an investigation of the State Department, which turned over a number of its confidential files to that committee. The subsequent release of some of the information contained in those files infuriated the president, and served as a prelude to a final showdown on the question of loyalty files. Within a matter of weeks the House Committee on Un-American Activities demanded pertinent confidential information from the Department of Commerce, which pertained to the prominent atomic scientist and director of the Bureau of Standards, Dr. Edward U. Condon.[14]

In June of 1947 two magazine articles had appeared under the by-line of J. Parnell Thomas which stated that Dr. Condon was a man to be watched. He was later the subject of an investigation by the Loyalty Board of the Department of Commerce and subsequently cleared of any suspicion on February 14, 1948.[15] On March 1 Chairman Thomas, in complete disregard of the determination made by the Commerce Department Loyalty Board, singled out Condon as "one of the weakest links in our atomic security."[16] One of the things Thomas held against Condon was his attempt to acquire a passport to Russia in 1947 in order to attend an international scientific celebration in Leningrad.[17] *The Nation* charged that Thomas, an advocate of military control of atomic energy, had hoped to discredit civilian control by his assault on the character of Dr. Condon.[18]

The heart of the accusations was Condon's acquaintance with certain people regarded as subversive by the FBI. The evidence to sustain such charges was supposedly included in a letter from J. Edgar Hoover to the secretary of the Department of Commerce, W. Averell Harriman, a portion of which was made public in the *Congressional Record*.

> Mr. and Mrs. Condon associated with several individuals connected with the Polish Embassy, among those. . .Ignace Zlotowski. . . .It is also known that Mr. and Mrs. Condon were in contact with several other persons closely associated with this alleged Soviet espionage agent.[19]

However, the part of the letter considered most critical was still in the possession of the Commerce Department. The house committee's request for that portion, and Secretary Harriman's refusal to release it, moved the president to take decisive action.

On March 13, 1948, Truman circulated a "Memorandum to All Officers and Employees in the Executive Branch of the Government," which directed that "all reports, records, and files relative to the loyalty of employees. . .shall be maintained in confidence."[20] The administration acted not without precedent, as the first such issue between a president and a congressional investigative committee occurred in the administration of George Washington, who refused to release reports relative to the disastrous expedition of General Arthur St. Clair.[21] After an examination of all the precedents that related to the executive's power to withhold information, the administration concluded that the president and the various department heads were not bound to disclose papers communicated to them, and that Congress could not compel the department heads to produce information in violation of the orders of the president.[22]

Tom Clark took special note of such precedents and felt that the president took the logical and necessary steps to halt congressional interference.[23] Alan Barth expressed a similar view but declared that such an executive decision "must be guided by a recognition that the executive and legislative branches belong to the same government and are supposed to function as partners."[24] Truman was apparently guided by such a recognition; but in view of the exorbitant demands made on the executive, it appeared that certain factions in Congress were not.

The reaction to the March 13 memorandum reflected a marked division of opinion. Certain members of Congress were quick to defend Truman for his decision to withhold the Condon files. Senator Barkley, for example, stated that the president should in all cases be the final judge of what was to be submitted to Congress in such delicate and important areas as loyalty and security.[25] Some conservative groups expressed a different view. John J. Sullivan of Bosworth, Sullivan and Company, Investment Bankers, protested vehemently the president's decision to withhold the FBI report on Condon.

> On one hand we are told that we must rearm because of the fear of an attack by Russia. . .on the other hand we are told in effect that we must do nothing to weed out of Washington the many Communists who are. . .doing much to sabotage the best interests of the United States.[26]

The large number of other letters that expressed views not unlike Sullivan's prompted Stephen Spingarn, a new member of the White House staff, to suggest that a form letter be drafted in order to explain in detail the president's ideas on the matter of confidential files. It was recommended that such a letter should contain three essential points: (1) That the administration was determined that no disloyal person should work for the government; (2) That the president's loyalty program was working with a quiet effectiveness to eliminate any disloyal employee; (3) That the president was always ready to cooperate to the fullest with any "responsible" congressional committee, but felt that an injustice would be done if loyalty files were released.[27]

Spingarn's final recommendation struck at the heart of the matter. It made it obvious that Truman did not regard those congressional committees engaged in investigations of subversive activity as "responsible" committees, and was therefore determined that they should not have access to confidential files. Such a stand was necessary but nevertheless regrettable, for it brought the president into direct confrontation with the Congress and negated any hope for the kind of harmony suggested earlier by Senator Barkley.

Since other presidents had taken similar positions without such serious impairment in their relations with Congress, it might seem that Truman lacked political tact in the way he handled the situation. But it should be remembered that at few other times in the nation's history was the political atmosphere more highly charged than in the late winter and early spring of 1948. An unreasoned fear pervaded the country—fear of the bomb, of the Communists, of the unknown. There were those who, if not the actual promoters of such fear, were ready to take advantage of it. Perhaps it would have been politically more feasible had the president quietly given his assent to congressional demands, but that was not the Truman way. As Tom Clark remarked, Truman's decisions were never based on political feasibility.[28] There were no ulterior motives in the president's decision to withhold information from Congress; it was an altogether courageous decision in the face of the obvious repercussions. It was based only on Truman's belief that the release of such information to what he considered irresponsible factions would damage the personnel involved, would undermine his own loyalty program, and would therefore serve no useful purpose. Certain members of Congress obviously did not concur with the president's view.

Newsweek reported in mid-April that the relations between the president and Congress had grown steadily worse by the day.[29] Earlier in that month, and three weeks after the Truman memorandum of March 13, the Committee on Un-American Activities demanded for the second time that Secretary Harriman release the loyalty records on Edward U. Condon. Harriman's refusal for the second time led Chairman Thomas of the House committee to predict that a showdown between the executive and Congress was imminent.[30]

The Thomas threat materialized with the introduction of House Resolution 522, an attempt on the part of Congress to force the president to relax his order of March 13. On April 22, 1948, the House of Representatives passed the resolution by a vote of 300 to 29 and "peremptorily" ordered Truman to release the Condon file. The vote was indeed a surprise, as was the large number of Democrats who voted with the majority.[31]

At a presidential press conference the following day, in an obviously petulant mood, Truman reminded the reporters of Thomas Jefferson's observation on John Marshall's statement in the Aaron Burr case: "The Chief Justice has made his decision, now let him enforce it." The president concluded that the House had made its decision and he would like to see them try to enforce it. Presidential Press Secretary Charles G. Ross later corrected Truman's faux pas when he stated that the president had actually cited Andrew Jackson's comment on Marshall's decision in the case of *The Cherokee Nation v. Georgia*.[32]

An editorial in the *Washington Post* on April 23 contended that the president had justifiable reasons to withhold the Condon letter and should have explained them in preference to his terse reference to Andrew Jackson.[33] Truman apparently came to that realization, for a message to Congress was prepared on May 4 which outlined in detail the basis for his decision not to comply with the congressional demand for information that pertained to Condon.

Truman stressed his belief that the release of such information would undermine the integrity of the loyalty program, prejudice the work of the FBI by the exposure of its sources of information, and prove unduly harmful to the individuals involved. He placed especial emphasis on the latter point, and insisted that it was "vital to the carrying out of the employee loyalty program that the rights of Government employees be effectively protected." After a careful evaluation of each point, and a reiteration of his desire to cooperate with Congress whenever possible, the president concluded that the "foregoing considerations convince me that disclosure of the letter to which House Resolution 522 is directed would be contrary to the national interest, and I must therefore decline to transmit it."[34]

The president's determined stand in the face of H. Res. 522 prompted the Congress to move toward more stringent action. Speaker Martin threatened legislation that would have the force of law. Such was already pending before the House Rules Committee in the form of a Joint Resolution, H. J. Res. 342, introduced by Representative Claire Hoffman, which would require the executive branch to turn over any records demanded by Congress.[35] The Hoffman bill, as it emerged from the Rules Committee, also contained provisions for the arrest of any member of Congress or the press who might divulge such confidential information.[36] After vigorous debate, the bill passed the House of Representatives by a vote of 219 to 142.[37]

The Nation charged on May 22 that certain members of Congress wanted the confidential reports for no other purpose than to continue their witch-hunt, and predicted that the Hofman bill would never make it through the Senate.[38] The prediction proved correct. The bill was referred to the Senate Committee on Expenditures but never reported out.[39] Although a crisis of significant proportions had been averted, another was pending.

On April 8, 1948, Senator William F. Knowland of California introduced an amendment to the Atomic Energy Act of 1946, S. 1004, which would permit the Senate to require an FBI investigation into "the character, associations, and loyalty. . ." of each presidential appointee to the Atomic Energy Commission.[40] The Knowland amendment passed the Senate on April 12.[41] It was immediately referred to the House where it was passed on May 3 in lieu of H. R. 5216.[42] Twelve days later Truman vetoed the bill because he felt it would "permit an unwarranted encroachment of the legislative upon the executive branch."[43]

In the debate that followed the veto Senator Claude Pepper sided with the president, and insisted that the Senate had no constitutional right to take such action in regard to presidential appointees. Senator Robert Taft contended that the Senate's assertion of its powers of confirmation was an executive function. In such a case, Taft argued, the FBI as an executive agency should be made available to the Senate.[44] On May 21, the Senate, by a vote of 47 to 29, fell just four votes short of overriding the president's veto.[45]

Legislation embodied in bills such as those proposed by Hoffman, Knowland, et al would have come close to congressional tyranny. The founding fathers were not unaware of such a possibility. Madison, in his Federalist Paper XLVIII, pointed out that "one hundred and seventy-three despots would surely be as oppressive as one."[46] When legislative bodies assert such power, as Alan Barth stated, "only the most vigorous and forceful countervailing power can contain them."[47] The president in his March 13 memorandum and in his veto of the Knowland bill had asserted such "countervailing power." He had won a battle but certainly not the war. Truman's trouble with the Eightieth Congress had just commenced.

In addition to its many investigations Congress also advanced vigorously its legislative power in the struggle with the Truman administration. It had been evident for some time that certain congressmen felt the Truman loyalty program was not being conducted with sufficient vigor and they were determined to force through more restrictive legislation in the loyalty-security field. On March 15, 1948, Representatives Karl Mundt and Richard Nixon, both members of the House Committee on Un-American Activities, introduced H. R. 5852, "A Bill to Combat Un-American Activities by Requiring the Registration of Communist Front Organizations, and for Other Purposes."[48]

In summary form, the Mundt-Nixon bill declared that anyone who attempted to establish a totalitarian dictatorship in the United States would be subject to a prison term of up to ten years, a fine of not more than $10,000, and would suffer automatic loss of citizenship. Communism, by legislative definition, constituted such a totalitarian dictatorship. The most important part of the bill was contained in its provision that required the Communist party and all of its front organizations to register with the Justice Department, to list their officers, and to account for all income and expenditures. The Communist party, but not its front organizations, would also be required to publish a membership list. Front organizations would be determined by the attorney general whose decisions would be subject to judicial review.[49]

One of the major controversies that raged over H. R. 5852

centered on whether the bill would outlaw the Communist party in the United States. Mundt insisted that it would not. He extolled the virtues of the bill and concluded that "only the Communists and their closest allies and associates—their dupes, their front organizations. . .have spoken out in opposition. . . ."[50] Raymond Moley, in his *Newsweek* column, praised the Mundt-Nixon bill as an excellent attempt to deal with the Communist problem, and stated that it went as far toward outlawry of the party as the committee dared.[51]

Jacob Javits of New York declared that the bill, whether so stated or not, would eliminate the Communist party, a move which he opposed. Nevertheless, Javits admitted that the very nature of the bill, supposedly designed to protect the internal security of the United States, made it difficult for any congressman to oppose.[52] Representative George G. Sardowski, Democrat from Michigan, also felt the Mundt-Nixon bill was a not-too-cleverly concealed attempt to destroy the Communist Party U. S. A. "The purpose. . .is obvious—it is to frighten everybody out of every organization except the Republican Party, the Democratic Party, and the Boy Scouts."[53]

In May of 1948, two hopefuls for the Republican presidential nomination, Harold Stassen and Thomas E. Dewey, debated the issue of whether the Mundt-Nixon bill would outlaw the Communist party. Stassen affirmed that it would and that he favored such action. Governor Dewey stated that he had some doubts about the constitutionality of the bill, but did not think that it would outlaw the party; he would oppose it, he said, if that were the case.[54]

The authors of H. R. 5852 continued to deny that their bill would ban any political party, but it is not too difficult to conclude that it would have had that effect. The Communist party—by legislative definition—was found to constitute a totalitarian dictatorship. The bill then provided drastic penalties that could be imposed on anyone who attempted to establish such a dictatorship. In that respect, the provisions of the Mundt-Nixon bill would make it virtually impossible for any party so considered to exist in the United States.[55]

Truman indicated on May 13 his disapproval of any legislation designed to suppress a political party. He expressed a persistent personal belief that "splinter" parties were harmless and should be left alone. Both Truman and his attorney general insisted that bills such as the Mundt-Nixon would serve only to drive the Communists underground and thereby increase the problem of detection. The president implied that he would veto H. R. 5852 if it passed the Congress.[56]

The Democratic National Committee, to provide for such a contingency, prepared a fact sheet which defended the administration's antisubversive program. The committee pointed out that the Communist party had reached its peak strength in the United States in 1932, after twelve years of Republican rule. It was further noted that Attorney General Clark had asked for certain improvements in existing laws on February 5, 1948, and the Congress had responded with the politically motivated Mundt-Nixon bill. In conclusion, the National Committee stressed the effectiveness of the president's loyalty program and its provisions to protect the individual.[57]

The Loyalty-Security Program created by Executive Order 9835, as noted in Chapter II, was a far from perfect instrument, and contained serious inequities. Nevertheless, the president had consistently stressed the need to safeguard individual liberties. That conviction emerged from almost his every comment on the program and ran deeper than mere political rhetoric. The congressional debates on the subject revealed no such consideration with regard to individual rights but rather stressed enforcement continually.

As the final House vote on H. R. 5852 neared in the late spring of 1948, the groups lined up for and against the bill provided a revealing study in contrasts. In favor of the Mundt-Nixon bill were the United States Chamber of Commerce, the American Legion, the Catholic War Veterans, the Veterans of

Foreign Wars, and, not least, the National Association of Retail Grocers. Those groups opposed to the bill were the AFL-CIO, the Americans for Democratic Action, the National Association for the Advancement of Colored People, the Civil Rights Congress, the Progressive Citizens of America, and a group whose support Truman could well have dispensed with, the Communist Party U. S. A.[58] The Democratic National Committee charged that H. R. 5852 was politically motivated. It would appear from the preceding lineup, however, that the primary contest was not so much between the Republicans and Democrats as between the forces on the right and those on the left.

In a full-scale debate on May 18, the House demonstrated a determined mood as it shouted down several efforts to modify H. R. 5852 and adopted by voice vote two amendments that would strengthen it. One amendment, offered by Richard Nixon, defined a particular political organization as Communist if "it is reasonable to conclude that it is under the control of the World Communist movement's directorship." The bill received unexpected eleventh-hour support from liberal Adolph Berle, Jr., who recommended a revision in the definition of communism which he felt was too broad. None was ever made.[59]

The House undertook its final debate on May 19, as Nixon accentuated the urgent need for the Congress to act decisively against communism in the United States.[60] Mundt implored his colleagues to remember that "we Republicans. . .promised the country to move effectively against Communism. . . ."[61] Few were surprised when H. R. 5852 easily passed the House of Representatives by a margin of 319 to 58..[62] There was an immediate and divided reaction to the House passage of the bill.

The *Los Angeles Daily News* reported on May 20 that "the House vote yesterday overwhelming [*sic*] approving the Mundt-Nixon Bill. . .is a public demonstration of lack of faith in a living democracy."[63] An editorial in the *Cleveland Plain Dealer* praised the House's action and declared that the bill would hurt no one other than the Communists. Anyone who opposed it, the editor stated, had followed the party line.[64] Senator Elbert D. Thomas pointed out to his colleagues in the Upper House that there were already twenty-seven laws in the statute books that would effectively do what was intended by the Mundt-Nixon bill. Thomas termed the bill dangerous and most probably unconstitutional.[65] The latter charge was in all probability what eventually doomed the Mundt-Nixon bill in the Senate.

Senator Alexander Wiley announced on May 25 that the Senate Judiciary Committee would open public hearings on H. R. 5852 on the 27th.[66] One of the major questions before the Senate committee involved the constitutionality of the House bill. In the course of the hearings, two Democrats, Tom Clark and John W. Davis, and two Republicans, Charles Evans Hughes, Jr. and Seth Richardson, all furnished written opinions backed by substantial evidence that the bill was unconstitutional. Their opinions evidently prevailed, as H. R. 5852 was never reported from the committee.[67]

In the House debate on H. R. 5852 Representative John A. Carrol of Colorado opposed the bill on the grounds that it was special-interest legislation at the expense of legislation required to meet the needs of the people.[68] Truman for some time had maintained that the best way to combat communism was through legislation that would improve the quality of American life rather than by restrictive measures inherent in such bills as the Mundt-Nixon.

> The menace of Communism lies primarily in those areas of American life where the promose [*sic*] of democracy remains unfulfilled. . . .If some of our people are living in slum housing, and nothing is done about it, that is an invitation to Communism.[69]

Senator Taft confirmed that the foregoing were in fact Truman's views when he assailed the president for one of his many attacks on the Eightieth Congress. Taft declared that Truman had always favored a "soft" approach to communism, and had opposed every attempt by the Congress to stop the spread of that ideology in the United States. "The only remedy he [Truman] can think of is the passage of social welfare laws. . . ."[70]

Although the president had survived the acrimonious debates of the regular session of the Eightieth Congress, those over the Condon file and the Mundt-Nixon bill, the worst was yet to come. The Republicans held their convention in the early summer of 1948, where they nominated Thomas E. Dewey as their presidential candidate and adopted a platform which incorporated much of Truman's domestic program.[71] Truman received the Democratic nomination on July 15 and delivered a short extemporaneous acceptance speech at two o'clock in the morning. In the course of the talk the president announced that the Republican Congress was to be called back into special session on July 26, "turnip day" in Missouri he noted, to afford them the opportunity to make good the promises outlined in their platform.[72]

The challenge was considered by many as a shrewd political move on Truman's part: the Republicans would be forced to confirm or in effect repudiate their own platform.[73] The Congress, of course, ignored the president's legislative recommendations and turned the special session into a sustained investigation of communism. The performance proved invaluable to the administration from a short-range political point of view, as it gave considerable validity to Truman's campaign charge that this was, in fact, the "do-nothing, no good Eightieth Republican Congress."[74] In the final analysis, however, and especially as it pertained to the Communists-in-government issue, the special session of the Republican Congress would prove to be Truman's "Long Parliament." The Pandora's box opened by the investigations provided a wealth of material for the Red hunters to use in harassing the president throughout his remaining years in office.

The session opened with two sets of congressional hearings. A special Senate subcommittee, chaired by Homer Ferguson, Republican of Michigan, investigated the operation of the government's loyalty-security program, while the House Committee on Un-American Activities busied itself with disclosures of Communist spy activities.[75] The latter committee's first star witness, ex-Communist courier Elizabeth Bentley, had been billed by the press as another Mata Hari. Though her physical appearance hardly matched the famous female spy's, her tales of intrigue created as much excitement. In her first public exposure on July 30 she named William W. Remington as a past member of the Communist spy ring in Washington. Remington had been suspended just six weeks before from his job as chairman of a Department of Commerce committee, which handled secret information from many different government offices. Bentley also mentioned "a man around the White House" from whom she had received information.

On the next day Bentley named Lauchlin Currie, who had served as one of Franklin Roosevelt's advisors, as her White House informant. In subsequent testimony she implicated Harry Dexter White from whom she claimed to have received information through Gregory Silvermaster, past employee at the Board of Economic Warfare. Both Currie and White denied the accusations in their entirety. Remington, however, admitted that he gave Bentley, *alias* Helen Johnson, certain pieces of information, but he declared that it amounted to no more than he would have given any member of the press.[76]

The Bentley revelations led to the appearance before the Ferguson subcommittee of Louis F. Budenz, an ex-Communist and a professor of economics at Fordham University. Budenz talked of many spy rings and estimated that the party had placed thousands of its spies in government jobs. In answer to a question from Senator John McClellan, Budenz concluded that it was impossible for any individual to be a member of the

Communist party and remain loyal to the United States.[77]

The Budenz and Bentley revelations were enough to cause dismay, but they fade into obscurity compared with the testimony of Whittaker Chambers, a confessed ex-Communist spy, before the House committee on August 3, 1948. On that day Chambers proclaimed that Alger Hiss, one-time boy wonder of the New Deal, had been an active member of the Communist party. At various times Hiss had been secretary to the late Oliver W. Holmes, an assistant counsel with the Nye Committee, an advisor to the president at Yalta, and active in both the Dumbarton Oaks and San Francisco conferences.[78]

The Hiss case has been examined time and again and it is not within the purview of this study to make a reexamination or to form an opinion as to the guilt or innocence of Alger Hiss. But the case, and in particular the reaction to it, must be examined in the light of its effect on the Truman administration from the moment the charges were first made until Truman left the presidency. After August 3, 1948, the terms "New Deal" and "Communism" became almost synonymous. The forces of conservatism made Alger Hiss not only the representative of sixteen years of liberal democratic rule, but also—and perhaps more importantly—"the symbol and living proof of their contention that the Truman administration was soft on Communism."[79] Truman's reaction to the Chambers-Hiss affair did not unfortunately serve to exonerate either himself or his administration of that charge.

Two days after Whittaker Chambers had made his sensational charges, Harry Truman issued the following statement in regard to the congressional investigations.

> The public hearings now underway are serving no useful purpose. On the contrary, they are doing irreparable harm to certain persons, seriously impairing the morale of Federal employees, and undermining public confidence in the government.[80]

The president should have stopped after these remarks. But at the same news conference on August 5, he characterized the congressional investigations as a "red herring," designed to distract attention from the Republican failure to act on his legislative program.[81] It was a typical Truman response, but it could not have come at a more inopportune time. Such a remark made the president the perfect target for the Fergusons, the Rankins, and all the other self-styled patriots who had been contending for some time that Truman was not really concerned with the problem of Communists in government. It also alarmed further a public already in shock from the many tales of Communist intrigue that had so recently come from the various congressional investigations.[82]

Dean Acheson relates in his *Memoirs* that members of the cabinet and White House staff lived in constant fear of presidential press conferences. Truman's hasty responses to reporters' questions, Acheson noted, "were a constant menace."[83] Actually, such openness was one of Truman's greatest strengths as a man. He "shot from the hip" with a kind of honesty which was, in the midst of so much political double-talk, like a breath of fresh air. Yet, his candor was assuredly a political liability and kept the president almost constantly in hot water. The congressional hearings may well have been a "red herring," but Truman should have known better than to say so. A more tactful response would have been to stress the effectiveness of his own loyalty program and point out that all of the individuals named before the congressional committees had been presented before a New York grand jury in 1947, and none indicted after months of testimony.[84] A detailed chronology of the operations of that special grand jury, as Assistant Secretary of Defense Marx Leva noted, "would reflect credit on the administration."[85]

Tom Clark admitted that the public exposures in 1948 served only to frustrate the Justice Department in its efforts to arrive at a sound basis for the prosecution of those previously named before the grand jury. He further confessed that someone in the Justice Department had furnished the congressional committees with the names of the individuals involved.[86] Although the source of the leak had never been discovered, it has been suggested that the FBI furnished much of the information.[87] Whatever the source, the committees obviously knew what witnesses to call. Chairman Ferguson, still not satisfied, demanded that the administration turn over the loyalty files on a number of people implicated by the committee's star witnesses.

On July 30, Senator Ferguson penned a letter to Secretary of Commerce Charles Sawyer in which he requested "all memoranda or documents relating in any way to the employment of William W. Remington."[88] Three days later Undersecretary of the Treasury E. H. Foley, Jr., notified the White House that Ferguson had asked for both personnel and loyalty files on "7 or 8" Treasury employees. Foley was advised to follow the procedure as outlined for the Department of Commerce; that he was to ask for a request in writing, respectfully to decline it, and then to turn the matter over to the president.[89]

Foley addressed a letter on August 5 to William P. Rogers, chief counsel for Ferguson's subcommittee. He noted that six of the individuals mentioned in the senator's request were former employees, and another was on involuntary leave pending adjudication of loyalty proceedings. Foley concluded that the Senate committee might freely examine any of the personnel files, but the department "would not be in a position to make available any information relating to the loyalty of an employee."[90] To cover the eventuality of any further requests for information on former employees, a letter was sent to all department heads to make it clear that the President's memorandum of March 13 was intended to apply to all records of former employees as well as to persons then employed in the federal service.[91]

Ferguson, clearly displeased with Truman's continued determination to withhold loyalty files, threatened to institute impeachment proceedings against the president. "Presidential arrogance," he declared, "is becoming intolerable."[92] Senator Clyde Hoey of North Carolina voiced approval of Truman's characterization of the spy proceedings as a "red herring," and concluded that far from being threatened with impeachment, the president should be commended for the effectiveness of his loyalty program.[93] Hoey's view, however, did not reflect the majority sentiment.

John Rankin continued to insist that the congressional investigations had proven conclusively that the Truman program was ineffective. The real policy of the chief executive, he remarked, was to "tell Congress one thing and do another." Rankin further charged that the president's refusal to make the loyalty files available to Congress denied the American people access to the truth.[94]

A *Washington Post* editorial of August 11 praised Truman for his stand against the Ferguson committee. The editor implied that the president was on dubious grounds constitutionally, but had upheld the spirit of that document.[95] A later and certainly contradictory editorial stated that Ferguson had asked for only employment records and not loyalty files. The president, it was concluded, should comply with such a request.[96] A member of the White House staff responded with the following short note: "Ferguson did so ask for all."[97]

Two separate articles, which appeared in the *Washington Post*, delineated the two points of view with regard to loyalty files. David Lawrence claimed not to understand the president's reluctance to release such files. He admitted that public disclosure of such information might prove painful to certain individuals but, he concluded, "it's the only way to get at the truth.[98] Walter Lippman offered a different view:

> It has been argued lately that though the injustice to individuals done in this inquiry is regrettable, the national interest is being served so well that it justifies the sacrifice

> of a few innocent persons. That argument is profoundly immoral. It is also profoundly unintellectual.[99]

It was unfortunate that the voices of those who cried for more stringent action drowned out effectively those which expressed the need for more protection of individual rights.

One of the more harmful effects of the congressional inquires resulted from the House committee's investigations in the field of atomic research. In early September, Truman received a letter from a number of atomic scientists who asserted that the Condon affair, and the committee's continued investigation into the scientific field, was so repugnant to the nation's scientists that it would require years to undo the damage.[100]

A *Washington Post* editorial also criticized the committee for its attacks on various scientists. Although the editor felt Truman might have used a better phrase than "red herring," he concluded nevertheless such a characterization of the committee's activities was justifiable. It was also noted that "scientists, being intellectuals, are naturally suspect to the 'know nothing' mentality of members of the Committee on Un-American Activities."[101] The House committee, undeterred by such criticism, continued its search for subversives.

Meanwhile, the Ferguson subcommittee report was released in early September. In general the committee concluded that the loyalty program within the executive branch had not been conducted with sufficient determination to rid the government of subversive or disloyal employees. It was therefore recommended that Congress take some action immediately, although it was noted that the president's continued refusal to release certain pertinent information would severely limit the power of the Congress to do so.[102]

There was some indication in the early part of September that the administration might relax its stand with regard to the withholding of confidential reports. Three days before the

Ferguson report was released, a suggestion was made within the administration that perhaps the president should offer to turn over all of the data on William Remington on condition that the information be kept in strictest confidence. It was further suggested that in the event the committee violated such confidence, the administration should immediately "blast loose that all Ferguson wants. . .is publicity."[103] No action was taken on the recommendation, but it was announced in the press on September 9 that Attorney General Clark and Senator Ferguson had planned to meet and discuss the differences that existed between the president and Congress. It was seen as a major move toward reconciliation on the part of the administration.[104]

At the conclusion of the conference, the press predicted that a compromise was about to be reached and that it had been "tentatively agreed that Attorney General Clark would urge Truman to relax his order withholding the records from Congress."[105] If Truman ever considered such a course, and there is no indication one way or the other, it was quickly shelved and the war of words continued.

On September 22, while on a campaign trip through California, Truman delivered his most stringent attack on the Committee on Un-American Activities, which he described as "more un-American than the activities it is investigating." Many of those who heard the speech voiced surprise at "the vehemence with which the President spoke."[106] A few days later the Justice Department issued a statement which voiced regret over the continued congressional investigations, but reiterated the department's determination not to attempt prosecution on the basis of hearsay evidence.[107] From that point on there was no further talk of any immediate reconciliation between the president and Congress.

As the congressional hearings abated toward the end of August there were speculations as to what effect they might have on Truman and his campaign for the presidency. An article in *Newsweek* declared that Democrats in general were convinced that the "red herring" remark and the continued refusal to release confidential files would hurt Truman in the November election. Many top Democrats, it was noted, had urged him to change his strategy before it was too late.[108] George Elsey indicated that the spy issue constituted the "administration's weakest link. . . ," and suggested the urgent need for strong counteraction. It could no longer be hoped, Elsey said, that public revulsion at the tactics employed by the congressional committees would make the spy issue backfire. It had become evident "that these tactics, however reprehensible. . .are in some ways more effective than the facilities of the Executive branch. . . .There is paydirt here, and the Republicans have no intention of being diverted by appeals from anguished liberals who see the Bill of Rights transgressed."[109]

The administration had made a concerted effort throughout 1948 to free itself from the persistent "soft on communism" charge. A major part of that effort called for the indictment of eleven top Communist leaders in late July under provisions of the 1939 Smith Act.[110] This action perhaps lessened the pressure for a time but disclosures arising in the special session quickly revived the issue. There was "paydirt here," and it seemed more than likely the Republicans would utilize the Communist problem to the full in the November campaign. Senator Wiley of Wisconsin summed up the Republican attitude in the following statement:

> The issue of the Administration's coddling of Reds and Red sympathizers in government is going to be a crucial issue in the coming political campaign. . . .The present administration. . .has served as a fertile breeding ground for Reds during the last sixteen years.[111]

Administration officials continued their efforts to repudiate such charges by emphasizing the positive results of the president's loyalty program. Secretary of Commerce Charles Sawyer, in an address before a Veterans of Foreign Wars encampment, claimed that the congressional investigations had revealed significant espionage activity during the war years, but had failed to show any weakness in the present loyalty-security program. Sawyer emphasized that not one subversive had been found after the investigation of almost two million federal employees.[112]

Truman's best defense of his administration on the Communist issue was made in an address delivered in Oklahoma City on September 28, 1948. The president once again emphasized his personal belief that the United States was strong enough to resist communism and was not endangered by Communist infiltration.

> The Republican Congress however, would like you to believe that none of these things are true. . . .They are holding public hearings and creating scare headlines and hysteria because they want you to overlook their own indifference to the country's real welfare. . . .[113]

The congressional investigations, Truman said, had uncovered no new evidence and had done irreparable harm to the individuals involved. He chided those responsible for the hearings, and asserted that he would continue to withhold confidential information from such irresponsible persons.

The president praised the loyalty program which he said had already indicated that 99.7 percent of federal employees were above suspicion. The program was delayed, he stated, because the Congress had failed to vote sufficient funds. Truman concluded the address with a statement that "the test of an American's patriotism is not how anti-Communist he may be. The German-American Bund was anti-Communist. So was Adolph Hitler."[114]

The Oklahoma City address, stripped of its political rhetoric, was a review of several points the president had stressed in the past: that this country was in no serious danger from Communist infiltration; that the most effective way to fight it was by an improvement in the quality of American life; and that the rights of the individual ought to be protected. On those points Truman had been consistent throughout.

Chairman Thomas of the Committee on Un-American Activities responded to the Truman address in a strongly worded letter of September 29. He charged that the president had been remiss in his duty and had continually thwarted the House committee's attempts to get at the truth. Thomas also challenged Truman's statement that all the information revealed before the congressional committees had been previously known to the administration. He invited the president to back up his statement with facts.[115] Had Truman intended to reply it would have been necessary for him to do so with all dispatch, for in a matter of weeks J. Parnell Thomas would be indicted for fraud and removed from the scene of action. In one of the great ironies of the time the grand inquisitor of the House committee, the man who had on numerous occasions driven witnesses frantic with his abrasive questions, himself refused, on November 8, 1948, to testify before a grand jury on the grounds that it might tend to incriminate him.[116]

Although Thomas was removed from the scene, the committee as well as the issue of Communists in government persisted. Historians have generally agreed that it was not a very significant issue in the campaign of 1948. However, a Gallup poll conducted in September revealed that eight in ten voters felt the spy hearings had unearthed valuable information and disagreed with those—a group that would have included Harry Truman—who charged that such hearings were no more than political in nature.[117] Certainly the polls were wrong about almost everything else in 1948, but it appears that the Communist threat might have been a viable campaign issue.

Dewey did raise the "soft on communism" charge on a number of occasions but only in the mildest of tones. In point of fact, the governor said about the same things as Truman did on the problem of native communism.[118] Perhaps Dewey was too decent a man to stir the witches' brew, or perhaps he felt it would do more harm than good. Whatever the cause, the Republican candidate in 1948, to his credit, simply did not exploit to the full the fear of internal Communist subversion.

The issues notwithstanding, few believed that Truman had more than an infinitesimal chance to continue in the presidency. Richard Rovere, in an article that appeared in *Harper's Magazine*, voiced the universal view of the 1948 election. The author was sympathetic toward the president and recognized the many problems he had faced, but indicated that Truman was, after all, just not big enough for the job. He concluded that "it will be impossible to get rid of him before election time but we will surely do it then."[119]

Rovere was no doubt as red-faced and perplexed as many others when Harry Truman emerged the winner in what has been correctly judged one of the great political upsets of all time. Journalists scurried about for weeks attempting to determine just where the polls went wrong. Truman's campaign strategy had, in fact, worked to perfection. "In a highly personal and emotional way, he sharply contrasted [the Democratic program] with the least popular aspects of the Eightieth Congress and skillfully identified that Congress with the Republican party in general."[120]

In retrospect, a Republican victory in 1948 might well have laid the Communist "bugaboo" to rest. Such was not to be the case. The issue grew and thrived and would continue to plague the president from his moment of triumph in November 1948 until he left the White House in 1953.

Truman had little time to savor his victory before he was thrust suddenly back into political hot water. On December 2, 1948, Whittaker Chambers produced the famous microfilm from the pumpkin on his Maryland farm. The film, allegedly given to Chambers by Alger Hiss, contained various items of diplomatic correspondence that dated back to 1937.[121]

The president, as his later contradictory statements indicated, was obviously shaken by the disclosures. He initially declared that all of the investigative machinery of the government should be employed to determine exactly who was responsible for the theft of the classified documents found on the microfilm. Then, in almost the same breath, he again characterized the committee hearings as a "red herring." Such confused thinking drew immediate criticism from the press which declared that the president should be at least as anxious as the House committee to find out what Chambers really knew.[122]

In private, administration officials expressed the opinion that the Chambers documents amounted to little more than harmless correspondence that would have been of no value to a foreign government. They noted, however, that the "general public rarely reads the views of first-rate experts. . . ." It was a fact that nations were going to spy; the question was whether it could be kept at a safe level. But antiadministration groups had attempted to show "that any success by any foreign agent in spying on our government is necessarily catastrophic. . . ."[123] The report concluded with a word of praise for Truman, and his opinion of the spy hunters in Congress.

> The President seems to have been almost the only person who had such people and their outpourings sized up right. He never gave them an inch. He might have added that not only their excitement, but themselves, were red herrings.[124]

Other sources had openly questioned the importance of the Chambers documents. The *Washington Post* reported that it was impossible to see how the publication of such bland diplomatic correspondence could in any way endanger world peace then or now.[125]

John Rankin attempted to answer such an opinion in the House committee's report on the Hiss proceedings. He pointed out that some of the recovered documents had been in code, which if it had been broken would have undermined our entire intelligence apparatus. Rankin added that "State Department officials have testified that publication of some of these documents even today. . .would endanger national security."[126] In conclusion, he praised the work of the House committee, and strongly suggested the need for legislation of the kind embodied in the Mundt-Nixon bill.[127]

There is little doubt that the discovery of the pumpkin papers, whatever their value, greatly enhanced the prestige of the Committee on Un-American Activities. Cabell Phillips, in a *New York Times* article, reported that the Justice Department had been "outsmarted by the House committee."[128] The conservative former Republican congressman, Hamilton Fish, wrote a letter to the president in which he attacked him for his continued denunciation of the House committee and its work. Fish made much of Alger Hiss and his various appointive positions and concluded his letter, in all capitals for emphasis, with the following demand: "LET NO GUILTY MAN OR WOMAN ESCAPE, NO MATTER HOW IMPORTANT OR POWERFUL, DEAD OR ALIVE."[129]

The reputation of the committee was somewhat tarnished when certain members on December 23 released testimony that pertained to Lawrence Duggan, who had just days before fallen or leaped to his death from his office window in New York. Karl Mundt's statement in connection with the incident, as reported by the *Washington Post* but denied by Mundt himself, did not help matters. When asked by a reporter if any further names would be released, the South Dakota Republican was reported to have replied, "We will give them out as they jump out of windows."[130] Both Mundt and Nixon later stated their regret over the Duggan incident and proposed a nine-point code of procedure to give greater protection to witnesses who would appear in the future.[131]

As the year drew to a close, there was still the general

uneasiness in the country that had characterized the American scene throughout 1948. The election had stilled the spy scare roused by the Bentley and Chambers revelations, but the discovery of the stolen microfilm and the uncertainty that surrounded it had just as surely revived the issue. The spy hunt, as it gained strength throughout December, promised to carry over into 1949.

NOTES

1. *New York Times*, June 20, 1948.
2. U.S., *Congressional Record*, 80th Congress, 2d sess., 1948, 94, pt. 10, p. A2530.
3. Quoted in Alan Barth, *Government by Investigation* (New York: Viking Press, 1955), p. 219.
4. Ibid., p. 61.
5. Stefan Kanfer, *A Journal of The Plague Years* (New York: Atheneum, 1973), pp. 40-41. The author, a film critic and associate editor of *Time* Magazine, has written a lucid account of show-business blacklisting. For a more detailed study, see John Cogley's two-volume work, *Report on Blacklisting*, published by the Fund for the Republic.
6. *New York Times*, October 21, 1947.
7. Eric Bentley, ed., *Thirty Years of Treason: Excerpts from Hearings before the House Committee on Un-American Activities, 1938-1968* (New York: Viking Press, 1971), pp. 120-21.
8. Ibid., pp. 153-60.
9. Kanfer, *The Plague Years*, pp. 74-75.
10. *New York Times*, October 28, 1947.
11. Ibid., November 4, 1947.
12. Ibid., October 10, 1947.
13. Truman to Claire Hoffman, October 21, 1947, Internal Security File, Elsey Papers, Truman Library.
14. Harry S. Truman, *Memoirs*, vol. 2, *Years of Trial and Hope* (Garden City, N.Y.: Doubleday, 1956), p. 282.
15. U.S., *Congressional Record*, 80th Congress, 2d sess., 1948, 94, pt. 4, pp. 4779-80.
16. *Newsweek*, March 15, 1948, p. 25.
17. U.S., *Congressional Record*, 80th Congress, 2d sess., 1948, 94, pt. 4, pp. 4779-80.
18. *Nation*, March 13, 1948, p. 303.
19. U.S., *Congressional Record*, 80th Congress, 2d sess., 1948, 94, pt. 4, p. 4778.
20. *See* Appendix D.
21. Barth, *Government by Investigation*, p. 31.
22. Conclusions, after study of precedents relating to the withholding of confidential papers, Internal Security File, Elsey Papers, Truman Library.

23. Interview with Justice Thomas C. Clark, Washington, D.C., August 22, 1969.

24. Barth, *Government by Investigation*, p. 39.

25. U.S., *Congressional Record*, 80th Congress, 2d sess., 1948, 94, pt. 3, p. 2930.

26. John J. Sullivan to the President, April 28, 1948, OF 252K, Truman Papers, Truman Library.

27. Memorandum, from Stephen J. Spingarn on the subject of a letter to explain the president's views on withholding confidential files, Internal Security File, Spingarn Papers, Truman Library. Stephen Spingarn joined the White House staff in 1948. He was one of the more liberal of the group and was particularly active in the loyalty-security field. Spingarn's background no doubt contributed to his liberalism. He was the son of Joel E. Spingarn, an outstanding liberal academician who was one of the leaders in the formation of the NAACP in 1909.

28. Interview with Justice Thomas C. Clark.

29. *Newsweek*, April 19, 1948, p. 22.

30. *New York Times*, April 8, 1948.

31. Ibid., April 23, 1948.

32. *Newsweek*, May 3, 1948, p. 18.

33. *Washington Post*, April 24, 1948.

34. Draft, presidential message to Congress on withholding Condon file, May 4, 1948, Internal Security File, Elsey Papers, Truman Library.

35. *New York Times*, April 25, 1948.

36. Ibid., May 6, 1948.

37. U.S., *Congressional Record*, 80th Congress, 2d sess., 1948, 94, pt. 5, p. 5822.

38. *Nation*, May 22, 1948, p. 563.

39. U.S., *Congressional Record*, 80th Congress, 2d sess., 1948, 94, pt. 13, p. 639.

40. Ibid., pt. 3, p. 4248.

41. Ibid., pt. 4, p. 4311.

42. Ibid., p. 5194.

43. Ibid., pt. 5, p. 5895.

44. Ibid., p. 6194.

45. Ibid., p. 6264.

46. Quoted in Barth, *Government by Investigation*, p. 7.

47. Ibid., p. 5.

48. U.S., *Congressional Record*, 80th Congress, 2d sess., 1948, 94, pt. 2, p. 2893.

49. Memorandum, To President from Clifford, Comments on Lowenthal's memorandum, "The Sedition Bills of 1949" Summary of Mundt-Nixon bill of 1948, Sedition Bills of 1949 File, Clifford Papers, Truman Library.

50. U.S., *Congressional Record*, 80th Congress, 2d sess., 1948, 94, pt. 10, p. A2659.

51. *Newsweek*, May 10, 1948, p. 88.

52. U.S., *Congressional Record*, 80th Congress, 2d sess., 1948, 94, pt. 5, p. 5866.

53. Ibid., p. 5878.

54. Memorandum, For the President from Clifford, Summary of Stassen-Dewey debate on Mundt-Nixon bill, April 29, 1949, Sedition Bills of 1949 File, Clifford Papers, Truman Library.

55. *Nation*, May 29, 1948, p. 594.

56. Article, *New York Herald Tribune*, May 14, 1948, Democratic National Committee Clipping File, Truman Library.

57. Fact Sheet No. 11, *Communism and Loyalty*, 1948, Democratic National Committee Clipping File, Truman Library.

58. Memorandum, To the President from Clifford, April 29, 1949, Sedition Bills of 1949 File, Clifford Papers, Truman Library.

59. *New York Times*, May 19, 1948.

60. U.S., *Congressional Record*, 80th Congress, 2d sess., 1948, 94, pt. 5, p. 6146.

61. Ibid., p. 6148.

62. Ibid., p. 6149.

63. Article, From *Los Angeles Daily News*, May 20, 1948, Democratic National Committee Clipping File, Truman Library.

64. Article, From *Cleveland Plain Dealer*, June 17, 1948, Democratic National Committee Clipping File, Truman Library.

65. U.S., *Congressional Record*, 80th Congress, 2d sess., 1948, 94, pt. 11, p. A3547.

66. U.S., *Congressional Record*, 80th Congress, 2d sess., 1948, 94, pt. 5, p. 6376.

67. Memorandum, To the President from Clifford, summary of Senate Hearings on Mundt-Nixon bill, 1948, April 29, 1949, Sedition Bills of 1949 File, Clifford Papers, Truman Library.

68. U.S., *Congressional Record*, 80th Congress, 2d sess., 1948, 94, pt. 5, p. 5869.

69. Statement, Truman on Communism, Box 14, Democratic National Committee Clipping File, Truman Library.

70. *New York Times*, June 12, 1948.

71. *Newsweek*, July 5, 1948, p. 21.

72. *U.S. News and World Report*, July 23, 1948, p. 67.

73. Ibid., August 6, 1948, p. 25.

74. Susan Hartmann, *Truman and the 80th Congress* (Columbia: University of Missouri Press, 1971), p. 202.

75. *New York Times*, September 12, 1948.

76. *Time*, August 9, 1948. One of the best accounts of the Bentley affair can be found in Earl Latham's book. Those named by Elizabeth Bentley continually denied her accusations, but Latham contends that most of what she said was correct. Remington was later sent to prison for perjury and subsequently killed in a fight among some inmates. Harry Dexter White died of a heart attack a few days after he testified before the House Committee on Un-American Activities in August 1948. There was speculation that White had died from an overdose of sleeping pills but that has never been confirmed.

77. *New York Times*, August 3, 1948.

78. *Time*, August 16, 1948, pp. 18-19. Alger Hiss was eventually convicted on two counts of perjury—that he had lied when he said he had never turned over any documents to Chambers, and when he denied that he had ever seen Chambers, *alias* George Crosley, after January 1, 1937. The most incriminating piece of evidence was the Hill typewriter on which the stolen documents were typed.

79. Cabell Phillips, *The Truman Presidency: The History of a Triumphant Succession* (New York: Macmillan Co., 1966), p. 372.

80. Statement by the President, August 5, 1948, OF 252K Truman Papers, Truman Library.

81. *New York Times*, August 6, 1948.

82. Eric F. Goldman, *The Crucial Decade and After: America 1945-1960* (New York: Alfred A. Knopf, 1966), p. 118.

83. Dean Acheson, *Present at the Creation: My Years in the State Department* (New York: W.W. Norton, 1969), p. 192.

84. Alonzo L. Hamby, *Beyond the New Deal: Harry S. Truman and American Liberalism* (New York: Columbia University Press, 1973), p. 380.

85. Memorandum, For Clifford from Marx Leva, August 4, 1948, Internal Security File, Elsey Papers, Truman Library.

86. Interview with Justice Thomas C. Clark.

87. Corliss Lamont, *Freedom Is as Freedom Does: Civil Liberties Today* (New York: Horizon Press, 1956), p. 61.

88. Homer Ferguson to Charles Sawyer, July 30, 1948, Internal Security File, Elsey Papers, Truman Library.

89. Memorandum, To Clifford from Elsey, August 2, 1948, Internal Security File, Elsey Papers, Truman Library.

90. E. H. Foley, Jr., to William Rogers, August 2, 1948, Internal Security File, Elsey Papers, Truman Library.

91. Donald Dawson to heads of Executive Departments and Agencies, August 5, 1948, OF 252K, Truman Papers, Truman Library.

92. *New York Times*, August 8, 1948.

93. Ibid., August 9, 1948.

94. U.S., *Congressional Record*, 80th Congress, 2d sess., 1948, 94, pt. 8, p. 9783.

95. *Washington Post*, August 11, 1948.

96. Ibid., August 15, 1948.

97. Note, From George Elsey, Internal Security File, Elsey Papers, Truman Library.

98. *Washington Post*, August 4, 1948.

99. Ibid., August 17, 1948.

100. Harrison Brown et al to Truman, September 6, 1948, White House Assignment, Spingarn Papers, Truman Library.

101. *Washington Post*, September 15, 1948.

102. *New York Times*, September 5, 1948.

103. Unsigned note, September 1, 1948, Internal Security File, Elsey Papers, Truman Library.

104. *New York Times*, September 9, 1948.

105. *Newsweek*, September 20, 1948, p. 19.

106. *New York Times*, September 23, 1948.

107. Statement, By the Department of Justice, September 29, 1948, White House Assignment File, Spingarn Papers, Truman Library.

108. *Newsweek*, August 30, 1948, p. 15.

109. "Random Thoughts," August 26, 1948, Internal Security File, Elsey Papers, Truman Library.

110. Harold Chase, *Security and Liberty: The Problem of Native Communism,*

1947-1955 (Garden City, N.Y.: Doubleday, 1955), p. 27.

111. U.S., *Congressional Record*, 80th Congress, 2d sess., 1948, 94, pt. 12, p. A4867.

112. Address, Secretary of Commerce Charles Sawyer, August 30, 1948, White House Assignment File, Spingarn Papers, Truman Library.

113. Draft, Presidential Message on Communist and National Security, September 24, 1948, White House Assignment File, Spingarn Papers, Truman Library.

114. Ibid.

115. Parnell Thomas to the President, September 29, 1948, OF 320B, Truman Papers, Truman Library.

116. *New York Times*, November 9, 1948.

117. *Washington Post*, September 5, 1948.

118. Irwin Ross, *The Loneliest Campaign: The Truman Victory of 1948* (New York: New American Library, 1968), pp. 298-99.

119. Richard H. Rovere, "President Harry," *Harper's Magazine* (July 1948) 197:30.

120. Hartmann, *Truman and the 80th Congress*, p. 210.

121. *Time*, December 13, 1948, p. 23.

122. *Washington Post*, December 10, 1948.

123. Article, "The So-Called Spy Bills," January 25, 1949, Internal Security Folder, Clifford Papers, Truman Library.

124. Ibid.

125. *Washington Post*, December 9, 1948.

126. U.S., *Congressional Record*, 80th Congress, 2d sess., 1948, 94, pt. 12, p. A5353.

127. Ibid., p. 5355.

128. *New York Times*, December 19, 1948.

129. Hamilton Fish to the President, December 23, 1948, OF 320B, Truman Papers, Truman Library.

130. *Washington Post*, December 24, 1948. Lawrence Duggan had served as chief of the Latin American division of the Department of State. Although he was accused by Whittaker Chambers, his involvement with the Washington spy ring was never confirmed. On December 24, Attorney General Clark stated that there was no substantial proof that Duggan was ever a Communist.

131. *New York Times*, December 28, 1948.

4
TRUMAN VERSUS THE EIGHTY-FIRST CONGRESS: JANUARY 1, 1949-AUGUST 1, 1950

The demagogues, crackpots, and professional patriots had a field day pumping fear into the American people.

Truman opened the new year with a plan for cooperation with the Eighty-first Congress in the enactment of his Fair Deal program. The Democratic success in the elections of 1948 had perhaps buoyed the president's hopes for a more tranquil and productive 1949.[1] Although the relations between Truman and Congress improved somewhat, it was another year of frustration for the administration. But, in retrospect, it can be seen as the best year Truman had until he left the presidency.

The Communist issue, although to some extent subdued when compared with the struggles of 1948, was still very much in evidence. Truman's old nemesis, the House Committee on Un-American Activities, was ever active and a force to be reckoned with, as communism had become its raison d'être. On January 1 the committee announced that the federal service was still infested with Reds and issued the call for more public vigilance and the enactment of the Mundt-Nixon bill.[2]

Before the end of January, events in China boded ill for the future of the Truman administration. On January 21, 1949, Generalissimo Chiang Kai-shek resigned his office and thereby signaled the total collapse of the Nationalist Chinese. There were no immediate repercussions but for those who had warned of Communist infiltration for years, the Nationalist defeat became the cause celèbre; the Truman administration, it would be concluded, had sold China down the river. Although the so-called China bloc would not coalesce until 1950, increased fear was manifest throughout 1949.[3]

In the course of the year many states established "little" un-American activities committees, loyalty oaths came into vogue, and investigations became the order of the day. Three ex-FBI agents continued their publication of a tabloid entitled *Counterattack* which presumed to identify suspected subversives in many areas.[4] In the South and elsewhere the Ku Klux Klan remobilized its forces to harass "the Communists, race-mixers, and atheists."[5] John Rankin charged in Congress that a major Communist goal was the integration of the races.[6]

Truman, as reported in the June 27, 1949 issue of *Time*, denounced such witch-hunts and compared them to the Alien and Sedition Acts of 1798. In the same issue, however, the observation was made that the various executive departments had certainly not been inactive in the anti-Communist field, especially the Justice Department which had instituted numerous proceedings against suspected Communists. Tom Clark, it was noted, had boasted in early June that "under President Truman more top-notch Communists have been convicted than during our entire history."[7]

In his inaugural address in January 1949 Truman devoted considerable attention to what he termed the Communist "threat to world recovery and lasting peace."[8] Such presidential warnings were for the most part directed at Communist expansion abroad. Truman had consistently played down the threat of internal subversion, an attitude the Red hunters were quick to challenge, particularly after the Chambers-Hiss affair. There is indication that Tom Clark did not always share the president's lack of concern. He several times expressed the need for more affirmative action against possible Communist infiltration.

A major part of that action involved the prosecution of the eleven Communists arrested and indicted in 1948. The trial began in January 1949 under the general charge that the eleven "had conspired in 1945 to form the present Communist Party structure and teach and advocate the violent overthrow of the United States Government."[9]

The proceedings ended in October with a verdict of guilty on all counts. In his charge to the jury, presiding Judge Harold Medina said that it was not necessary for the state to show the existence of a "clear and present danger" before it took action; that it was sufficient to prove that an evil thing existed.[10] Ten of the convicted received prison sentences of five years each and $10,000 fines. The eleventh had his prison sentence reduced to two years in recognition of his service in World War II.[11]

The trial, with ample attention from the press, certainly added to the already overcharged atmosphere of the time, but it did not free the administration from the accusation that it was soft on communism. Liberals condemned the proceedings from the outset. It was dangerous, the editors of the *New Republic* said, to try men only for the principles they espoused; the best way to beat communism was by practicing democracy.[12] Those were the same ideas that Truman had expressed on many occasions, ideas which are difficult to reconcile with the prosecution of the eleven Communists.

There is no indication that Truman did not altogether concur with his attorney general in the indictment of the Communist leaders, although the main impetus for the proceedings may well have come from the Justice Department rather than the White House. On other matters that involved loyalty-security there was evidence of a considerable divergence of opinion between Clark and others within the administration.

In January 1949 Clark dispatched a letter to Senator Pat McCarran, conservative Democrat from Nevada, in which he asked Congress to pass the "toughest anti-spy laws in American history."[13] Among other things, the attorney general requested a law that would legalize wiretaps, and provide that "information thus obtained would be admissable in evidence. . . ." Clark indicated that such a request had "been drafted to carry out the recommendations of the Interdepartmental Intelligence Committee."[14] McCarran, never noted for any outspoken defense of individual liberties, urged caution in regard to Clark's request because it "touches upon many things which heretofore we have regarded as exceedingly sacred to the individual."[15]

One week later a memorandum appeared under the authorship of Clark Clifford entitled "The So-called Spy Bills." He stressed that such legislative proposals deserved the prompt attention and concern of every member of the administration. "The President indicated to me a week ago yesterday that it is the Republicans who are avid for such bills. . .the hysteria-mongering brach [*sic*] of the Republican party. . . ." Clifford devoted abundant space in the memorandum to a thorough denunciation of wiretapping. It had been demonstrated time and again, he said, that the final result of such investigative procedure had been in all cases "disgraceful and disastrous."[16]

In July 1946, in a memorandum to Truman, Tom Clark noted that Franklin Roosevelt had approved the use of wiretap devices and he requested permission to continue the practice. The attorney general neglected to mention Roosevelt's obvious reservations about such surveillance or the late president's clear intention that wiretaps be limited to cases which involved possible espionage or sabotage by foreign agents. Truman, who apparently felt that he was only being asked to follow an F.D.R. directive, expressed his approval at that time.[17] The request for wiretap legislation in 1949, however, appears to have originated in the Justice Department, and when viewed in conjunction with the Clifford memorandum of January 25 suggests a definite conflict of opinion within the administration.

S. 595, which incorporated the various legislative requests submitted by Clark, was reported from the Senate Judiciary Committee on May 27.[18] It was not debated until August 1950, at which time McCarran pointed out that the wiretap provision had been removed from the bill. A provision that would require persons trained in espionage by a foreign government to register with the Justice Department, and another that would provide punishment for anyone found in possession of stolen government documents, were retained.[19] A similar wiretap bill in the House, H. R. 4703, suffered the same fate as S. 595. "The members of the [House] Sub-committee on the Judiciary felt that it would be improvident and improper to accept the recommendations of these various intelligence units concerning wire tapping."[20]

There was additional evidence of discord between the White House and the Justice Department in connection with H. R. 10, the Hobbs bill, which was introduced in January 1949 and designed "to facilitate the deportation of aliens from the United States" and "to provide for supervision and detention pending eventual deportation. . . ."[21] The administration manifested concern over certain provisions in the bill when it emerged in the spring of 1950, especially those provisions which pertained to the detention of aliens.

On May 20, 1950, Truman learned that the Justice Department had pushed the Hobbs bill in spite of his own previous objections to such legislation. Stephen Spingarn was detailed to speak for the president and to relay his concern to the attorney general. Spingarn suggested that the civil rights section of the Justice Department ought to restudy H. R. 10 in an effort to establish a balance between internal security and individual rights.

Attorney General J. Howard McGrath, when he had replaced Clark after the latter's appointment to the Supreme Court in August 1949, received Spingarn's message with surprise since the Hobbs bill had been initiated by Tom Clark, with, he assumed, the president's approval. McGrath indicated that he would take prompt action to correct the iniquities in the Hobbs bill for "he knew the president's deep conviction of the need for protecting individual rights because the President had frequently spoken to him about it."[22] The attorney general's intentions may have been good but he lacked the initiative to do anything. He was content to allow his assistant, Peyton Ford, to run the department. Ford, a hard-line holdover from Clark's tenure, showed little inclination to cooperate with the president.[23]

Undoubtedly evidence of such a lack of coordination between the various executive departments hurt the administration in its effort to head off the even more drastic measures proposed by Congress. In particular, there appears to have been a conflict of views between Truman and his then attorney general, Tom Clark, who seemed determined to take a much tougher line than Truman felt either necessary or advisable.

In early March 1949, Clark instituted proceedings against an employee of the Justice Department. Judith Coplon, twenty-seven years of age and employed as a political analyst in the foreign agents registration section, was arrested on March 4 with a handbag full of notes abstracted from confidential documents within the department. Coplon had presumably passed such information to her Russian paramour, a United Nations employee, Valentin A. Gubitschev.[24]

Coplon was indicted in federal court on two counts: one for participation in espionage, and the other for the theft of government documents. She was subsequently found guilty on both and received a sentence of forty months to ten years on the first, and one to three years on the second, the sentences to be served concurrently. She was then escorted to New York to face a joint conspiracy trial with Gubitschev.[25] Clark, it was observed in the press, had been forced to expose various undercover agents in order to win the Coplon trial. The presiding judge, Albert Reeves, had informed the attorney general that the government, if it expected to prosecute, would be required to produce the evidence.[26]

On the day prior to the arrest of Judith Coplon, two of the more prominent Communists on trial, Eugene Dennis and William Z. Foster, declared that in the event of war, the Communist Party U.S.A. would work to defeat the "war aims of American imperialism." The next day, and the day of the Coplon arrest, Truman branded both Dennis and Foster as traitors to their country.[27] The combination of events shook a nation already on the verge of Red hysteria, and hastened the inevitable introduction of more antisubversive legislation.[28]

March 8, 1949, might well be remembered as antisubversive day in Congress. No less than three major bills were introduced, all of which closely resembled the Mundt-Nixon bill which had expired at the end of the Eightieth Congress. In the Senate, Karl Mundt and Olin D. Johnson of South Carolina introduced S. 1194, a bill "to protect the United States against certain un-American and subversive activities."[29] Senator Homer Ferguson introduced S. 1196, which differed only in minor details from the Mundt-Johnson bill. Both were referred to McCarran's Senate Judiciary Committee.[30] In the House, Richard Nixon introduced H. R. 3342, a companion to the Mundt bill, which was referred to the House Committee on Un-American Activities.[31]

On March 10 Representative Francis E. Walter, Democrat of Pennsylvania, sponsored H. R. 3435, an amendment to the Nationality Act of 1940, which would deprive native-born American Communists of their citizenship and make them liable to deportation.[32] Other antisubversive legislation included H. R. 1002, introduced by Edward H. Rees of Kansas, which would have directed Communist front organizations to identify themselves on any matter sent through the mail, and H. J. Res. 9, authored by Charles E. Bennett of Florida, which redefined treason to include: (1) affiliation with any group that advocated the overthrow of the government by force, and (2) any collaboration with a foreign agent for the purpose of overthrowing the government by force.

The primary bills, S. 1194, S. 1196, and H. R. 3342, all closely resembled the 1948 Mundt-Nixon bill in their provisions for registration, membership lists, and financial accounting. One important difference placed the power to determine Communist-front organizations in the hands of a three-man Subversive Activities Commission outside the Department of Justice. In addition, the authors contended that the 1949 version tightened the provisions that would curtail Communist activities, provided for more drastic penalties, and removed the statute of limitations from any treasonable acts in time of peace. An effort was also made to remove any doubts as to the constitutionality of such legislation, although "it does not appear. . .that these attempts have been successful or even substantial."[34]

The administration's concern was evidenced in an April 29 memorandum by Clark Clifford, in which he stated his views on all antisubversive legislation and his recommendations for executive counteraction. Clifford initiated the memo with the following general comments:

> It is one thing for a nation to take basic counterespionage and security measures necessary to protect its existence. . . . It is another thing to urge or tolerate heresy hunts at every stump and crossroads to smoke out and punish nonconformists of every shade and stripe of opinion different than that of the majority. I'm afraid we are moving increasingly in that direction. . .to riddle the barn door in order to hit the knothole.

He further deplored the increased antisubversive activity on the part of many states, accompanied by a nationwide tendency to associate loyalty with orthodoxy. Many had come to support the false assumption "that change. . .is subversive and those who urge it are either Communists or fellow travelers."[35]

After a review of the various bills before Congress, Clifford concluded that the administration should vigorously oppose all such legislation. He remarked, however, that it would be difficult to beat "something with nothing." In that respect he recommended that the president consider, as an administrative alternative to the Mundt-Ferguson-Nixon bills, a proposal made in 1947 by Truman's Civil Rights Commission. Such a proposal would entail both the Congress and the state legislatures enacting legislation that required the registration of all organizations whose objective was to influence public opinion. Such legislation, Clifford commented, would prohibit nothing and would pertain to any organization, right or left, subversive or nonsubversive. The theory behind such a proposal, he stated, was to provide for a free and open marketplace of opinion in which it was felt that truth would prevail.[36]

Clifford's advice evidently went unheeded. The administration made no move, until it was too late, to introduce any measure by way of a substitute for the congressional antisubversive bills. No stretch of the imagination can conclude—nor is it the intention of this author to do so—that any administrative alternative would have substantially altered the situation. The nature of right-wing extremism at the time may well have cast doubt on the possibilities. Yet, by the same logic, the lack of any positive response left the president on the defensive and negated any hope that the administration might forestall the eventual passage of a major congressional bill to deal with internal communism.

By early summer the anti-Red crusade had taken on all the aspects of a three-ring circus. The Justice Department was busy with its prosecutions of Judith Coplon and the Communist leaders; state legislatures were enacting spy laws at a record pace; the Hiss-Chambers perjury trial was still in the headlines; and, not least, the House Committee on Un-American Activities had extended its investigative power to include the field of education. Over one hundred colleges and universities were ordered in June to submit textbooks to the committee for examination.[37] The chancellor of Cornell University, Edmund E. Day, satirically suggested that if the members of the House committee really wanted to examine a particular college's textbooks, "they had better take courses there. . . ."[38]

Education in general received its share of attention, with emphasis in particular on the question of Communist party members teaching in the nation's schools. The National Education Association concluded that they should not be allowed to do so, but denounced the tendency to label as Communist anyone who voiced opinions that differed from the majority.[39] Truman stated, in answer to a reporter's question, that he "didn't feel that those who advocated overthrow of the Government should teach the nation's young people."[40] Henry S. Commager in a *New Republic* article admitted that Communists might not be good teachers but claimed that he could see no benefit, and much harm, that might result from any attempt to purge the schools. Such an endeavor, Commager noted, would only reveal "evidence of lack of faith in the intelligence and integrity of the American people.[41] The search continued, however, as more and more states—twenty-six by October 1949—resorted to the loyalty oath as a means of preventing the employment of Communists in the public schools and colleges.[42]

The Senate also manifested concern over possible Communist influence in education, particularly with regard to fellowships granted by the Atomic Energy Commission. The commission chairman, David Lilienthal, was taken to task after Hans Freistadt, a University of North Carolina student and supposedly an avowed Communist, was awarded such a fellowship. Lilienthal defended the Freistadt award on the grounds that no classified information was involved in the program. He soon retreated, however, and promised that henceforth a non-Communist affidavit would be required.

Senator Joseph C. O'Mahoney of Wyoming indicated that he would prepare a law to that effect, and one that would also require an FBI check of all applicants for AEC fellowships.[43]

Stephen Spingarn expressed his belief in the administration's openly opposing the O'Mahoney amendment, because it would subject AEC fellows to a stricter security check than that imposed on government employees. He suggested that Truman might voice his objections to the amendment at his next press conference. "The O'Mahoney amendment is symptomatic of the increasing and almost hysterical unreason which tends to obscure and complicate sane discussion of loyalty and security problems."[44] In spite of administration opposition and of charges from the floor of the Senate that the O'Mahoney proposal would destroy the fellowship program, the amendment passed the Upper House on August 2, 1949.[45]

Truman continued to compare the period to the late 1790s, but contended that it was only postwar hysteria and would soon pass.[46] The analogy was somewhat faulty—the 1790s hysteria was engendered by fear of a war rather than a result of one—but the basic assumption was correct. The fear would pass, but not until it had sapped the strength of the Truman administration, damaged its domestic program, and done incalculable harm to a number of individuals. The administration's failure to make some positive response would prove fatal in the long run. Congress continued to press for action.

In July the Senate Judiciary Committee combined the best and worst features of the Mundt, Ferguson, and Johnson bills into one major piece of antisubversive legislation, S. 2311.[47] The bill was not reported from the committee in 1949 but nevertheless posed a major threat to the president's effort to retain executive control of the loyalty program.

Truman's comments on S. 2311 were essentially the same as those he had made in 1948 on the Mundt-Nixon bill. He opposed a ban on any political party, did not feel fringe parties represented any great danger, and considered the government had sufficient laws to protect itself against internal subversion.[48] Others in the administration concluded that "S. 2311 is almost certainly unconstitutional in some respects and will be entirely ineffective to achieve its purposes."[49] The Justice Department, in its review of the bill, noted that the conviction of the eleven Communist leaders for conspiracy "to organize the Communist party as a society which teaches and advocates the overthrow of the government by force," raised the most important of the constitutional questions presented in the Senate bill. The department could not recommend enactment of S. 2311, it was said, until the court of appeals ruled on that conviction.[50]

The liberal press exhibited immediate opposition to the new antisubversive bill. The *Washington Post* referred to it as "an outright sedition bill, comparable to nothing ever enacted by the Congress of the United States since the odious Sedition Act of 1798."[51] The *New York Times* labeled it an infringement of the rights of every American citizen.[52] The old charge also persisted, that any such legislation, in addition to its establishment of guilt by association and thought control, would drive the Communists underground and thereby increase the problem of detection.[53] The supporters of S. 2311 ignored all such opposition and continued to push for enactment.

In spite of congressional preoccupation with the spy problem, there were a few positive achievements in the first session of the Eighty-first Congress: rent control was extended, the minimum wage was increased to seventy-five cents an hour, and the armed services were unified.[54] But most of the Fair Deal remained unfulfilled as the conservatives continued to harp on the evils of big government and the welfare state, and there appeared little hope of a change in that point of view in the next election year. It was predicted, however, that the Republicans would need more than the "big-government" issue if they hoped to make substantial gains in the congressional elections.[55] And they indeed found another, for 1950 marked the dramatic appearance of Senator Joseph R. McCarthy.

In January 1950, a news story described the merger, under the sponsorship of the American Legion, of sixty organizations for the expressed purpose of fighting communism. The Ku Klux Klan's crusade against the NAACP, B'nai B'rith, and the Federal Council of Churches of Christ was discussed in the same news story. Stephen Spingarn observed, in connection with the article, that one of the major policies of the Truman administration had been to move decisively against communism but to do so in an unhysterical way.

> It is something else again when it becomes a crusade or holy war entirely devoted to the negative aspect of attacking Communism and detached from the positive aspect of building up democracy so that. . .it will be invulnerable to the challenge of Communism. . . .In short, a successful organization to fight Communism must have a positive program for improving democracy. . .otherwise, it is going to find that it has some very slimy characters indeed, among its most articulate supporters.[56]

Spingarn's thoughts were more prophetic than he knew.

On January 24, 1950, the ordeal of Alger Hiss came to an end with his conviction on a charge of perjury. At a press conference the following day, Secretary of State Dean Acheson, a long-time friend of Hiss, stated firmly, "I do not intend to turn my back on Alger Hiss."[57] Such words served as the catalyst to solidify the China bloc, that group of individuals who contended that responsibility for the loss of China could be traced directly to the Communist sympathizers in the Department of State, and inevitably to the whole Red-infested Democratic administration. Within a matter of three weeks, the group would find a leader in the bullish and crude junior senator from Wisconsin—the self-acclaimed "tailgunner Joe" McCarthy.

Senator McCarthy launched his campaign at Wheeling,

West Virginia, on the evening of February 9, 1950. In a speech before a group of Republican ladies at a Lincoln Birthday dinner, McCarthy announced:

> I have here in my hand 57 cases of individuals who would appear to be either card-carrying members or certainly loyal to the Communist Party, but who nevertheless are still helping shape our foreign policy.[58]

The thirty-seven-year-old McCarthy had been elected to the Senate in the Republican surge of 1946. His record for 1949 did indicate considerable activity—he introduced some thirty-eight bills mostly of a minor nature—but gave no hint that he had any more than a passive interest in the Communist, antisubversive field.[59]

Richard Rovere, author of a critical biography, states that McCarthy "was in many ways the most gifted demagogue ever bred on these shores. No bolder seditionist ever moved among us—nor any politician with a surer, swifter access to the dark places of the American mind."[60] Dean Acheson, on the other hand, viewed McCarthy as "essentially a small-town bully, without sustaining purpose, who on his own would have soon petered out."[61]

McCarthy was not on his own for long however. He soon became the agent and spokesman for fundamentalist conservatism—referred to as the "cutting edge" by Earl Latham.[62] It was Joe McCarthy who would perform what he once defined himself as the "bare-knuckle job" on the Truman administration, aided and abetted by the conservative Taft-led Republicans.[63]

On the evening of February 20, McCarthy repeated his charges on the floor of the Senate. He utilized the power of the sergeant-at-arms to encourage the senators to stay and listen as he laboriously plodded through eighty-one separate cases of what he termed treasonable activity in the State Department. It was clear from the exchange between the senator from

Wisconsin and others that he was uncertain just how many suspects he had named at Wheeling. For convenience, perhaps, he finally settled on eighty-one. McCarthy's subsequent refusal to designate any of them by name drew fire from Majority Leader Scott Lucas, who charged that McCarthy had cast a shadow of guilt on the entire State Department.[64]

Nine days before his speech on the Senate floor, McCarthy had wired the president and demanded that he order Acheson to release the State Department files; "Failure on your part will label the Democratic Party of [*sic*] being the bedfellow of international Communism."[65] Truman remained silent for the moment, but it was soon decided to give McCarthy a forum to prove his charges, with the full expectation that, given enough rope, the senator would surely hang himself.

On February 22, the Senate adopted S. Res. 231 which established a subcommittee of the Senate Committee on Foreign Relations to "investigate whether there are employees in the State Department disloyal to the United States." It was to be composed of Democrats Millard Tydings of Maryland as chairman, Theodore F. Green of Rhode Island, and Brien McMahon of Connecticut. Republican members were Henry Cabot Lodge of Massachusetts and Bourke Hickenlooper of Iowa.[66] In his *Memoirs* Dean Acheson views the appointment of the Tydings committee as a serious error on the part of the administration. Such hearings, Acheson noted, furnished McCarthy with a platform from which to broadcast his charges to the nation.[67]

McCarthy took ample advantage of this platform. He attracted, as expected, a generous measure of support from right-wing journalists and broadcasters, men such as Westbrook Pegler and Fulton Lewis, Jr.[68] In addition, those in the media who disliked him the most unwittingly contributed to the senator's fame. "They exposed his past and denounced his present, and above all gave him column after column of coverage. They suffered what one critic described as phobophilia: They were in love with their enemy."[69]

In the course of the debate on S. Res. 231, the Republicans successfully attached to it an amendment which empowered the subcommittee to subpoena all confidential files on those individuals charged by McCarthy. Truman reacted to the implied threat at his press conference on February 24 with the announcement that under no circumstances would he comply with such a subpoena if one were issued. He maintained a firm "come and get it" attitude as he once again reminded reporters of Andrew Jackson's comment. McCarthy decried what he termed such complete presidential arrogance.[70]

The subcommittee hearings commenced in early March as Tydings promised "neither a witch hunt, nor a whitewash."[71] McCarthy was the first witness to appear and was soon able to seize the initiative since both Lodge and Hickenlooper pressed the chairman to allow the senator to present his case. In the initial stage the hearings centered on six relatively obscure individuals. Later, McCarthy implicated some of more renown such as Philip C. Jessup, United States Ambassador-at-Large and a specialist in Far Eastern Affairs; John Stewart Service, who had been cleared before a State Department Loyalty Board of charges made in 1946; and Owen Lattimore, director of the Walter Hines Page School of International Relations at Johns Hopkins University and at that time on a special United Nations mission to Afghanistan.[72] Jessup and Service were recalled from their foreign service posts to answer the charges, and received substantial support from both the Justice Department and the White House.

The most spectacular charge was against Lattimore whom McCarthy referred to as the "top Soviet espionage agent in the State Department."[73] McCarthy informed the subcommittee that he would rest his entire case on the Lattimore charge.

> I am telling you that this is the one case in which I think we can easily have a determination by this committee as to whether or not my charges are well founded or not. I think for the balance of the investigation you should know that.[74]

Owen Lattimore, although not a widely known public figure, was recognized among scholars as an expert on Far Eastern affairs. He had served from 1934 to 1941 as editor of the magazine *Pacific Affairs*, a publication of the Institute of Pacific Relations. In World War II he worked as a deputy director of the Office of War Information in the Pacific and served at one time as a political advisor to Chiang Kai-shek.[75]

Tydings accepted the McCarthy challenge and ordered Lattimore recalled from his foreign assignment to appear before the committee. On April 6 Tydings announced that the committee, with the exception of Hickenlooper, had viewed a summary of the Lattimore files in the presence of J. Edgar Hoover and had found no evidence to indicate that Professor Lattimore was or ever had been disloyal to the United States.[76]

Rovere observes that McCarthy sensed almost at once that he had committed a serious blunder with his emphasis on Lattimore. It would have been difficult for the professor ever to have been the most prominent spy in the State Department since he had never been employed there.[77] At a press conference, Dean Acheson revealed that he had no recollection of ever having met Lattimore.[78] McCarthy had quite obviously missed the mark, but that fact failed to deter him in the least, for he quickly pressed the attack in another direction and continued to challenge the committee to check the complete files on all those he had named.[79]

There was an announcement in the press on March 2 that Truman had decided to reverse his three-year stand and allow the Tydings subcommittee to examine the loyalty files. It was reported that the case of Klaus Fuchs, the British scientist convicted of treason, had convinced the president of the necessity to prove that there were no such individuals in the State Department.[80] The announcement was premature, for Truman had made no such decision, although the possibility was under consideration. The continued refusal to allow access to the files would, the president was aware, bring renewed charges that subversives were under the protection of the administration.[81] He also wanted to aid the committee but felt if an exception were made at that point, it would be most difficult to deny such papers to any other committee in the future. The president faced a difficult decision.

On March 14, Senator Tydings asked Truman to set forth the conditions under which the files might be made available to the Senate committee. Spingarn suggested that the president inform Tydings that he had decided to open the files in order to resolve once and for all the serious charges made against the State Department, and had been assured that the committee would use them with discretion. It was further suggested that a special room be set aside in the White House where only committee members would be allowed to examine a summary of each file in the presence of a presidential representative.[82] Truman remained unconvinced and the loyalty files remained closed.

Truman had evidently been impressed with the Justice Department's persistent argument that the release of such confidential information would adversely effect the investigative procedure of the department. He was also not unreceptive to opinion expressed in the press, such as a March 22 editorial in the *Washington Star.* It was there noted that the president's loyalty program did not at that time present a serious threat to the reputations of innocent people but might do so if loyalty files were released to just anyone.[83]

On the same day, March 22, Truman received an official request from Tydings for the loyalty files on all those individuals named by McCarthy from the floor of the Senate on February 20. The president replied on March 28 that he would be unable to make such files available for the reasons he had explained in the past. Truman indicated his earnest desire to cooperate with the committee and stated that the Richardson Loyalty Board had been instructed to recheck each of the cases and to submit a report which would be made available to subcommittee members.[84]

The reaction to the president's decision reveals the marked division of opinion on the matter. Tydings announced that he was required by the amendment included in the Senate Resolution to issue a subpoena for the files; he expected the president to ignore it. Homer Ferguson characterized Truman's decision as a cover-up, and Senator Kenneth Wherry, Nebraska Republican, called it "shocking and shameful."[85] The *Milwaukee Journal* congratulated the president on his determined stand not to release information which would have "opened up Pandora's box overflowing with hearsay, gossip, rumor, conjecture and outright lies. . . ."[86] McCarthy, as might have been expected, asserted that Truman had refused to release the information because he knew it would substantiate the senator's charges.[87]

There was little doubt that Truman and the whole of his administration were stunned by the McCarthy attack. The savages were on the attack and there seemed to be no effective way to oppose them. In the spring of 1950, Truman set up a special force, composed of Herb Maletz and Max Lowenthal, to issue instant rebuttals to McCarthy's endless charges.[88] Democrats in general were frightened out of their wits that McCarthy—on the loose with a blunderbuss—might turn up another Alger Hiss, which would certainly deliver the death blow to the Democratic administration. Former Secretary of State Henry Stimson stated that Joe McCarthy had no wish to get rid of Communists but was rather, "hoping against hope that he will find some."[89]

Columnist Drew Pearson reported that McCarthy had rapidly drained away whatever public support Truman had left. Most people believed, Pearson stated, that where there is smoke there must be fire, and McCarthy had certainly created enough of the former. Pearson also claimed that many felt that the president had failed to offer positive leadership and in the process had lost control of the situation.[90]

Truman did attempt to rebuke McCarthy at every possible

opportunity, especially at press conferences and in various speeches. The most notable of the press appearances occured in Florida on March 30, 1950, when Truman angrily charged that "the greatest asset that the Kremlin has is Senator McCarthy," and asserted that "the policy of the Republican party has endorsed the antics of Mr. McCarthy."[91] It was the kind of response the press had come to expect from Truman, but his remarks served no purpose other than allowing him to vent his emotions.

A more significant attempt to counter the McCarthy attack came on April 24, 1950, in the president's address before the Federal Bar Association. It was for the most part a reiteration of points he had made on numerous occasions but should be viewed as a sensible, straightforward, and eloquent appeal for a return to sanity. He stressed that improvement in the quality of American life was "the strongest anti-Communist weapon in our whole arsenal. . . ." and he closed with a "call on all fair-minded men and women to join in this good fight."[92]

It would do the president an injustice to criticize his appeal to reason, but it must be considered as insignificant in the face of the barbarous attack then underway against the administration. There had been a number of suggestions made in the past for a more positive response, but unfortunately no action had been taken. Truman continued to rest his greatest hope for exoneration on the Tydings subcommittee, which was still in the process of trying to reach some conclusion in the midst of an almost daily barrage of charges.

Republican Senator William E. Jenner of Indiana, one of the most vindictive voices raised in the Senate in those days, repeatedly referred to the subcommittee hearings as a "white wash."[93] Bourke Hickenlooper charged that Truman had attempted to shift the blame on to J. Edgar Hoover for his own refusal to allow the committee to see the loyalty files.[94] Senator Tydings pleaded only for a truce that would allow the subcommittee to conclude its hearings in a less hysterical atmosphere.[95] Such irresponsible and reckless charges as those that had been thrown about by McCarthy, Jenner, Wherry, and others prompted Theodore F. Green to comment that "we are not so much imperiled today by what the 'noisy' and 'troublesome' Communists can do to us as by what they may induce us, through the McCarthy's, to do to ourselves."[96]

The charges and countercharges continued unabated and had no doubt much to do with the sudden and unexpected announcement from the White House on May 4 that the president had reversed his decision and would allow the subcommittee to view the files under the conditions suggested earlier by Spingarn.[97] Two days later Senator McCarthy delivered an address before a young Republican group in Chicago, in which he charged that the loyalty files about to be released had in fact been purged of all derogatory information. He continued to name Owen Lattimore as the architect of the United States policy in China, despite considerable evidence to the contrary, and concluded with an attack upon the integrity of the president of the United States.[98]

Some weeks later, in a letter to the president, McCarthy restated his charge that the State Department's files had been systematically stripped in 1946 of all derogatory evidence. The Department characterized such accusations as false and malicious and stressed that the so-called "stripping" consisted of a reorganization of personnel files that did not pertain in any way to loyalty.[99]

A short time after Truman's reversal, Senator Tydings requested that the president appoint a "panel of distinguished citizens" to assist the committee in its consideration of the loyalty files. It was suggested that Truman advise Tydings that the appointment of such a panel at that time might discredit the Richardson Loyalty Board and also interfere with the president's own plan "to set up a Presidential Commission on Internal Security and Individual Rights the jurisdiction of which will include but not be limited to considering the adequacy of the Government's Loyalty-Security Program. . . ." It was further proposed that the president inform the senator that the Richardson board would give priority to the McCarthy charges, would prepare a complete report of its conclusions, and would meet and discuss such a report with the Senate committee.[100] There was ample discussion about the advisability of a presidential commission, and it is regrettable that no more came of it at that time. The appointment of a nonpartisan body of distinguished citizens to study and evaluate the loyalty program might well have blunted the congressional attack and restored some measure of confidence in the government's security procedures.[101]

By the early summer of 1950 it was evident that public confidence in the administration's loyalty program had reached an all-time low. When the program was first launched there had been loud and persistent charges that it was too harsh and a threat to individual freedom. The pendulum, however, had swung the other way by June 1950. McCarthy's charges implied, and many had come to believe it, that the loyalty boards, if not outright dishonest, were too lenient and ineffectual.[102] As the administration struggled to remove such doubt, J. Edgar Hoover, one of the more important and influential members of that administration, did in effect much to increase the doubt.

It had been evident for some time that certain members of the White House staff were unhappy with the FBI director's statements on the strength of the Communist party in the United States, which only served to "keep the pot bubbling and play directly into the hands of the self-styled super patriots of the McCarthy variety."[103] Stephen Spingarn voiced particular displeasure with Hoover's article, in a June issue of *U. S. News and World Report*, which detailed the dangers of the Communist fifth column. Spingarn maintained that Truman had presented the true picture, that the administration had adequately handled the problem of Communists in the United

States. Nowhere in Hoover's statement, Spingarn declared, "is there any suggestion that we are licking or even hurting the CPUSA. On the contrary, the whole suggestion is that they are getting more and more dangerous." It was obvious, Spingarn said, that the director had employed such "scare tactics" in order to get more money from Congress.[104]

Tom Clark admitted that Hoover often used the Communist issue for just that purpose, but quickly added that such tactics did not constitute anything dishonorable. Clark pointed out that Hoover's longtime concern with internal communism, dating back to the Palmer raids in 1920, explained much of the director's preoccupation with the issue after World War II.[105] Some effort should have been made to check Hoover's remarks but in view of his overwhelmingly independent base of power, any such attempt would probably have failed. It was yet another instance of discord within the Truman administration, which the president could ill afford at that particular time.

The long-awaited report of the Tydings committee was submitted, regrettably on a partisan basis, in mid-July and, as expected, completely repudiated every charge McCarthy had made.

> At a time when American blood is again being shed to preserve our dream of freedom we are constrained fearlessly and frankly to call the charges, and the methods employed to give them ostensible validity, what they truly are; a fraud and a hoax perpetrated on the Senate of the United States and the American people. . . .[106]

The report was presented to the Senate on July 20 where, after bitter debate, it was approved by a vote of 45 to 37. Even the Republican liberal, Wayne Morse of Oregon, and the moderate Margaret Chase Smith of Maine, voted to sustain McCarthy.[107] Mrs. Smith, along with six other Republican senators that included Morse, had earlier been among the few in the Senate who had dared to challenge McCarthy when they signed a "Declaration of Conscience" which deplored the tactics employed by the Wisconsin senator. In an extraordinary speech from the floor of the Senate, Mrs. Smith criticized the Democratic administration's failure to move effectively against communism, and stressed the need for a Republican victory in November. "But I do not want to see the Republican Party ride to political victory on the Four Horsemen of Calumny—fear, ignorance, bigotry, and smear."[108]

Henry Cabot Lodge indicated that he had not signed the Tyding's report because the subcommittee simply did not have sufficient time to make a full and complete investigation. The loyalty files, Lodge said, were in an unfinished state but still so long and complicated that he confessed a complete inability to understand them. He also observed that the committee members had been allowed to examine the files only in the White House and were not permitted to take notes.[109] Earlier, on April 3, Lodge had introduced S. 338 "To Provide For Establishment of a Commission to Investigate Charges of Disloyalty in the State Department." It was to be composed of twelve members selected on a nonpartisan basis with half of that number chosen from outside the government.[110] Until a thorough investigation could be conducted by such an impartial commission, Lodge concluded that he could not state with certainty that all of McCarthy's charges were false.[111] Lodge's objections were at least of a reasonable nature. Such could not be said for those voiced by some other senators.

The most vicious attack on the subcommittee's report in general, and on Tydings in particular, was delivered on July 21 by Senator Jenner who characterized the Tydings investigation as a "scandalous and brazen whitewash." Jenner then proceeded with a personal attack so vile and repugnant that he was at one point declared out of order. The Indiana Republican was however allowed to continue and finally concluded his polemic with a declaration that Tydings would soon receive a medal from Joe Stalin with an inscription, "Thanks from good old Joe for a job well done."[112] Such an exhibition demonstrated the kind of "shameful and nihilistic orgy," as Acheson termed it, to which the country was being subjected at that time.

Although editorial comment on the Tydings report was generally favorable, there were some who were less well-disposed. The strongest denunciation came from the *Chicago Daily Tribune* which attacked not only the Tydings subcommittee but the whole New Deal—Fair Deal era.[113] The *Washington Times Herald* viewed the report as a typical Democratic sleight of hand. "What else could we expect? This is the party of lies." It was concluded that the best way to spot a Communist was to single out "those who support the Tydings Report."[114]

The *Milwaukee Journal* praised the committee's work but concurred with Senator Lodge concerning the need for a non-partisan body to study the whole loyalty program.[115] A similar view was expressed in the *Christian Science Monitor*.[116] The *St. Louis Post Dispatch* reported that the committee had performed a valuable service to the nation by "blowing Senator McCarthy out of the water. . . ."[117] A wishful thought, no doubt, but far from correct. Harry Truman would bear the cross of Joe McCarthy for the remainder of his years in office.

The Tydings report represented at best an illusory victory for the administration, but it did at least offer Truman a brief opportunity to make a definite move to recapture the initiative which the conservatives had held since the special session of 1948. The administration remained inactive however, seemingly paralyzed by the McCarthy onslaught and the other cataclysmic events of 1950. Time had about run out and Congress was pressing toward the passage of an all-inclusive, antisubversive bill.

On March 21, 1950, the Senate Judiciary Committee favorably reported S. 2311 by a vote of 10 to 1. The lone dissenting vote was cast by William Langer who said the bill "would constitute the greatest threat to American civil liberties since the Alien and Sedition Laws."[118] The *Washington Post* admitted that the bill had been cleaned up a bit in committee but "still entails sweeping and arbitrary invasions of American liberties. . ."[119] The Justice Department continued to voice objections to the bill on constitutional grounds.[120] In the midst of the debate on S. 2311, the United States was shaken, on June 25, 1950, by the news that North Korean Communist troops had swept across the Thirty-eighth parallel into South Korea. Truman's historic decision to order United States military forces to the aid of South Korea sharply increased the demand for congressional action on the antisubversive legislation. The Taft-led Minority Policy Committee of the Senate met shortly after the invasion and demanded passage of the Mundt-Ferguson bill.[121]

Administration officials took notice of the Republican demand and concluded that "Congress is in a mood to pass very drastic legislation indeed in the antisubversive field." It was suggested that Senator Lucas be asked to lend his support for S. 595, the bill introduced in 1949 by Tom Clark, minus the wiretap provision, as a substitute for the Mundt-Ferguson bill. It was also recommended that a provision be attached to S. 595, or even a separate bill, which would provide for the registration of all subversive organizations, both right and left. The proposal was similar to the one made by the president's Civil Rights Commission in 1947 and alluded to earlier in the memorandum from Clark Clifford.[122]

As the Mundt-Ferguson bill gained favor through the latter part of July, it was observed in the *Washington Post* that Truman faced a difficult political hurdle. The bill was favored by most Republicans and a rather significant number of Democrats; a presidential veto, it was noted, would be difficult to defend politically.[123] Truman stated unequivocally, however, that "he would veto any legislation such as the Mundt-Nixon bill which adopted police-state tactics and unduly encroached on individual rights, and he would do so regardless of how politically unpopular it was. . .election year or no election year."[124] The president soon had the opportunity to prove that he meant what he said.

NOTES

1. *New York Times*, January 6, 1949.
2. Ibid., January 2, 1949.
3. Dean Acheson, *Present at the Creation: My Years in the State Department* (N. Y.: W. W. Norton, 1969), pp. 303-7.
4. Stefan Kanfer, *A Journal of the Plague Years* (N.Y.: Atheneum, 1973), In June 1950, the authors of *Counterattack*, in collaboration with Vincent Hartnett, published *Red Channels*, which contained "the most effective blacklist in the history of show business." pp. 105-6.
5. Cabell Phillips, *The Truman Presidency: The History of a Triumphant Succession* (N.Y.: Macmillan Co., 1966), pp. 372-73.
6. U.S., *Congressional Record*, 81st Congress, 1st sess., 1949, 95, pt. 14, p. A4014.
7. *Time*, June 27, 1949, p. 13.
8. *New York Times*, January 21, 1949.
9. *Time*, January 31, 1949, p. 20.
10. Ibid., October 24, 1949, p. 22.
11. *New Republic*, October 31, 1949, pp. 7-8.
12. Ibid., February 7, 1949, p. 6.
13. *Newsweek*, January 24, 1949, p. 19.
14. U.S., *Congressional Record*, 81st Congress, 1st sess., 1949, 95, pt. 1, p. 442.
15. Ibid.
16. Memorandum, "The So-Called Spy Bills," January 25, 1949, Internal Security Folder, Clifford Papers, Truman Library.
17. Memorandum, For the President from Tom Clark, July 17, 1946, National Defense Folder, Spingarn Papers, Truman Library.
18. U.S., *Congressional Record*, 81st Congress, 1st sess., 1949, 95, pt. 1, p. 6942.
19. U.S., *Congressional Record*, 81st Congress, 2d sess., 1950, 96, pt. 9, p. 11944.
20. Ibid., pt. 3, p. 3404.
21. U.S., *Congressional Record*, 81st Congress, 1st sess., 1949, 95, pt. 1, p. 1949.
22. Memorandum, For the files from Spingarn, May 20, 1950, National Defense Folder, Spingarn Papers, Truman Library.
23. Alonzo L. Hamby, *Beyond the New Deal: Harry S. Truman and American Liberalism* (N.Y.: Columbia University Press, 1973), pp. 394-95.
24. *Time*, March 14, 1949, p. 28.
25. Ibid., July 11, 1949, p. 18. The Coplon conviction was later reversed on a technicality.
26. *U.S. News and World Report*, July 8, 1949, pp. 22-23.
27. *Washington Post*, March 4, 1949.

28. *New Republic*, March 21, 1949, pp. 7-8.

29. U.S., *Congressional Record*, 81st Congress, 1st sess., 1949, 95, pt. 2, p. 1972.

30. Ibid., p. 1965.

31. Ibid., p. 2034.

32. Ibid., p. 2213.

33. Memorandum, For the President from Clifford, April 29, 1949, Comments on Max Lowenthal's memorandum, "The Sedition Bills of 1949," Internal Security Folder, Clifford Papers, Truman Library.

34. Ibid.

35. Ibid.

36. Ibid. Clifford indicated in a letter to this author that he did not play a very prominent role in the formulation of administration policy in the loyalty-security field. Although the memo suggests that Clifford did attempt to play such a role, he was probably correct in his contention that he did not. The memo in question was authored, in its entirety, by Clifford's administrative aide, Stephen Spingarn. (Interview with Stephen Spingard, August 9, 1971).

37. *U.S. News and World Report*, June 24, 1949, p. 22.

38. *Time*, July 4, 1949, p. 39.

39. Ibid., June 20, 1949, p. 52.

40. *Washington Post*, June 10, 1949.

41. H. S. Commager, "Red-Baiting in the Colleges," *New Republic* 121 (July 25, 1949): p. 12.

42. *New Republic*, October 10, 1949, p. 15.

43. *Time*, May 30, 1949, p. 14.

44. Memorandum, For Clifford from Spingarn, July 27, 1949, Internal Security Folder, Spingarn Papers, Truman Library.

45. U.S., *Congressional Record*, 81st Congress, 1st sess., 1949, 95, pt. 8, p. 10564.

46. *Washington Post*, June 17, 1949.

47. U.S., *Congressional Record*, 81st Congress, 1st sess., 1949, 95, pt. 8, p. 10564.

48. Memorandum, For Loyalty and Subversive Activities File, From Spingarn, August 11, 1949, Spingarn Papers, Truman Library.

49. Comments, "Constitutional and Practical Aspects of S. 2311," OF 2750, Truman Papers, Truman Library.

50. Peyton Ford to Pat McCarran, January 4, 1950, National Defense Folder, Spingarn Papers, Truman Library.

51. *Washington Post*, August 23, 1949.

52. *New York Times*, August 24, 1949.

53. *New Republic*, September 12, 1949, p. 10.

54. *U.S. News and World Report*, October 21, 1949, p. 18.

55. Ibid., November 18, 1949.

56. Memorandum, For Murphy from Spingarn, January 31, 1950, Internal Security Folder, Spingarn Papers, Truman Library.

57. Acheson, *Present at the Creation*, p. 360.

58. B. J. Bernstein and A. J. Matusow, eds., *The Truman Administration: A Documentary History* (N.Y.: Harper & Row, 1966), p. 404.

59. U.S., *Congressional Record*, 81st Congress, 1st sess., 1949, 95, pt. 17, pp. 379-80.

60. Richard Rovere, *Senator Joe McCarthy* (New York: Meridian, 1960), p. 3.

61. Acheson, *Present at the Creation*, p. 370.

62. Earl Latham, *The Communist Controversy in Washington: From the New Deal to McCarthy* (N.Y.: Atheneum, 1969), p. 423.

63. Acheson, *Present at the Creation*, p. 363. Acheson contended that Taft, frustrated by the GOP defeat in 1948, decided to give McCarthy Republican backing and support. Taft, Acheson declared, felt McCarthy "should keep talking and if one case doesn't work out, he should proceed with another." p. 364.

64. U.S., *Congressional Record*, 81st Congress, 2d sess., 1950, 96, pt. 2, pp. 1952-81.

65. Telegram, To President from McCarthy, February 11, 1950, OF 3371, Truman Papers, Truman Library.

66. Theodore F. Green Papers, Tydings Subcommittee Correspondence, Library of Congress.

67. Acheson, *Present at the Creation*, p. 363.

68. Robert Griffith, *The Politics of Fear: Joseph R. McCarthy and The Senate* (Lexington: University Press of Kentucky, 1970), p. 71.

69. Ibid., p. 142.

70. *Washington Post*, February 24, 1950.

71. *Time*, March 6, 1950, p. 17.

72. Latham, *The Communist Controversy in Washington*, p. 272.

73. Phillips, *The Truman Presidency*, pp. 384-85.

74. Quoted in Latham, *The Communist Controversy in Washington*, p. 279.

75. Alan Barth, *Government by Investigation* (N.Y.: Viking Press, 1955), p. 96.

76. Phillips, *The Truman Presidency*, p. 386.

77. Latham, *The Communist Controversy in Washington*, p. 279.

78. *Time*, April 10, 1950, p. 18.

79. Phillips, *The Truman Presidency*, p. 382.

80. Article, *New York Herald Tribune*, March 2, 1950, Internal Security Folder, Elsey Papers, Truman Library.

81. *Washington Post*, March 6, 1950.

82. Suggested message, To Tydings from President, March 15, 1950, Internal Security Folder, Spingarn Papers, Truman Library.

83. Editorial, From the *Washington Star*, March 22, 1950, Internal Security Folder, Elsey Papers, Truman Library.

84. Truman to Tydings, March 28, 1950, Internal Security Folder, Spingarn Papers, Truman Library.

85. *Washington Post*, March 28, 1950.

86. Article, *Milwaukee Journal*, April 12, 1950, Democratic National Committee Clipping File, Truman Library.

87. *New York Times*, April 10, 1950.

88. Interview with Stephen Spingarn, Washington, D. C., August 9, 1971.

89. *Time*, April 10, 1950, p. 18.

90. *Washington Post*, May 8, 1950.

91. Truman's statements, presidential press conference, March 30, 1950, Joe McCarthy File, Lloyd Papers, Truman Library.

92. Presidential address, Federal Bar Association, April 24, 1950, PPF 200, Truman Papers, Truman Library.

93. U.S., *Congressional Record*, 81st Congress, 2d sess., 1950, 96, pt. 5, p. 5699.

94. Ibid., p. 5709.

95. Ibid., p. 5711

96. *Washington Post*, April 26, 1950.

97. *New York Times*, May 5, 1950.

98. U.S., *Congressional Record*, 81st Congress, 2d sess., 1950, 96, pt. 15, pp. A3426-27.

99. Press Release, Department of State, July 12, 1950, Internal Security Folder, Spingarn Papers, Truman Library.

100. Memorandum, To the President from Spingarn and Murphy, May 24, 1950, OF 252K, Truman Papers, Truman Library.

101. Griffith, *The Politics of Fear*, p. 109.

102. *New York Times*, June 4, 1950.

103. Memorandum, For Admiral Dennison from Spingarn, June 19, 1950, Internal Security Folder, Spingarn Papers, Truman Library.

104. Remarks, Spingarn on J. E. Hoover's article in *U.S. News and World Report*, June 28, 1950, National Defense Folder, Spingarn Papers, Truman Library.

105. Interview with Justice Thomas C. Clark, Washington, D. C., August 22, 1969.

106. Bernstein and Matusow, eds., *The Truman Administration*, p. 412.

107. U.S., *Congressional Record*, 81st Congress, 2d sess., 1950, 96, pt. 8, p. 10686.

108. Quoted in Acheson, *Present at the Creation*, p. 364. The other five to cosponsor Mrs. Smith's resolution were Republican Senators Tobey of New Hampshire, Aiken of Vermont, Ives of New York, Thye of Minnesota, and Hendrickson of New Jersey. Democrats Lehman of New York and Humphrey of Minnesota supported the resolution.

109. U.S., *Congressional Record*, 81st Congress, 2d sess., 1950, 96, pt. 8, pp. 10775-79.

110. Theodore F. Green Papers, McCarthy Loyalty-Security File, Library of Congress.

111. U.S., *Congressional Record*, 81st Congress, 2d sess., 1950, 96, pt. 8, p. 10779.

112. Ibid., p. 10791.

113. Article, *Chicago Daily Tribune*, July 19, 1950, Democratic National Committee Clipping File, Truman Library.

114. U.S., *Congressional Record*, 81st Congress, 2d sess., 1950, 96, pt. 16, p. A5245.

115. Article, *Milwaukee Journal*, July 18, 1950, Democratic National Committee Clipping File, Truman Library.

116. Article, *Christian Science Monitor*, July 19, 1950, Democratic National Committee Clipping File, Truman Library.

117. Article, *St. Louis Post Dispatch*, July 18, 1950, Democratic National Committee Clipping File, Truman Library.

118. *New Republic*, March 27, 1950, p. 7.

119. *Washington Post*, April 3, 1950.

120. Ibid., March 22, 1950.

121. *New Republic*, July 14, 1950, p. 8.

122. Memorandum, To Murphy, Dawson, Elsey from Spingarn, July 20, 1950, National Defense Folder, Spingarn Papers, Truman Library.

123. *Washington Post*, August 1, 1950.

124. Memorandum, For the Files on Internal Security from Spingarn on conversation with President concerning possible presidential message to Congress on subject of Internal Security, July 22, 1950, National Defense Folder, Spingarn Papers, Truman Library.

5
PASSAGE OF THE McCARRAN INTERNAL SECURITY ACT

. . . Congress, in an atmosphere of emotion and excitement, chose to go along with the advocates of extreme measures.

The birth of the Mundt-Nixon bill in 1948 gave notice of a major effort on the part of certain members within Congress, notably Richard Nixon, Karl Mundt, Homer Ferguson, and, as of 1950, Pat McCarran, to enact into law a major antisubversive bill. Several reversals had not deterred the group, as legislation that closely resembled the original Mundt-Nixon proposal had been introduced in each succeeding session of Congress. The administration's consistent response to such congressional activity was: to denounce legislation of that type as unconstitutional and a threat to individual liberty; to insist that present laws were sufficient to deal with the problem of subversion; and to emphasize the positive aspects of the president's loyalty-security program.

The congressional hearings on communism in August and September of 1948 did much to weaken public confidence in the loyalty program, and strongly hinted at the need for a review of the whole procedure. Although contemplated, no such review was undertaken at that time. The Red hysteria which had grown throughout 1949, the McCarthy assault in early 1950, and finally the outbreak of the Korean War in June

1950, all enhanced chances for the enactment of a congressional antisubversive bill and forced the administration (at last) to take some affirmative action in August 1950. It was, in retrospect, an ill-fated, eleventh-hour attempt.

The increased tempo of congressional activity in July 1950 had already prompted Spingarn and others to encourage the passage of S. 595, and a revised form of H. R. 10, as administration alternatives to S. 2311, the Mundt, Ferguson, Johnson bill, which had been gaining favor throughout the month of July.[1] On August 1, Judge Learned Hand, of the United States Court of Appeals in New York, upheld the 1949 conviction of the eleven Communist leaders. The judge ruled the Communist party to be a dangerous conspiracy which did, in its operation, represent a "clear and present danger" to the United States.[2] Such a judicial stamp of approval on the 1940 Smith Act gave credibility to the administration's contention that the antisubversive laws already in existence were sufficient to deal with any possibility of internal subversion.

On August 8, armed with Judge Hand's decision, Truman addressed the Congress on the subject of the new antisubversive bills and his own recommendations for protecting the security of the nation without unnecessary encroachments on the rights of individual citizens. The president initiated his address with a reaffirmation of his regular assertion, that the most effective defense against communism was to be found in a "functioning democracy which succeeds in meeting the needs of the people." He admitted that strong government action was required to protect the nation, but insisted that such action "must not be so broad as to restrict our liberty unnecessarily, for that would defeat our own ends. Unwise or excessive security measures can strike at the freedom and dignity of the individual which are the very foundations of our society—and the defense of which is the whole purpose of our security measures."

Truman warned that proposals broad and vague enough to be dangerous were at that moment before the Congress and should be rejected. All that was needed, he said, was additional legislation to strengthen those statutes already in existence. The president recommended laws (1) to extend the statute of limitations for peacetime espionage beyond the current three-year limit, (2) to require persons who received instruction from foreign governments in the techniques of espionage to register under the foreign agents registration Act,(3) to broaden authority to establish security regulations for the protection of military and national defense installations, and (4) to require aliens who were about to be deported to maintain contact with the Justice Department at all time.[3]

An editorial in the *Washington Star* praised Truman for his refusal to be swept along on the wave of hysteria, and admired his appeal to reason.[4] The *Washington Post* referred to Truman's "statesmanlike message" in which, it was said, he had "grasped the great dilemma of our society—the dilemma of protecting our liberties while safeguarding our security. . . ."[5] The message indicated—the *Chicago Sun Times* concluded—that "Harry S. Truman is all-American, on the first team with Washington, Madison, and Jefferson."[6]

Meanwhile, Senator Pat McCarran had successfully blended a number of congressional proposals into one all-inclusive antisubversive bill, S. 4037, which was introduced by the Nevada Democrat on August 10.[7] The McCarran bill incorporated the most important provisions of such bills as: S. 2311, which contained the registration and publication provisions of the Mundt, Ferguson, and Nixon proposals; S. 1832, McCarran's own bill which authorized the Justice Department to bar from immigration, or deport, a large variety of "subversive" aliens; S. 595, the Justice-sponsored bill designed to tighten existing safeguards against espionage; H. R. 10, which provided for detention of aliens about to be deported; and S. 3096, a bill to establish a new bureau of passports and visas.[8]

To combat such legislation and to facilitate the promotion of his own proposals, Truman named Charles Murphy to serve as his liaison between the White House and Capitol Hill. On August 11, Stephen Spingarn, in Murphy's absence, informed Senate Majority Leader Scott Lucas that there was to be no compromise on the "Mundt-Nixon bill—that as a matter of high principle, he [Lucas] stand on the President's recommendations even though he were [*sic*] going to be defeated in trying to hold that line." Spingarn also discussed the matter with Harley Kilgore, John McCormick, and others on the Hill.

Assistant Attorney General Peyton Ford expressed a certain displeasure with the president's determination not to support any legislative proposals in the loyalty-security field other than what he had proposed in his August 8 message. Such a stand, Ford said, appeared inconsistent with the president's previous indication that he would not object to the preparation of a Justice Department registration bill for Senator Lucas. The assistant attorney general was informed that the president had no objections to a draft of such legislation, but it should be noted, Spingarn said, "that no such bill had any administration backing or approval. . . .The President told me to hold the line on this matter."[9] A later memorandum to Millard Tydings included the president's proposals and reemphasized his belief that there was no need for any additional legislation.[10]

The battle lines had been drawn. Spingarn's messages and hurried trips between the White House and Capitol Hill represented only a small portion of a major effort on the part of the administration to rally its forces for the showdown. It was a noble but belated attempt. Those interested members of Congress had planned, coordinated, and revised their program over a period of two years; it seemed improbable that the administration, as late as August 1950, could mount an effective counterattack. Also, the evident lack of cooperation between the various executive departments and the administration's supporters in Congress did not help.

On August 17, Senators Warren Magnuson, Scott Lucas,

Francis J. Myers, Harley Kilgore, Estes Kefauver, Frank Graham, Theodore F. Green, Paul Douglas, Hubert Humphrey, and Herbert Lehman sponsored S. 4061, a bill which incorporated the president's earlier recommendations.[11] Karl Mundt and others in Congress were quick to charge that the administration bill represented an obvious attempt to "water down" the stronger congressional proposals.[12] It made little difference, for S. 4061 was submitted to the Senate Judiciary Committee where Chairman McCarran quietly slipped it into a pigeonhole from whence it would never emerge.[13]

On that same day, August 17, the Judiciary Committee, by a vote of nine to three, favorably reported S. 4037, or "that chamber of horrors" as it was referred to by administration officials. The three members who dissented were Kilgore, Graham, and the Republican "radical," William Langer. Both Kilgore and Graham had been among the cosponsors of the president's bill; another sponsor, Warren Magnuson, surprisingly voted with the majority. All bills that dealt with the problem of security, Magnuson declared, should at least be heard before the whole Congress.[14]

The McCarran bill ran thirty-two pages in length and appeared from the outset as something of an administrative monstrosity. As indicated earlier, it was an all-inclusive, omnibus bill which incorporated provisions from many other pieces of antisubversive legislation. One of the most significant parts of the proposal provided for the creation of a five-man Subversive Activities Control Board, which would be empowered to classify any group of individuals who belonged to one of two types of Communist organizations:

1. A Communist-action organization which was defined as any group controlled by a foreign government or a foreign organization such as the Comintern.
2. A Communist-front organization which was defined as "any organization in the United States which (A) is substantially directed, dominated, or controlled by a Communist-action organization and (B) is primarily

> operated for the purpose of giving aid and support to a Communist-action organization, a Communist foreign government, or the world Communist movement."[15]

Under such vague criteria, almost any organization, regardless of its intent, might well have been designated as subversive. Who, for example, could have derived a precise definition from the phrase "substantially directed. . .by a Communist-action organization"? There had been charges made in the past that such registration procedure would, in effect, outlaw the Communist party in the United States. The contention was even more believable after the circuit court decision which upheld the conviction of the eleven Communist leaders. Indeed, it would appear that the whole scheme was to require registration of a particular organization and then charge it with a violation of the Smith Act.[16] The administration continued to hold stubbornly to its belief that there were already sufficient laws in the antisubversive field; the addition of the McCarran suggestions, it was said, would only confuse matters.[17] The search for supporters of that point of view intensified.

J. V. Fitzgerald, in an August 18 memorandum, remarked what a "big boost" the president's recommendations would receive if J. Edgar Hoover spoke out with a strong public endorsement.[18] Four days later Spingarn made such a request of Hoover, and asserted that a statement of support by the FBI director "might contribute notably to unsnarling the unholy mess which has developed with respect to all this internal security legislation."[19] No such endorsement was ever made, as Hoover, for reasons known only to himself, chose to remain silent.

On August 21, Spingarn dispatched a letter to Attorney Joseph E. Rosen, a member of the board of governors of the National Counter-Intelligence Corps Association. Included in the letter were copies of the president's message of August 8 and the Senate bill which incorporated his requests of that date. Spingarn indicated that a public statement of support of the president's recommendations, by the board of governors of the CIC, would help discredit the "super-patriots and headline hunters who really don't care a continental about anything but their own personal advancement."[20] A similar letter had been sent to Stanley M. Goodrich, a former counterintelligence agent, who was requested, if he agreed with the president, to write letters to Senators Margaret Chase Smith, Robert Taft, Pat McCarran, and Representative Joseph Martin expressing his support for the administration bill.[21] The increase in such correspondence evidenced an earnest attempt on the part of the administration to build some base of support for the president's recommendations.

Truman's view received an endorsement on August 21 when Paul H. Jensen, a staunch Republican and former wartime counterintelligence officer, thoroughly denounced both the Mundt-Ferguson and McCarran bills in the course of a radio interview. He characterized both as "amateurish attempts at counterintelligence designed to catch headlines but not spies." Jensen concluded the interview with an announcement of his support for the administration bill.[22]

On numerous occasions, Truman had compared the climate of opinion in 1949-1950 to that of the period before the passage of the first Alien and Sedition Acts. In the summer of 1950 a "Study of Witch Hunting and Hysteria in the United States" was prepared in order to illustrate the comparison. In late August, Truman submitted the completed work to Alben Barkley, Sam Rayburn, Scott Lucas, and John McCormick, with the hope that it would perhaps sway a few opinions.[23] There was no indication that it did so, as the McCarran bill, despite the extensive effort directed against it, continued to gain supporters.

The administration forces were evidently aware almost from the first that their cause was hopeless. A statement from

Spingarn is indicative. "The outlook is very gloomy. It looks as if the President's recommendations will be badly licked. . . ."[24] Truman's military aide, General Harry H. Vaughn, expressed precisely the same view.[25] The contest did not abate, however, as Truman continued to threaten a veto of any such measure as S. 4037.[26] McCarran asserted that the president would not have "the temerity" to veto such a bill. The Nevada Democrat must have known from experience that Truman usually meant what he said on such matters.[27]

The political climate in the late summer of 1950 seemed to demand some kind of drastic action. The "old Curmudgeon," Harold L. Ickes, in a September 2 letter to Theodore F. Green commented on such times: "The moral climate seems to me to be getting worse and worse."[28] It was, indeed: the hysterical fear of internal Communist activity had grown to a point where it seemed probable that the American people would accept any measure, no matter how restrictive, so long as it struck a blow against the hated Reds. Hundreds of letters in the president's correspondence file express that sentiment all too clearly. The following excerpt from "average citizen" Lee Mansfield's letter to Truman, dated September 7, 1950, serves as an example.

> I think it should be made a national law that anybody that even thinks of Communism should be strung up by their neck until dead. . . .If you are the honorable man I think you are, you will feel the same toward Communism as I do, or any clear thinking American Citizen.[29]

Such demands for action coming from the people were perhaps what convinced a number of Truman's supporters in Congress that a drastic move on the part of the administration was urgently needed to stop the McCarran steamroller. That conviction led to the presentation of an extraordinary, and certainly drastic, proposal at a White House conference on September 6.

Senators Harley Kilgore, Paul Douglas, Frank Graham,

Hubert Humphrey, Herbert Lehman, Estes Kefauver, and Clinton Anderson proposed, at the meeting, to introduce an "emergency detention" amendment which "would provide for the internment of persons believed likely to commit acts of espionage or sabotage. . . . The authority thus conferred would come into effect in time of war. . . ." The seven senators informed Truman that such a move, to be offered as a substitute for all or part of S. 4037, offered the only hope to overtake the McCarran lead. Truman "told them to go ahead and make the move and he would reserve judgment on their proposal until the bill reached him."[30] On the same day, September 6, the Kilgore bill, S. 4130, was introduced in the United States Senate.[31]

What would prompt seven supposedly liberal senators to propose such an extreme measure, and one that appeared to be at least as undesirable as the bill they opposed? Those men were certainly not antagonistic toward American ideals of fair play, nor was there any reason to suppose that they were simply caught up in the reactionary climate of the time. It would not seem unreasonable to suggest, as an explanation for their action, that the senators viewed their proposal as an emergency measure, aimed specifically at hard-core subversives, saboteurs, and the like, and one that would never be implemented except in time of the most extreme national emergency. They may have also presumed, and perhaps correctly so, that in the event of such an emergency, the government would exercise arbitrary powers with or without legislative sanction. Certainly Lincoln's assumption of extraordinary powers in the Civil War period might well have served as a precedent for such an idea.

On the other hand it was felt that the McCarran bill, which the Kilgore group termed a "blunderbuss," would offer little real security, and would undoubtedly lead to serious violations of individual liberties.[32] The basic assumption, of course, was that the Kilgore bill, if enacted into law, would be enforced with discretion, while the McCarran bill would not. Humphrey, Lehman and the others might well have heeded the words of one of their own, Estes Kefauver, when he spoke out in opposition to the McCarran bill.

> I think that in considering a bill of this kind we have got to consider the uses which might be attempted to be made of it by someone who did not have regard for constitutional privileges and for the Bill of Rights.[33]

The same might also have been said for any piece of legislation designed to incarcerate American citizens without due process of law.

The strategy employed by the senatorial group involved the substitution of the Kilgore bill, S. 4130, for all of the McCarran bill or the substitution of the detention proposal, in the form of an amendment, for the registration section of S. 4037. Title I of the Kilgore bill incorporated the president's recommendations already embodied in S. 4061, which remained in the Judiciary Committee. Title II provided for the arrest and detention of "dangerous" Communists in the time of an internal security emergency. The president would be empowered to declare such an emergency in the event of an invasion or the threat of imminent invasion, a declaration of war by the United States, an insurrection in aid of a foreign enemy, or the pronouncement of an internal security emergency by a concurrent resolution of Congress.[34]

Senator Douglas insisted that S. 4130 addressed itself to the substance and not the shadow of internal subversion, and that it contained adequate provisions to protect the rights of the individual. Douglas included an editorial which certainly did not favor the Kilgore bill but found it preferable to the McCarran alternative.

> There is no use blinking at the fact that this bill [Kilgore] contemplates the creation of concentration camps. . . . It

> is legislation of a most drastic character, never before enacted or even seriously contemplated in the United States. . . . Nevertheless, the proposal seems to us markedly preferable to the McCarran measure.[35]

Thus by September 1950 matters had reached the point at which the only seeming choice was to determine the lesser of two evils.

The debates on the McCarran and Kilgore bills presented a study in paradox, as liberals and conservatives switched roles dramatically: the liberals adopted the tougher line while the conservatives became defenders of individual rights. Humphrey, Lehman, and others pictured the McCarran bill as completely unworkable—"a political palliative," as Humphrey termed it—and one that would not accomplish its stated purpose. The Kilgore proposal, Humphrey said, would allow the government to seize dangerous subversives immediately.[36] "The FBI knows where they are," and "can pick them up like that" [with a snap of his fingers].[37]

The McCarran-Mundt group at first charged that the detention camp proposal was an attempt by the administration to create the illusion that it wanted to do something about internal communism.[38] The same group would later declare the Kilgore bill not only unconstitutional but un-American as well, and a threat to individual liberties. A Karl Mundt statement adequately summarized the conservative argument against the Kilgore proposal:

> While I sincerely welcome the support of the Kilgore group in trying to do something about Communism. . .let us not tear the Constitution to shreds; let us not out-Hitler Hitler; let us not out-Stalin Stalin; let us not establish concentration camps in America. . . .[39]

On August 12, Senate Majority Leader Scott Lucas offered the detention camp proposal as a substitute for the registration section of the McCarran measure. Lucas admitted that there was a need for some anti-Red bill, in view of the Korean emergency, but recorded his disapproval of the registration provisions in S. 4037.[40] Homer Ferguson asserted that the Lucas proposal marked "the first time in the history of America that an attempt had been made in the Congress to infringe the constitutional rights of citizens."[41] The Lucas amendment was subsequently rejected by a vote of 45 to 29.[42]

Lucas immediately, in a somewhat strange move, offered a second amendment, the same as the first, but this time as an *addition* to the McCarran bill. McCarran argued strongly against such an addendum on the grounds that it would only furnish the president with an excuse to veto the bill.[43] The second amendment was also rejected but by the much slimmer margin of 37 to 35.[44]

At that point in the proceedings, Harley Kilgore offered his bill as a substitute for the whole of the McCarran bill. After a short period of debate, the Kilgore substitute bill, S. 4130, was rejected by a vote of 50 to 23.[45] The Senate was apparently receptive to any amendment that might strengthen S. 4037, such as the second Lucas proposal, but was quite adamant in not accepting any replacement that would weaken the legislation. Still more surprises occurred when the detention proposal was presented a fourth time.

Within a matter of hours after the rejection of S. 4130, Senator McCarran offered a detention amendment to his own bill, an amendment which he claimed had been purged of the unconstitutional features contained in the Kilgore proposal. The McCarran amendment did represent a watered-down version since it did not provide for suspension of habeas corpus. It carried by a voice vote.[46]

As the Senate approached a final vote on the McCarran omnibus bill, Senator Lehman, one of the few presidential supporters who remained consistent throughout those strange proceedings, offered the following comment: "I am going to vote against this tragic, this unfortunate, this ill-conceived legislation. My conscience will be easier, though I realize my political prospects will be more difficult."[47] Lehman's words evidently passed unheeded, as the Senate overwhelmingly passed, by a vote of 70 to 7, H. R. 9490, which contained the same language as the Senate bill. McCarran insisted on retention of the Senate's amendments and issued the call for a conference with the House.[48]

The roll-call vote on S. 4037 presents some interesting comparisons. Of the seven senators who voted against the proposal, only Kefauver, Lehman, Green, and Graham had actively supported the president's recommendations. Conspicuous among the seventy who favored the bill were Harley Kilgore, Paul Douglas, Scott Lucas, and Hubert Humphrey, all supporters of the administration.[49] Senator Humphrey's yea vote was especially curious when viewed in the context of his comments on the bill the day before the final vote. "The Congress of the United States will regeret the day it ever passes S. 4037. It will prove to be one of the darkest pages in American history."[50] Humphrey's remark was certainly typical of the confused efforts on the part of the administration to stop the McCarran bill.

On September 14, the House of Representatives, by a vote of 324 to 8, agreed to a resolution to appoint a conference committee to resolve the differences between the House and Senate versions of the internal security bill. Representative Adolph Sabath voiced the hope that the conference committee might still substitute the Kilgore proposal but concluded that it was improbable. He did call on the committee at least to come up with a bill the president would sign. Representatives John Rankin and Edward H. Rees pleaded for agreement on a strong bill as quickly as possible.[51]

The conference committee submitted its report on September 20. Although the committee did make a few significant changes, the bill remained generally intact. It eliminated a provision that placed a three-year time limit on the act and imposed more severe penalties than were included in the original version of H. R. 9490.[52] The Senate agreed to the report by a roll-call vote of 57 to 7;[53] the House concurred by a margin of 313 to 20.[54] In the debate on the report, Senator Spessard L. Holland of Florida viewed the final version of the bill as "the product of more than two years of the hardest kind of work. . . ."[55]

The passage of the Wood-McCarran Act was indeed the culmination of a long and persistent effort on the part of congressional conservatives to enact a major antisubversive law—an effort which dated back at least to the introduction of the Mundt-Nixon bill in March 1948. In a last-minute flurry of action, the Truman administration had attempted to head it off, but the effort came much too late and offered far too little.

Truman had repeatedly asserted that he would veto any legislation not in accord with the Bill of Rights, and he left little doubt that he considered the McCarran bill in that category. At his press conference on the fourteenth, however, the president refused to state categorically that he would veto the bill. This was interpreted as a departure from his previous position and led to a number of hurried calls to the White House, most notably from the twenty representatives and seven senators who had risked their political lives in their vote against the bill, and Senator Humphrey who had surprisingly voted for it. They were informed that the president had not changed his opinion but wanted to wait for the conference committee's report before he made a final determination. On the sixteenth, Truman received a tentative report from the committee. From that moment he appeared to have his mind set on a veto.[56]

On the twentieth Truman received a letter from Lehman, Kefauver, and James E. Murray. The three senators voiced concern that the McCarran Act would create more problems than it would solve. "We are convinced that you with your fine feeling for the liberties and also the security of our country, know the dangers better than we." They urged the president to veto the Wood-McCarran Act and at the same time to announce the appointment of a commission to study the whole problem of internal security.[57] Other prominent Democrats such as Sam Rayburn and Alben Barkley, both frightened over the political consequences of a veto, strongly urged Truman to sign the bill. The president replied that he could not, in good conscience, add his name to such a law.[58]

With the prospect of a Presidential veto imminent, Spingarn prepared a memorandum on September 20 entitled "Political and moral reasons for a Presidential veto of the Wood-McCarran Anti-Subversive bill." Spingarn maintained that a veto was doubtless preferable from a long-range, 1952, political view. The president would receive little credit if he signed such a bill; on the contrary, the charge would immediately be made that he had simply yielded to congressional pressure. In addition, a presidential approval would alienate and conceivably drive the liberals into a third party. If the veto was upheld, the president would be vindicated at once; if the veto was overridden, a constitutional test of the law might be accomplished before 1952 which, it was felt, would expose the unconstitutional features of the Act, justify the veto, and pave the way for a more sensible bill regardless of the consequences.

Spingarn also noted that "the signing of the bill would represent an action of moral appeasement on a matter of highest principle." It was infinitely better, he said, to take a stand when the first moral aggression occurred. If not, it would surely prepare the way for other such transgressions. In conclusion, Spingarn concurred with those who had proposed that the president include in his veto message an announcement of his intention to appoint a commission of distinguished citizens to review the loyalty-security program.

> The announcement of such a commission would not only be extremely helpful in securing the votes required to uphold a veto, but it would provide a strong basis for the reconsider-

> ation of this type of legislation in the next session. . .and would. . .put the initiative into the hands of the administration. . . .[59]

The approved conference bill reached the White House early in the afternoon of the twenty-first. After he had rejected three drafts of a proposed veto message Truman added his comments to a fourth and returned it for revision. The fifth and final draft was discussed at a cabinet meeting the next morning. Truman requested that the finished copy of the message be double-spaced to make it easier to read. In a cover sheet on each copy he urged the members of Congress to read and consider carefully the message. Such an unprecedented move, Spingarn concluded, "was an indication of the deep conviction of the President on this subject."

The veto was delivered to the House of Representatives at 4:00 P. M. on Friday, September 22. Despite the president's plea for consideration, the House, without debate, voted 286 to 48 to override.[60] However, a momentary delay in Senate action provided the administration with one last desperate opportunity to forestall passage of the Act.

Late in the evening of the twenty-second, Truman contacted Hubert Humphrey, who had confessed to a change of heart since his vote for S. 4037 on September 12, and asked the freshman senator to lead the fight to sustain the veto in the Senate. The hastily preparesd strategy called for a filibuster by Humphrey, Douglas, Lehman, and Langer, with the expectation that such a delay might prevent Senate action before the scheduled adjournment of Congress at midnight on the twenty-third. There was also a ray of hope that a delay in the Upper House would afford time to build up public support against the bill. The latter, however, constituted little more than wishful thinking.

The Senate remained in session throughout the night as the senators meticulously poured over each point in the president's message. At 5:30 A.M., William Langer, as a result of the strain from the all-night encounter, collapsed and was rushed to the hospital. Humphrey and the others carried on until 2:30 P.M., at which time the president, with the issue no longer in doubt, released them from any further obligation. At 4:00 P.M., on September 23, 1950, the Senate voted 57 to 10 to override the veto.[61]

Truman's nine-page message deserved more attention than either house of Congress apparently gave it. The following principal objections emerged from the president's point-by-point critique:

1. It would aid potential enemies by requiring the publication of a complete list of vital military and national defense facilities.
2. It would require the Department of Justice and the FBI to waste vital time and energy in an attempt to carry out its unworkable registration provision.
3. It would deprive the United States of the assistance of many aliens in intelligence matters.
4. It would antagonize friendly governments.
5. It would place the government of the United States in the business of thought control.
6. It would make it easier for subversive aliens to become naturalized citizens.

The central theme of the message, however, reveals clearly the president's concern for individual liberties. The following quotation represents only one of many extensive passages devoted to that particular subject:

> We can and we will prevent espionage, sabotage, or other actions endangering our national security. But we would betray our finest traditions if we attempted. . .to curb the simple expression of opinion. This we should never do. . .for it would make a mockery of the Bill of Rights and of our claim to stand for freedom in the world.[62]

Truman's arguments were persuasive, a fact attested to by

many who opposed him. But, it was election time, and many who might otherwise have voted with the president could not find the courage to do so. Political expediency quite obviously took precedence over integrity on that particular day in Congress.

Press opinion on the veto was divided. The *Cincinnati Times Star* of September 23 wholeheartedly denounced the president's action. Truman, it was concluded, had decided to oppose the bill rather than admit—by his signature—that the administration had been soft toward the Communists.[63]

An editorial in the *Washington Star* admitted that the new Internal Security Act contained many errors, but it reasoned that the administration's refusal to do anything constructive about the threat of internal communism had forced the Congress to take drastic action.[64] The usually hostile *Chicago Tribune* concluded that the veto furnished conclusive evidence that the Truman administration had become the captive of the Communists.[65]

New York Times columnist Arthur Krock stated that Truman had been soundly defeated because it was a known fact that his administration had been lax in its attempts to keep subversives out of government, and because some of the most violent protests against the bill had come from "pinkos."[66] A *New York Times* editorial, however, described the veto as "an act of genuine courage. . . ."[67]

There was praise from other quarters. Ralph Edwards, a wartime counterespionage agent, congratulated the president for his stand against a bill which, Edwards said, would prove totally inadequate to protect the nation's security and would seriously jeopardize basic American rights.[68] One of the more thoughtful and balanced evaluations of the Truman veto was contained in an article in the October 7 issue of *America*, a Catholic weekly.

> Mr. Truman's veto message may be open to question on a number of the points he raises. What is not open to question

> is the spirit that prompted the veto. . . .He was stressing a firm confidence in our free institutions, in their power to draw upon their own internal resources to meet and defeat totalitarianism without yielding to the totalitarian seduction.[69]

There was certainly no reason to doubt either the president's motives or his courage. Truman felt that the McCarran Act, phrased in such broad and loose language, would prove more of a hindrance than a help. The veto was an honest expression of that feeling and represented one of the notable acts of Truman's political career. The president could have killed the McCarran Act with a pocket veto, but instead he chose to voice his objections. Such outspoken presidential disapproval, even though it failed to achieve its purpose, was nevertheless important because it offered strength to others who opposed restrictive legislation.[70]

Truman was vindicated to an extent when the Act proved to be as unenforceable as he had predicted it would be. The passage of such legislation, as again the president had warned, encouraged many state and local governments to enact similar laws. One such law in New Rochelle, New York, led to the following report.

> Under a local 'little McCarran' law, Communists living in or passing through New Rochelle, N. Y. were ordered to register by midnight, September 28. Midnight passed in suburban New Rochelle with only one registration; an elderly, civic-minded Republican who thought the regulation was for 'commuters.'[71]

The attempt to enforce such a registration law in the state of Maryland—the Ober Act—prompted the following headline in a Baltimore newspaper: "Ober Act Catch: Three Quakers No Communists."[72]

There were other less humorous circumstances which accompanied the 1950 Internal Security Act. The apparent inability to interpret the Act's provisions contributed, from the first, to the persistent charge that such a law was in fact "helping the cause it intends to harm."[73] The *Washington Post* concluded that the formulation of regulations to fit such "cockeyed nonsense" posed a near hopeless task for State Department officials;[74] the *Chicago Sun Times* suggested that the law should have been termed "an act for the Eternal Stupidity of Pat McCarran."[75]

There was also evidence of ineptitude in the enforcement of certain provisions of the Act, especially those which involved immigration restrictions. On October 23, it was reported that Friedrich Gulda, an Austrian pianist, and Fedora Barbieri, an Italian mezzo-soprano, had been detained on Ellis Island due to their past connections with Fascist groups. Gulda had been forced, at the age of ten, to join a Hitler youth organization; Barbieri had attended a Fascist school, as all Italian children were expected to do.[76] Such literal interpretations of the law—if continued—would have barred entrance to almost anyone who had ever lived under a one-party regime.[77]

The heart of the Internal Security Act, its registration provision, was ignored from the outset.[78] McCarran accounted for such disobedience by insisting that the law had not been properly administered.[79] Zechariah Chafee, in his book *The Blessings of Liberty*, asserted that such a charge was false. Both the president and the Subversive Activities Control Board appointed by Truman in October, had performed their duties in good faith. They were, the author declared, simply faced with an impossible task. Chafee also noted the waste in time and human resources. After five years of operation, not one organization had registered under the Act, nor had any received a final order to register.[80] The author wondered at the value of such

> a law which after five years of steady labor has produced for the protection of the United States three administrative orders still under review by the courts, no final orders, no registrations, and 40,200 pages of testimony.[81]

The fear and hysteria that had given birth to the McCarran Act also had a significant effect on the November congressional elections. The concern over communism, in evidence for years, was intensified by the outbreak of the Korean War. An elderly farm couple in Ohio just before the election demonstrated by their remarks, the frustration felt by many:

> Why doesn't Truman get rid of those Communists in government?. . .With our boys dying in Korea, he won't kick out the people who are fighting us—it makes me sick![82]

The Republicans conducted an aggressive campaign unlike that of 1948. Robert Taft, as he stumped through his native state of Ohio, delivered one blast after another at the "spy-riddled" Truman administration. Joe McCarthy labored hard for a number of Republican candidates. His campaign of innuendo worked most effectively in Maryland against Millard Tydings, the Democratic candidate McCarthy was most anxious to destroy. The Wisconsin senator's repeated charges that Tydings had "whitewashed" the Reds played a significant part in the election of a relatively obscure Maryland lawyer named John Marshall Butler. Butler was later charged, and for that reason refused his seat in the Senate for a short time, with having countenanced the distribution of a doctored photograph which pictured Tydings with Communist leader Earl Browder.[83]

McCarthy also contributed to Richard Nixon's election to the United States Senate from California. In a ruthless mudslinging campaign, Nixon charged continually that his opponent, Helen Gahagan Douglas, sympathized with Communist causes. Attention was drawn to the fact that her votes in the House had often corresponded with those of the suspected pro-Communist, Vito Marcantonio of New York. Harold Ickes remarked of the campaign that Nixon had "demonstrated how low a man can sink when his ambitions outrun his scruples. . . ."[84]

There were other notable Democratic casualties in November 1950. Frank Graham, one of the senators who had spoken out in favor of Truman's recommendations, was soundly defeated in the Senate race in North Carolina. In Illinois, Democratic Majority Leader Scott Lucas lost his bid for reelection to Everett M. Dirksen.[85] An obviously disheartened Lucas—never a strong supporter of the president—attributed his defeat to Truman's "cockiness."[86]

Truman had suffered a grievous defeat with the formidable vote to override his veto of the McCarran Act. Without benefit of clairvoyance, the president might well have predicted the outcome in November. The trend, as the *New York Times* reported, was indisputably Republican.[87] If Truman sensed that fact he gave little indication of it; he put himself far out on a limb by predicting a Democratic landslide.[88] As it turned out, the Democratic losses were actually small compared to other off-year elections. Statistically in fact, it might have been construed, with the aid of a vivid imagination, as a victory of sorts. But "the nature of the Democratic defeats was more important than their numbers," as liberals and moderates lost their seats in both Houses of Congress.[89]

Many factors contributed to such an outcome. There was a general overall annoyance with the whole Fair Deal concept of government; there was also the war and its many problems. Still a primary factor, if not *the* factor, in the president's unpopularity was the persistent fear that the Truman administration had become a fertile breeding ground for Communists and their stooges. The issue, enlivened by the Hiss affair, intensified by the McCarthy charges, and manifested in the passage of the McCarran Internal Security Act, had robbed the administration of its vitality and rendered it nearly helpless. In early 1951, Truman made his last significant attempt to regain the initiative in the loyalty-security field.

NOTES

1. Memorandum, For Murphy, Dawson, and Elsey from Spingarn, July 20, 1950, National Defense Folder, Spingarn Papers, Truman Library.

2. *Time*, August 14, 1950, p. 11.

3. Presidential message to Congress, August 8, 1950, OF 262, Truman Papers, Truman Library.

4. Article, *Washington Star*, August 9, 1950, Democratic National Committee Clipping File, Truman Library.

5. *Washington Post*, August 9, 1950.

6. Article, *Chicago Sun Times*, August 11, 1950, Democratic National Committee Clipping File, Truman Library.

7. U.S., *Congressional Record*, 81st Congress, 2d sess., 1950, 96, pt. 9, p. 12145.

8. Congressional Quarterly Service, *Congress and The Nation: 1945-1964* (Washington, D.C.: Congressional Quarterly Service, 1965), p. 1655.

9. Memorandum, For the File on Internal Security from Spingarn, on the subject of action to carry out the President's recommendations, August 8, 1950, Spingarn Papers, Truman Library. In regard to the proposed drafting of a registration-type bill, it should be remembered that Spingarn, as late as July 20, had suggested the same type bill, supposedly with the president's support. The circuit court decision which upheld the conviction of the eleven Communists no doubt played a part in the changed point of view.

10. Memorandum, For Tydings from Spingarn, August 16, 1950, Internal Security Folder, Spingarn Papers, Truman Library.

11. U.S., *Congressional Record*, 81st Congress, 2d sess., 1950, 96, pt. 9, p. 12693.

12. Article, *Chicago Tribune*, August 18, 1950, Democratic National Committee Clipping File, Truman Library.

13. Cabel Phillips, *The Truman Presidency: The History of a Triumphant Succession* (N.Y.: Macmillan Co., 1966), p. 375.

14. Memorandum, For the File from Spingarn, on subject of McCarran "blockbuster" Internal Security Bill, August 17, 1950, National Defense Folder, Spingarn Papers, Truman Library.

15. Zechariah Chafee, Jr., *The Blessings of Liberty* (Philadelphia: J. B. Lippincott, 1956), pp. 119-20.

16. Phillips, *The Truman Presidency*, p. 374.

17. File of existing laws relating to the National Security and their recent enforcement, August 18, 1950, Internal Security Folder, Spingarn Papers, Truman Library.

18. Memorandum, For Steelman from Fitzgerald, August 18, 1950, Internal Security Folder, Spingarn Papers, Truman Library.

19. Memorandum, For J. Edgar Hoover from Spingarn, August 22, 1950, Internal Security Folder, Spingarn Papers, Truman Library.

20. Spingarn to Joseph E. Rosen, August 21, 1950, Internal Security Folder, Spingarn Papers, Truman Library.

21. Spingarn to Stanley M. Goodrich, August 18, 1950, Internal Security Folder, Spingarn Papers, Truman Library.

22. Views of Paul H. Jenson on effective legislation to deal with Communism, August 22, 1950, Internal Security Folder, Spingarn Papers, Truman Library.

23. Memorandum, For Barkley, Rayburn, Lucas, McCormick, from the President, August 28, 1950, Internal Security Folder, Spingarn Papers, Truman Library.

24. Memorandum, For General Landry from Spingarn, August 24, 1950, Internal Security Folder, Spingarn Papers, Truman Library.

25. Vaughn to Captain Watson Miller, August 25, 1950, Internal Security Folder, Spingarn Papers, Truman Library.

26. *Nation*, September 2, 1950, p. 202.

27. Article, *Washington Star*, September 6, 1950, Democratic National Committee Clipping File, Truman Library.

28. Ickes to Green, September 2, 1950, McCarthy File, Theodore F. Green Papers, Library of Congress.

29. Lee Mansfield to the President, September 7, 1950, OF 275C, Truman Papers, Truman Library.

30. Memorandum, For Internal Security File from Elsey, September 6, 1950, Internal Security File, Elsey Papers, Truman Library.

31. U.S., *Congressional Record*, 81st Congress, 2d sess., 1950, 96, pt. 10, p. 14229.

32. Ibid., p. 14419.

33. Ibid., p. 14239.

34. U.S., *Congressional Record*, 81st Congress, 2d sess., 1950, 96, pt. 11, p. 14414.

35. Ibid., p. 14416.

36. Ibid., p. 14420.

37. Ibid., p. 14487.

38. Article, *Washington Times Herald*, September 10, 1950, Democratic National Committee Clipping File, Truman Library.

39. U.S., *Congressional Record*, 81st Congress, 2d sess., 1950, 96, pt. 11, p. 14439.

40. Ibid., p. 14585.

41. Ibid., p. 14585.

42. Ibid., p. 14587.

43. Ibid., pp. 14587-93.

44. Ibid., p. 14594.

45. Ibid., p. 14606.

46. Ibid., p. 14623.

47. Ibid., p. 14627.

48. Ibid., p. 14628.

49. Ibid.

50. *Newsweek*, September 25, 1950, pp. 34-36.

51. U.S., *Congressional Record*, 81st Congress, 2d sess., 1950, 96, pt. 11, pp. 14849-55.

52. Arthur Sutherland, "Freedom and Internal Security," *Harvard Law Review* (January 1951) 64:395. This article contains one of the best contemporary evaluations of the McCarran Act—from a legal point of view.

53. U.S., *Congressional Record*, 81st Congress, 2d sess., 1950, 96, pt. 11, p. 15260.

54. Ibid., p. 15297.

55. Ibid., p. 15250.

56. Memorandum, For the File from Spingarn, Chronology of events on veto of Wood-McCarran Act, September 25, 1950, Internal Security Folder, Spingarn Papers, Truman Library.

57. Lehman, Kefauver, and Murray to the President, September 20, 1950, Internal Security Folder, Spingarn Papers, Truman Library.

58. Memorandum, For the File from Spingarn, Chronology of events on veto, September 25, 1950, Internal Security Folder, Spingarn Papers, Truman Library.

59. Memorandum, For the File from Spingarn, "Political and moral reasons for veto," Internal Security Folder, Spingarn Papers, Truman Library.

60. Ibid.

61. Phillips, *The Truman Presidency*, pp. 376-77.

62. *See* Appendix E.

63. Article, *Cincinnati Times Star*, September 23, 1950, Democratic National Committee Clipping File, Truman Library.

64. Article, *Washington Star*, September 24, 1950, Democratic National Committee Clipping File, Truman Library.

65. Article, *Chicago Tribune*, October 30, 1950, Democratic National Committee Clipping File, Truman Library.

66. *New York Times*, September 26, 1950.

67. Ibid., September 25, 1950.

68. Memorandum, For Murphy from Spingarn, Remarks by Ralph Edwards, September 29, 1950, OF 275A, Truman Papers, Truman Library.

69. Memorandum, For Record from Spingarn, Article by Father Keenan, October 9, 1950, Internal Security Folder, Spingarn Papers, Truman Library.

70. Interview with Stephen J. Spingarn, Washington, D. C., August 9, 1971.

71. Memorandum, For the File from Spingarn, October 5, 1950, Internal Security Folder, Spingarn Papers, Truman Library.

72. Ibid.

73. *Christian Century*, October 18, 1950, p. 1219.

74. *Washington Post*, October 20, 1950.

75. Article, *Chicago Sun-Times*, October 22, 1950, Democratic National Committee Clipping File, Truman Library.

76. *Newsweek*, October 23, 1950, p. 88.

77. *New Republic*, November 6, 1950, p. 7.

78. Ibid., November 13, 1950.

79. *Washington Post*, December 12, 1950.

80. Zechariah Chafee, Jr., *The Blessings of Liberty*, pp. 132-33.

81. Ibid., p. 135.

82. Quoted in Samuel Lubell, *The Future of American Politics*, 2d ed. (Garden City, N.Y.: Doubleday, 1952), p. 164.

83. Phillips, *The Truman Presidency*, pp. 390-91.

84. Quoted in Alonzo L. Hamby, *Beyond the New Deal: Harry S. Truman and American Liberalism* (New York: Columbia University Press, 1973), p. 422.

85. Robert Griffith, *The Politics of Fear: Joseph R. McCarthy and The Senate*

(Lexington: University Press of Kentucky, 1970), p. 123. Griffith suggests that the Communist issue has been exaggerated to the exclusion of a general dissatisfaction with the Democratic administration.

86. *Time*, November 20, 1950, p. 21.
87. Ibid., November 13, 1950, p. 19.
88. Ibid., November 6, 1950, p. 22.
89. Hamby, *Beyond the New Deal*, p. 421.

6
THE APPOINTMENT OF THE NIMITZ COMMISSION

I had hoped that Congress would be as anxious as I am to make sure that our procedures for maintaining the security of the government services are working effectively.

The story of the birth—and subsequent death—of the President's Commission on Internal Security and Individual Rights was essentially one of a series of near misses. The idea for such a commission had been thoroughly discussed in the past; for various reasons, no action was taken on the earlier proposals. A review of the background would seem both appropriate and pertinent to the January 1951 appointment of the commission.

The revelations concerning Communist spy activity which developed from the House and Senate investigations in July and August of 1948 prompted an urgent meeting of various officials of the executive branch on August 6, to discuss possible counteraction. Those present included Clark Clifford, Tom Clark, Peyton Ford, George Elsey, and Charles Murphy. Prominent among the various possibilities discussed was a suggestion that the "president should refer the whole matter, with documents, to a bipartisan commission like the Hoover Commission."[1]

It was reported in a national weekly toward the end of August that a large number of important Democrats, concerned over reactions to Truman's "red herring" remark of August 5, had urged the president to change his strategy. High on the list of suggestions was the appointment of a special presidential commission to study and evaluate the various procedures employed to deal with problems of internal security.[2] A similar suggestion was contained in a letter to the president from Sidney Walchok, a local chairman of the Americans for Democratic Action, on September 27, 1948. Walchok concluded that a review of the whole problem was needed in order to get the issue of anti-Communism into proper perspective.[3]

The congressional investigations in the late summer of 1948 had placed the administration in an almost untenably defensive position; the appointment of a bipartisan commission seemed to present a way out. But the unexpected Democratic victory in November had assauged anxieties and, it was evidently felt, negated any need for a presidential commission. The president had reclaimed the initiative by his unexpected victory, but it proved a triumph of short duration. The Red hunters continued to harass the Democratic administration.

Subdued but persistent pressure from both the right and left led in September of 1949 to a revival of the commission idea. George Elsey discussed a proposal presented by Max Lowenthal who had voiced concern over the operation of the loyalty program. Lowenthal was a long-time friend of the president, who served in an advisory capacity from time to time. Elsey disagreed with Lowenthal's contention that the program represented "one of the greatest blots on the President's record. . . . ," but he did approve of the commission proposal.

> If the President is to appoint such a commission, he should do it at a time like the present, when the Executive Branch is not under fire from Congress or any other source on loyalty matters.[4]

The previous pages attest to Elsey's perceptiveness in his plea for the appointment of a Lowenthal-type commission.

In November 1949, there was further discussion on the proposal. It was noted that Attorney General J. Howard McGrath, although not opposed to the idea, did not feel the time was right for such a commission. McGrath, it would seem, was not so perceptive and Elsey was quite evidently disappointed. "This leaves us exactly where we have been for too long."[5]

The staff continued to press the matter as is indicated by a January 12, 1950 memorandum from Charles Murphy to the president. Murphy noted that the bulk of the investigative work under the loyalty program had been almost completed, that from that point on the work load would be less, and that it therefore appeared an appropriate time for a review of the whole program. He recommended that the proposed commission be staffed with "such persons as John Lord O'Brien [O'Brian], former Senator Robert M. LaFollette, Jr., Milton Eisenhower. . .etc."[6]

The earnest attempt on the part of the staff to take advantage of the lull in the attack on the administration proved unsuccessful as there is no indication of any serious move to appoint a presidential commission. The storm broke anew on February 22, 1950, when Joe McCarthy fired his opening salvo at Wheeling, West Virginia. On that same day, a penciled note was circulated among the White House staff. "It was decided by Spingarn and Elsey that we should not press for a commission to review the operation of the loyalty program, in view of the poor circumstances now. . . ."[7] The implications of such a missed opportunity appear enormous. Had a commission been appointed in the fall of 1949, as Lowenthal and others suggested, it might have diluted the venom of the attack that came later. There would, however, be other opportunities for administration counteraction.

In the course of the Tydings subcommittee investigations, Senator Henry Cabot Lodge, one of the two Republican members of the committee, proposed that a nonpartisan board be appointed jointly by the Executive and Congress to give its full and complete attention to a study of the McCarthy charges. Lodge contended that the Tydings group had neither the time nor the expertise to deal with the problem effectively. Such a board would be composed of four members appointed by the president and four each by the House and Senate; the political makeup would consist of six Republicans and six Democrats. Several Senators voiced interest in the Lodge proposal, but no further progress was made.[8]

On May 22, a *Washington Post* editorial, entitled "The Road Back to America," proposed the establishment of a "Commission on National Security." The commission, bipartisan and staffed by well-known and competent citizens outside the government, could take a fresh look at the problem and submit a report to the American people.[9] Congressional reaction, though varied, was generally favorable.[10] Indeed, the desire for some kind of commission was increasing daily and coming from many different sources.

On May 23, Senator Tydings requested the president to appoint a panel of distinguished citizens to assist the Senate subcommittee with its evaluation of the confidential files just released. Murphy and Spingarn suggested that Truman decline this request because, among other things, it would interfere with the proposed appointment of a special presidential commission. Such a special group, it was stated, would be sufficiently broad to cover any charges made against government employees, and could, at the same time, examine all legislation in the loyalty-security field. The memorandum seems to indicate that the appointment of a presidential commission was imminent.[11] Still no action was taken although the idea continued to gain adherents.

Representative Helen G. Douglas, in the course of a radio broadcast on June 1, urged the need for the creation of a nonpartisan group of citizens to explore and examine the whole question of un-American activities and civil rights. Such an examination, Mrs. Douglas felt, might help to quell the distasteful hysteria that had swept the nation—hysteria which the congresswoman said had been nurtured to a great extent by the actions of the United States Congress. The representative from California indicated that she would recommend that the president appoint such a commission, and that it be headed jointly by Herbert Hoover and Eleanor Roosevelt.[12]

Meanwhile, members of the White House staff continued to press for action on the commission proposal. Spingarn viewed the loyalty program as a "reasonably judicious compromise in the never-ending struggle between freedom and security," but reasoned that the time had come for a review of the whole procedure. "It is my understanding," he said, "that a proposal for a presidential commission to examine and report on the loyalty program is already receiving consideration."[13]

One of the more thoughtful and deliberate appeals for a special commission was contained in a June 19 memorandum for the president from George Elsey.

> Upon further consideration, I have come firmly to the view that the President should recommend to the Congress that it enact legislation to establish a Commission on Internal Security and Individual Rights. . . .Some such step as this is necessary to offset the serious consequences of the irresponsible attacks which Republicans are making against the Government. . . .These attacks have very harmful effects. . . .They increase the likelihood of repressive legislation. They shake the confidence of the people in this country in their Government. A bipartisan commission. . . seems to present the best prospects for putting an end to all this. The fact that the President and the Congress would have to agree in advance upon the establishment of such a commission would be a great help in getting general acceptance of it. . . .Nothing less than such a commission as this would be adequate to the job.[14]

Elsey's appeal, no doubt, provided much of the impetus for a Blair House meeting on June 22 to discuss the proposal. Present, in addition to Truman and his staff, were such notables as Vice President Alben Barkley, Speaker Sam Rayburn,

House Majority Leader John McCormick, Senators Millard Tydings, Brien McMahon, Theodore F. Green, and Attorney General J. Howard McGrath.[15] Although the opinions for and against a proposed commission appeared evenly divided, members of the president's staff concluded that the favorable opinions predominated. The only question that remained was whether the commission would be appointed by the president or by Congress. In any case, it was felt that Truman should present the proposal in a message to Congress.[16]

In the course of the meeting, the president read the fourth draft of a proposed message which called for the creation, by Congress, of a bipartisan commission. Those present said it was a "splendid message," but several, notably Rayburn, Barkley, and McGrath, did not feel the time was right for such a move. The president assured them that he had made no firm decision on the matter.[17]

If the president had intended to act on the proposal, he would have been hard pressed to find the time to do so. Three days after the Blair House meeting, the Korean emergency demanded Truman's full attention and the commission idea was momentarily laid to rest.

Spingarn, Murphy, and Elsey, however, continued to urge the president to take some affirmative action. In a memorandum of July 11, the latter group recommended that the president take advantage of the temporary lull in the congressional attack to announce the appointment of a nonpartisan commission. "The creation of such a commission now might well be considered a statesmanlike response to the tensions and fears caused by the Korean aggression rather than to McCarthy." It was urgent, the staff asserted, that action be initiated at once to offset the increased demand engendered by the war for repressive legislation. Finally, it was recommended that another meeting be called to discuss the proposal, evidently with the hope that the appeal for a commission could be made in conjunction with the soon-to-be-released Tydings report.[18]

Although no action was taken on the memorandum, the release of the Senate subcommittee's report on July 20 offered the best opportunity since the late summer of 1949 for Executive action.

Spingarn, in a most important memorandum of July 20, argued convincingly that the administration should move quickly, while McCarthy "is in eclipse. . . ." In addition, Spingarn noted the growing popularity of the "Mundt-Nixon" bill and Truman's repeated assertion that he would veto such legislation. It was felt that a veto, given the climate of opinion at that time, would create serious political problems. It would be better, Spingarn said, to see that such a bill never reached the president's desk.

> I hate to be in the position of the boy who cried 'wolf' too often but I cannot help feeling that a decision on this commission proposal is pretty pressing and should not be overlooked.[19]

The proposal was "overlooked" at that time as the president, on August 8, presented his legislative proposals to strengthen the antisubversive laws already in existence. However, a later conversation between Spingarn and Averill Harriman reveals that the commission idea was not entirely dead:

> He [Harriman] told me that he was very strong for the proposal and that he thought we were going to regret not having included it in the August 8 message.[20]

No further action was contemplated until the McCarran Act emerged from the conference committee in its final form. The Truman veto message contained no mention of a possible commission although mention had been suggested. Members of the president's staff remained undiscouraged, however, and continued to push the idea. On November 22, Elsey noted, in a memo to Murphy, that Clark Clifford had promised to speak with the president on the subject.[21] Clifford's arguments must have been persuasive, for Truman, two years after the commission idea was first proposed, finally moved to take some affirmative action.

Three days after the meeting with Clifford, Truman, in a letter to Herbert Hoover, asked the former president to chair the proposed commission. The president pointed to the persistent charges over the past years of Communist infiltration, and suggested that a bipartisan presidential commission, headed by someone of Hoover's stature, would "not only restore the confidence of the people in the organization of the Government but could help the foreign policy situation very much."[22]

Hoover's reply on the twenty-sixth of November, though courteous, left little doubt that he did not approve of such a commission. The ex-President doubted the existence of many "card-carrying" Communists in government, and suggested "that the current lack of confidence arises from the belief that there are men in government (not Communists) whose attitudes are such that they have disastrously advised on policies in relation to Communist Russia." Hoover indicated that a statement by the president that such men had been relieved of their positions would do more to placate public opinion than any informal presidential commission.[23]

In his reply to the former president, Truman expressed his regret over Hoover's decision not to serve as chairman, but defended the commission proposal. Such a bipartisan group would be staffed with the most competent people available, and, far from the informal group alluded to by Hoover, would conduct a review of every phase of the loyalty-security question. To facilitate such a study, all pertinent loyalty files in the possession of the executive branch of government would be made available to the members of the commission. The president admitted that he had purposely avoided congressional participation in the commission for fear that it would become strictly partisan. "This is not a question which should be made the subject of a partisan debate in the Congress, which I am afraid might be likely if the establishment of such a commission were referred to the Congress."[24]

Disappointed but still determined, Truman, in a January 4, 1951 letter, asked retired Admiral Chester W. Nimitz to serve as chairman of the proposed commission.[25] Nimitz accepted on January 9, apparently undisturbed by having been the second choice.[26] The President's Commission on Internal Security and Individual Rights was officially created with the issuance of Executive Order 10207 on January 23, 1951.[27] Truman made the following general comments as he announced the appointments.

> We must continue to protect our security within the framework of our historic liberties, without thought of partisan advantage or political gain. To keep these great problems from falling into the arena of partisanship, I am appointing this commission of distinguished citizens on a nonpartisan basis.[28]

Other members of the commission included Anna Lord Strauss, former president of the National League of Women Voters; Right Reverend Carl Morgan Block, Protestant Episcopal Bishop of California; Republican ex-Senator John A. Danaher of Connecticut; Harvey S. Firestone, chairman of Firestone Tire and Rubber Company; William E. Leahy, a Washington attorney; Russell C. Leffingwell, chairman of J. P. Morgan and Company; Charles H. Silver, vice president of the American Woolen Company; and the Most Reverend Emmet M. Walsh, Coadjutor Bishop of the Catholic Diocese of Youngstown, Ohio.[29] The president's order was greeted as "a step. . .that many a Democratic politician heartily wished he had taken long ago. . . ."[30]

The appointees, although they represented a broad cross section of the country, were for the most part conservatives. The *Washington Post* complained that "the commission members lack identification in the public mind with the defense of civil liberties." For that reason it was suggested that someone of the stature of John Lord O'Brian be appointed to serve as counsel to the commission.[31] Roy Wilkins voiced his regret that no Negro had been appointed, especially since so "many Negroes had been persecuted" under the old loyalty program.[32] Despite these criticisms, Truman held high hopes for the success of the Nimitz Commission. Certain members of Congress, however, were not so optimistic.

Views expressed by Senator Homer Ferguson were representative of those others in Congress who had for so long opposed Truman on the issues of loyalty and security. Such a commission, Ferguson argued, was "bound to create strained relations between the Executive and Congress." In particular, the Michigan Republican exhibited extreme jealousy of the powers to be given the commission which had so recently been denied Congress; i.e., access to confidential files within the executive departments. In conclusion, Ferguson charged that the commission amounted to little more than an attempt "to cloak the subject with confusion in the hope that nothing effective will be done about security risks in Government service."[33]

In the minds of some congressmen, the president's commission appeared to be in conflict with the recently appointed McCarran subcommittee, which had been created specifically to keep watch on the administration's execution of the 1950 Internal Security Act.

The Nation asserted that "the President's Commission is as necessary and as promising as the McCarran subcommittee is useless and threatening."[34] The editor of the *Christian Science Monitor*, in response to Ferguson's charge that the Nimitz group would only confuse matters in the loyalty-security field, concluded that "Congress long since has proved itself unable to rise consistently above partisanship and headline hunting in dealing with these same serious matters."[35] In fact, press opinion on the commission was not only favorable but voiced some hope that "sanity and balance" might at last be restored "in an area of our national thinking that has gone dangerously off its rockers."[36] The *Washington Post* voiced approval but pointed out that they had pleaded for the appointment of such a commission in May 1950.[37] The same view was expressed in the *New York Times*—that the commission was a fine idea but should have been appointed many months before.[38]

The Nimitz Commission was officially sworn in on February 12. The president, in his remarks at the ceremony, stressed the urgent need to weigh the security requirements of the nation against the basic rights of the individual. The Bill of Rights, Truman said, "is still the principal part of the Constitution of the United States so far as the individual in this country is concerned. . . ." The president again promised that the Nimitz Commission would have access to all confidential files.[39] Those in Congress who had long been denied the right to examine such files were determined to deny the commission the same privilege.

On February 14, Nimitz notified Truman that the commission had experienced difficulty with certain conflict-of-interests statutes that restricted the number of responsibilities an individual could assume within the federal bureaucracy. If no exception could be made, he said, such statutes would severely limit the present and future services of members and employees of the commission. In particular, the admiral noted that it would be virtually impossible to secure competent legal counsel, who would "wish to be precluded from appearances before the Federal Courts and the Departments and Commissions not only throughout the period of his service with the Commission but for at least two years thereafter." Nimitz suggested the important need for some exemptive legislation.[40] This was not an uncommon request because Congress had, in the past, provided such legislation to exempt from the conflict-of-interest laws, persons appointed to special commissions.

Representative Francis E. Walter, on February 26, introduced H. R. 2829, "a bill to exempt the members and certain employees of the President's Commission on Internal Security and Individual Rights from the operation of certain conflict-of-interest statutes."[41] The bill passed the House on March 19;[42] it was referred to McCarran's Senate Judiciary Committee on March 20.[43]

McCarran, quite obviously determined from the beginning to bury the exemption bill, submitted it to a subcommittee composed of Herbert R. O'Connor of Maryland, Willis Smith of North Carolina, and Homer Ferguson of Michigan. John Danaher sought and arranged a meeting with the Senate group to discuss the matter. Danaher's report indicated that the subcommittee members were unhappy that Truman had appointed such a commission at the very time when various congressional committees had revived their investigations in the field of loyalty. More especially, the subcommittee was upset because the president's commission would be allowed to examine the loyalty files. On a question of whether the commission would release such files to Congress, Danaher replied in the negative. Ferguson in turn threatened legislation that would force the commission members "to be answerable to the Congress as well as the President." The ex-senator from Connecticut thereupon declared that he would resign rather than allow himself to become a "guinea pig" in a power struggle between the president and Congress.

Danaher reminded the senators that Public Law 391 had provided an exemption for the Hoover Commission and that he could see no reason why the same privilege should not be extended to the Nimitz group. Ferguson replied that Congress had appointed the Hoover Commission and had every right to grant such an exemption to one of its own creations.[44] Such an affirmation on the part of Ferguson indicated that Senate opposition to an exemptions bill was based on little more than petty jealousy.

As the Senate continued to procrastinate over the exemption

proposal, a question arose which seemed to fall within the purview of the commission's authority. On February 15, 1951, the new chairman of the Loyalty Board, Hiram Bingham, recommended the following change in the standard for dismissal of governmental employees:

> The standard for the refusal of employment or the removal from employment in an executive department or agency on grounds relating to loyalty shall be that on all evidence, there is a reasonable doubt as to his loyalty to the Government of the United States.[45]

The proposal involved a serious misapplication of an important precept of American criminal law. "The stricture that a reasonable doubt of an accused's guilt should result in his going free, when applied in this manner to the loyalty program, meant that reasonable doubt of an employees loyalty should result in his immediate dismissal."[46]

Bingham defended his request on the grounds that the War and the president's declaration of a national emergency demanded such drastic alteration. Truman at his press conference on February 16 stressed that the proposal would be given careful consideration by his Commission on Internal Security and Individual Rights.[47] However, the continued inability of the commission to function induced the president, in April 1951, to approve the change. It was an unfortunate decision because it led to a significant increase in the very kind of abuses Truman had hoped to eliminate.[48]

Had the Nimitz Commission been free to make the determination, its decision would apparently have been not unlike the president's. Correspondence in the commission files strongly hints that many of the members leaned heavily on the side of enforcement as opposed to judicious protection of individual rights. Excerpts from a March 20 letter from R. C. Leffingwell to Nimitz present a fair example:

> Both those who are disloyal or of doubtful loyalty, and those who are security risks, should be subject to summary removal by the agency head without any *right* of appeal, I think. . . . I get the impression that Congress has been too responsive to the views of the employees' associations and the civil liberties associations. . . . I think employee tenure and civil rights generally have to be subordinated to the right of the nation to defend itself. . . .[49]

On April 30, the Senate Judiciary Committee issued its disapproval of the House exemption bill, H. R. 2829, a move which, for all practical purposes, doomed the president's commission. On May 12, members of the commission submitted their resignations to the president.[50] Truman, still determined to work for the activation of his commission, refused to accept the resignations.

On the twelfth, Truman dispatched a letter to Senator McCarran, whom he had come to detest personally, in which he pleaded for further consideration on the exemption proposal. The letter included all pertinent data on the commission to that date, and contained, in addition, a long list of precedents for the exemption of other commissions from such restrictive statutes.[51] The *Washington Post* asserted that "the Senate cannot permit his [Truman's] defeat on this question without crass disregard of its responsibility to the country and to the individual citizen."[52] The editor doubtless misjudged Senator McCarran.

While the president awaited the senator's reply, a report circulated of a possible effort on the part of the administration to by-pass the Senate Judiciary Committee on the matter of exemption. The Senate had just approved a resolution that provided for immunity from the conflict-of-interest statutes for a Washington attorney, Robert Murphy, to serve as the counsel for the Senate Election Committee in its probe of the 1950 senatorial campaign in Ohio. The strategy would have involved the attachment of the president's appointees to the Murphy resolution in the House of Representatives. The Senate Judiciary Committee would be avoided, and it was hoped that the whole Senate would then reapprove the resolution with members of the commission attached.[53] It would have been a desperate move at best, and no more came of it. The Senate Judiciary Committee remained the president's only hope.

Senator McCarran, in his reply to the president on May 26, offered no consolation. He indicated that O'Connor, Smith, and Ferguson were "all honorable men," that they had reported the exemption bill without recommendation, and that the full Judiciary Committee had followed with a 6-3 vote against a favorable report. The chairman saw no reason for any further consideration. As for the precedents, McCarran pointed out that too many exemptions would erode otherwise worthwhile statutes. The Nevada Democrat concluded with the observation, for whatever it was worth, that "the present request for exemption from those statutes is the first that has been made to Congress in behalf of a Presidential Commission, created in the absence of any prior legislative directive."[54] McCarran's refusal to reconsider the exemption proposal was, as the *Washington Post* had charged earlier, "a slick, cynical piece of obstructionism."[55] Truman continued to hold up on accepting the resignations of Nimitz and the others, as he hoped for some kind of miracle—perhaps the only thing that could have saved his commission by the late spring of 1951.

As the Nimitz group remained inactive, Truman began to express noticeable concern over the conduct, or misconduct, of various loyalty boards. The president's alarm was increased on receipt of a memorandum from Francis Biddle, which outlined several abuses especially in the Fourth Regional Board in Washington, D. C.[56] Truman expressed his anxiety in a May 24 memorandum to Charles Murphy:

> I have been very much disturbed with the action of some of these boards and I want to find some way to put a stop to their un-American activities.

The president indicated that he hoped the Nimitz Commission would be able to handle such matters but, quite evidently dejected, he noted that "it looks now as if we are not going to get any Nimitz Commission."[57]

On July 4, in a letter to James S. Lay, executive secretary of the National Security Council, Truman expressed his continued concern over the actions of certain loyalty boards. The president requested that the council conduct a full and complete investigation of the manner in which the program was being administered.[58]

> We must never forget that the fundamental purpose of our Government is to protect the rights of individual citizens and one of the highest obligations of the Government is to see that those rights are protected in its own operations.[59]

Such correspondence offers ample evidence of Truman's concern for individual rights. It was a fact which stood out among whatever mistakes or oversimplifications he made in regard to the question of loyalty and security. The president was woefully late in his appointment of the Commission on Internal Security and Individual Rights, but once it was appointed, he was not prepared to give it up without a fight. Despite rather clear evidence that the commission would never be allowed to operate, Truman continued to hold on as he struggled with the many other problems of 1951; the war, congressional investigations, Joe McCarthy, and, not the least, a recalcitrant general.

It had been evident since the massive Chinese intervention in Korea in late November, 1950, that the United Nations commander, General Douglas MacArthur, strongly disagreed with the administration's policy of a limited conflict. Disregarding a presidential directive of December 6, 1950, which ordered the U. N. commander to restrict his statements, MacArthur continued to advocate his own position openly. The final break came with the release of MacArthur's statement of March 24 which represented—according to Acheson—"insubordination of the grossest sort to his commander in chief."

If the president still had any doubts, the release, on April 5, of MacArthur's March 20 letter to Representative Joseph W. Martin, Jr. must surely have disabused him. The letter openly attacked the administration's policy in Korea, and convinced Truman that the general would have to be relieved. Orders to that effect were released on April 11. In the aftermath, Acheson relates, "we settled down to endure the heavy shelling from press and Congress that the relief was bound to and did produce."[60] History may exonerate Truman for his decision to relieve Douglas MacArthur but the average American citizen in 1951 did not. The triumphant return of the general, his speech before a joint session of Congress, and the long congressional hearings that followed would haunt the already embattled president until he left office in 1953.

Meanwhile, the issue of internal communism continued to thrive, aided to a great extent by an influential member of the administration. On March 19, FBI Director J. Edgar Hoover warned that the Communist threat to the nation's internal security "looms large. . . ."[61] The director testified before the House Appropriations subcommittee on April 28 that Communists in the United States posed a more dangerous threat than did the Nazi fifth column of World War II—that the FBI was ready, at a moment's notice, to pick up some 14,000 dangerous Reds.[62]

Hoover's revelations probably inspired Congress to revive its investigations into Communist activity in the nation. In late March, the House Committee on Un-American Activities reopened its investigation of Hollywood. One of the first witnesses was actor Larry Parks, late of the *Al Jolson Story*, who confessed to the committee that he had drifted into a Communist cell organization in 1940, attended a few meetings, but eventually, in 1945, had left the party. Parks readily admitted his error in judgment but contended that it was unfair to blame him in 1951 for what he had done largely out of sympathy for the underprivileged in 1940.[63] Several committee members and many others sympathized with Parks, among the latter John Wayne, president of the Anti-Communist Motion Pictures Alliance.[64] Nevertheless the actor's open admission of past membership in the Communist party served to ruin an otherwise promising career. Two other film personalities, Howard da Silva and Gale Sondergaard, took a more belligerent attitude but fared little better.[65] The search for Communists intensified.

Senator McCarthy had remained in the limelight and in February 1951 he characterized the Republican victory in November 1950 as a "mandate to stand as a solid wall against the slow poison of socialism and the dagger death of Communism."[66] In June, McCarthy's vicious and uncalled-for attack on General George C. Marshall astounded many even of his own Republican colleagues who, if not giving outright support, had certainly acquiesced in McCarthy's tirades in the past. The attack on Marshall aroused the freshman senator from Connecticut, Democrat William Benton on August 6 to call for a resolution for the expulsion of Senator McCarthy on charges of "perjury, deceit, fraud, and lack of fitness to hold office."[67]

William Benton was an articulate man with impressive credentials. Although new to Congress, he was one of the few who dared to challenge McCarthy from the Senate floor. His subsequent resolution prompted an investigation that lasted until a final report, unfortunately of negligible value, was issued on January 2, 1953. It was a weak effort but still the only sustained attempt in Truman's last years to "do something" about McCarthy.[68]

Truman, although bruised and battered from his encounters with McCarran, MacArthur, and McCarthy, was still on his feet in August 1951. On the fourteenth of that month, the old familiar "give 'em hell Harry" rang out in a speech before the American Legion, when he blasted the scaremongers who were "chipping away at our basic freedoms just as insidiously and far more effectively than the Communists have ever been able to do." Truman pleaded for a return to "real Americanism" and urged the Legionnaries to "rise up and put a stop to this terrible business. . . ." and "expose the rotten motives of those people who are trying to divide us and confuse us and tear up the Bill of Rights."[69]

McCarthy followed up the president's speech with a renewed attack:

> If only Mr. Truman realized that the disgrace and shame is not to find them [Communists] high in government but the disgrace and shame come when politicians of little minds and less morals try to protect them. . . .[70]

The Legion speech was a noble and fighting effort, but, in essence, the president's last hurrah in 1951. On October 3, Admiral Nimitz recommended to the president that the commission, obviously dead since June, not be reactivated. Nimitz felt that the issue, "if carried over into the Presidential campaign year, might actually do harm to the cause which is so close to the President's heart, namely, protecting the rights of individuals." The admiral also remarked that there was actually less need for the commission in view of the recent Supreme Court decision which upheld the dismissal of Dorothy Bailey, the first government employee released under the 1947 loyalty order. Both Elsey and Murphy concurred with the Nimitz recommendation and suggested that the president reassign employees of the commission, appoint a special consultant on internal security matters, and wait for the report from the National Security Council.[71]

On October 15, Truman received a letter from Patrick M. Malin, executive director of the American Civil Liberties Union, who pleaded "that the Nimitz Commission not be abandoned, and difficult as they are, efforts be renewed to seek the means which would allow the Commission to function."[72] But the president had reluctantly decided that the cause was hopeless. He abandoned the commission plan on October 27 with the observation "that Congress was not interested as he was in making sure that Constitutional rights were not weakened in the drive against treason. . . ."[73]

Since the Nimitz Commission was never allowed to function, it would be impossible to determine just what effect it might have had on the loyalty question. It does not seem likely that there would have been any miraculous change as late as 1951. But in view of the fear and hysteria, the nation needed and deserved such a study as might have been provided by the Nimitz group. Had the commission been appointed at a more appropriate time, say in September 1948, the fall of 1949, or on several occasions during 1950, the outcome might conceivably have been more satlsfactory.

The year 1951, which had opened on a somewhat hopeful note, ended in frustration. The commission had expired, the Korean peace talks were stymied at Panmunjom, and the ever-present uneasiness over internal communism was certainly not pacified. A Gallup poll released on December 29 indicated that Truman's popularity had dropped to an all-time low. Only 23 percent of the American people approved of the president's performance.[74] The situation was to show little improvement in 1952.

NOTES

1. Memorandum, For Clifford from Elsey, consensus of opinion at meeting on August 6, 1948, Internal Security File, Elsey Papers, Truman Library. The highly regarded Hoover Commission, appointed by Congress on a nonpartisan basis in 1947, was given the task of evaluating various organizational procedures within the executive branch of government. The commission submitted its report, with recommendations, in 1949.

2. *Newsweek*, August 30, 1948, p. 15.

3. Sidney Walchok to the President, September 27, 1948, OF 252K, Truman Papers, Truman Library.

4. Memorandum. For Clifford from Elsey, September 19, 1949, Internal Security File, Elsey Papers, Truman Library.

5. Memorandum, For Spingarn from Elsey, November 8, 1949, Internal Security File, Elsey Papers, Truman Library.

6. Memorandum, For the President from Murphy, January 12, 1950, Internal Security File, Elsey Papers, Truman Library.

7. Note, On Delaying appointment of Presidental Commission, February 22, 1950, Internal Security File, Elsey Papers, Truman Library.

8. *New York Times*, April 4, 1950.

9. *Washington Post*, May 22, 1950.

10. Ibid., May 23, 1950.

11. Memorandum, For the President from Murphy and Spingarn, May 24, 1950, OF 252K, Truman Papers, Truman Library.

12. Excerpt, From radio broadcast by Helen Douglas, June 1, 1950, Internal Security File, Spingarn Papers, Truman Library.

13. Memorandum, For Dawson from Springarn, June 17, 1950, Internal Security File, Spingarn Papers, Truman Library.

14. Memorandum, For the President from Elsey, June 19, 1950, Internal Security File, Elsey Papers, Truman Library.

15. Memorandum, For the Files from Spingarn, meeting on proposed commission on Internal Security and Individual Rights, June 23, 1950, National Defense File, Spingarn Papers, Truman Library.

16. Memorandum, Pros and cons on proposal to establish a special commission, June 22, 1950, National Defense File, Spingarn Papers, Truman Library.

17. Memorandum, For the Files from Spingarn, June 23, 1950, National Defense File, Spingarn Papers, Truman Library.

18. Memorandum, For the President from Elsey, Murphy, and Spingarn, July 11, 1950, National Defense File, Spingarn Papers, Truman Library.

19. Memorandum, For Murphy, Dawson, and Elsey from Spingarn, July 20, 1950, National Defense File, Spingarn Papers, Truman Library.

20. Memorandum, For the File from Spingarn (n.d.), National Defense File, Spingarn Papers, Truman Library.

21. Memorandum, For Murphy from Elsey, November 22, 1950, Internal Security File, Elsey Papers, Truman Library.

22. Truman to Hoover, November 25, 1950, OF 2750A, Truman Papers, Truman Library.

23. Hoover to Truman, November 25, 1950, OF 2750A, Truman Papers, Truman Library.

24. Truman to Hoover, December 7, 1950, OF 2750A, Truman Papers, Truman Library.

25. Truman to Nimitz, January 4, 1951, OF 2750A, Truman Papers, Truman Library. According to Truman, he "chose Admiral Nimitz for this task because in previous discussions I had had with him he expressed himself vigorously about the

need of protecting fully every individual right. He was not only our greatest naval strategist in the Pacific and a forthright leader of men but also a devout patriot. . . ." Truman *Memoirs*, 2: 285-86.

26. Nimitz to Truman, January 9, 1951, OF 2750A, Truman Papers, Truman Library.

27. Executive Order 10207, January 23, 1951, OF 2750A, Truman Papers, Truman Library.

28. Statement, By the President on announcing appointment of Nimitz Commission, January 23, 1951, OF 2750A, Truman Papers, Truman Library.

29. Letters, Officially appointing members of Commission, January 30, 1951, OF 2750A, Truman Papers, Truman Library.

30. *Time*, February 5, 1951, p. 8.

31. *Washington Post*, January 27, 1951.

32. Roy Wilkins to the President, February 6, 1951, OF 2750A, Truman Papers, Truman Library.

33. U.S., *Congressional Record*, 82nd Congress, 1st sess., 97, pt. 1, pp. 680-81.

34. *Nation*, February 3, 1951, p. 99.

35. Article, *Christian Science Monitor*, January 27, 1951, Democratic National Committee Clipping File, Truman Library.

36. *New York Times*, January 28, 1951.

37. *Washington Post*, January 25, 1951.

38. *New York Times*, January 25, 1951.

39. Truman's remarks at swearing-in ceremonies for Presidential Commission, February 12, 1951, Democratic National Committee Clipping File, Truman Library.

40. Nimitz to the President, February 14, 1951, OF 2750A, Truman Papers, Truman Library.

41. U.S. *Congressional Record*, 82nd Congress, 1st sess., 1951, 97, pt. 2, p. 1496.

42. Ibid., p. 2609.

43. Ibid., p. 2642.

44. Danaher to Nimitz, March 2, 1951, Nimitz Personal File, Records of President's Commission on Internal Security and Individual Rights, Truman Library.

45. Bingham to Harry B. Mitchell, February 15, 1951, OF 252K, Truman Papers, Truman Library.

46. Alan Harper, "The Free Speech Issue in Post-World War II Reconstruction" (Paper read before the American Historical Association, Pacific Coast Branch, Los Angeles, California, August 27, 1964.)

47. Bingham to Nimitz, February 16, 1951, Nimitz Personal File, Records of President's Commission, Truman Library.

48. Alonzo L. Hamby, *Beyond the New Deal: Harry S. Truman and American Liberalism* (N.Y. Columbia University Press, 1973), p. 468.

49. Leffingwell to Nimitz, March 20, 1951, Nimitz Personal File, Records of President's Commission, Truman Library.

50. Congressional Quarterly Service, *Congress and the Nation: 1945-1964* Washington, D.C.: Congressional Quarterly Service, 1965), p. 1656.

51. Truman to McCarran, May 12, 1951, OF 275A, Truman Papers, Truman Library.

52. *Washington Post*, May 14, 1951.

53. Ibid., May 15, 1951.

54. McCarran to the President, May 26, 1952, OF 2750A, Truman Papers, Truman Library.

55. *Washington Post*, May 2, 1951.

56. Memorandum, For the President from Biddle (n.d.), OF 2750A, Truman Papers, Truman Library.

57. Memorandum, For Murphy from Truman, May 24, 1951, OF 2750A, Truman Papers, Truman Library.

58. Harry S. Truman *Memoirs*, vol. 2: *Years of Trial and Hope* (Garden City, N.Y.: Doubleday, 1956), pp. 288-89.

59. B. J. Bernstein and A. J. Matusow, eds., *The Truman Administration: A Documentary History* (New York: Harper & Row, 1966), p. 37.

60. Dean Acheson, *Present at the Creation: My Years in The State Department* (N.Y.: Norton, 1969), pp. 512-24.

61. *Washington Post*, March 19, 1951.

62. *New York Times*, April, 28, 1951.

63. *Washington Post*, March 22, 1951.

64. *Newsweek*, April 2, 1951, p. 21.

65. *Time*, April 2, 1951, p. 94.

66. Ibid., February 19, 1951, p. 18.

67. Cabell Phillips, *The Truman Presidency: The History of a Triumphant Succession* (N.Y.: Macmillan 1966), pp. 393-94.

68. Robert Griffith, *The Politics of Fear: Joseph R. McCarthy and the Senate* (Lexington: University Press of Kentucky, 1970), pp. 153-59. Benton had no illusion that he could gain enough votes for exclusion, but he hoped that the exposure might lead to the senator's defeat in the election of 1952.

69. Truman's American Legion Speech, August 14, 1951, PPF 200, Truman Papers, Truman Library.

70. *Newsweek*, August 27, 1951, p. 20.

71. Memoandum, For the President from Elsey, October 5, 1951, Internal Security File, Elsey Papers, Truman Library.

72. Patrick Malin to the President, October 15, 1951, OF 2750A, Truman Papers, Truman Library.

73. *Washington Post*, October 28, 1951.

74. Ibid., December 30, 1951.

7
1952: THE FINIS

. . . There never should have been competition on the anti-Communist issue between Congress and the Executive. . . .

Truman divided his State of the Union message of January 9, 1952, into what he termed the positive and the negative aspects of the past year. On the credit side the president pointed out that the United States had successfully turned back the tide of Communist aggression in Korea and not been in the process forced into a wider conflict. He stressed, however, that the situation remained hazardous and would demand perserverance on the part of the American people. Next on the credit side, the president declared the economy was in excellent shape. On the debit side, he admitted Russia's continued military productiveness and the incompleteness of the United States defense preparations, although they had greatly progressed. Conspicuously absent from the message was any mention of internal security.[1]

One week after the president's annual address, *Newsweek* reported that the issue of internal communism was on the wane, though still in evidence—as it surely was.[2] McCarran's Senate committee hearings into the affairs and influence of the Institute of Pacific Relations, in progress since July 25, 1951, were still in session, with attention focused on Owen Lattimore. The hearings, which were not concluded until June

20, 1952, did reveal the presence of Communist sympathizers within the institute but failed to prove the existence of any conspiracy in the formation of American foreign policy.[3] In March, Lattimore stated unequivocally that "I am not and have never been a Communist, a Soviet agent, a sympathizer or any other kind of promoter of communism or Communist interests."[4]

Besides pursuing the Lattimore affair, Joe McCarthy, now at the peak of his political power, was as diligent in his search of Communists as ever. On January 29, the senator reached into the ranks of the White House when he announced that Philleo Nash, a member of Truman's staff, had been a member of the Communist party. McCarthy revealed that his information had come from a number of points "developed by the FBI."[5] Truman was quick to defend his staff member, and denounced McCarthy in perhaps his strongest public language on the senator up to that time, as a "pathological character assassin and a liar. . . ."[6]

Senator William Jenner continued his attack on the president's persistent refusal to release certain loyalty files, particularly those relative to John Carter Vincent. A letter from Truman, inserted in the congressional record, reveals the consistency he had maintained in that matter.[7] Jenner was not impressed, and continued, unsuccessfully, to try to force the president to relax his order against the release of confidential files.

Truman's most significant battle with the Congress in 1951 developed over the passage of the controversial McCarran-Walter immigration bill. Although bearing only slightly on the issue of internal communism, overtones of that issue were clearly evident and it therefore deserves attention.

On March 24, 1952, Truman addressed Congress on the matter of displaced persons. Specifically, he asked Congress:—

1. to provide aid for the unfortunate victims of oppression who are escaping from Communist tyranny behind the iron curtain;

> 2. to continue our participation in the international effort. . . .to assist in the migration and resettlement throughout the world of a substantial number of persons from the overpopulated areas of Western Europe; and
> 3. to authorize additional immigration into this country, on a limited basis, to aid in alleviating the problems created by Communist tyranny and overpopulation in Western Europe.[8]

Congress responded with the McCarran-Walter omnibus bill, S. 2550, which would supposedly codify the amalgam of United States immigration laws. Representative Francis E. Walter's bill differed only slightly from McCarran's Senate bill which had developed after two and one half years of hearings and the words in which, McCarran proudly announced, exceeded both those of the Old and New Testament.

The debates on the new immigration bill closely paralleled those that preceded passage of the 1950 Internal Security Act. McCarran continually charged that the same groups that had opposed the Internal Security Act—Communists and their sympathizers—also opposed the McCarran-Walter bill. Karl Mundt voiced the same sentiments, and pointed specifically to the National Lawyers Guild which he described as the "foremost legal bulwark of the Communist Party. . . ."[9]

Opposition to the McCarran-Walter bill was led by Senators Hubert Humphrey and Herbert Lehman who introduced a substitute, S. 2842, on March 12. The bill was referred to the Senate Judiciary Committee from which it would never emerge.[10] Lehman particularly denounced the McCarran bill as one that produced "a philosophy of fear, suspicion, and distrust of foreigners outside our country, and of the aliens within our country."[11] Senator William Benton referred to the McCarran bill as a "codification of the bad features" of all other bills.[12] Brien McMahon inferred that S. 2550 would most certainly encourage a presidential veto. "No self-respecting President would sign a bill embracing such outlandish provisions as contained in this bill."[13]

Truman's legislative advisor noted certain merits in the Mc-

Carran proposal: it would remove racial barriers to naturalization, extend quotas to certain Asiatics for the first time, abolish discrimination based on sex, and facilitate the immigration of persons whose services are "urgently needed" in the United States. But, in the final analysis, it was concluded that "the bill is restrictive and repressive in spirit."[14]

The opponents of S. 2550 fought long and hard but their chance to stop the bill was negligible at best. On May 21, Senator Lehman offered an amendment as a substitute for the whole of the McCarran bill and it was promptly rejected by a vote of 51 to 27.[15] On the next day, the Senate passed the Walter bill, H. R. 5678, in lieu of S. 2550, and requested a conference with the House.[16] The conference report was submitted to the House on June 10 and approved by a vote of 203 to 53.[17] The Senate agreed on June 11.[18]

The president's correspondence, which urged approval of disapproval of the bill, paralleled that received on the Internal Security Act. Donald Nelson, national commander of the American Legion, exhorted the president to sign the McCarran-Walter bill.[19] Mrs. James Patton, president of the Daughters of the American Revolution, also urged approval.[20] One of the more thoughtful letters that requested a presidential veto came from Arthur Klein, representative of the 19th District of New York.

> I believe you will agree that the only course you can consistently follow is to veto this bill and thus continue your record of opposition to measures which would restrict the liberties and opportunities of the American people.[21]

As late as June 12, there was still doubt as to whether the president would exercise his veto power. Charles Murphy noted on that date that "apparently, there is actually a considerable amount of good in along with the bad. . . ."[22] Nonetheless both Lehman and Humphrey expressed concern that Truman might not follow through on his promised veto. Murphy assured them that the president simply wanted to see if the bill had been cleaned up sufficiently in committee to warrant his consideration.[23]

Stephen Spingarn has stated that when a bill was presented to Truman, his question was always, "is there more good than bad?"[24] The bad no doubt predominated in the case of the McCarran-Walter Act and the president delivered his veto message to Congress on June 25, 1952. Truman took notice of the desirable provisions, but stated that they "come before me embedded in a mass of legislation which would perpetuate injustices of long standing against many other nations of the world. . . .The price is too high, and in good conscience I cannot agree to pay it."[25] On Thursday, July 3, the House, as expected, voted 278 to 113 to override the president's veto. The best hope to sustain it rested in the Senate. The debate was vigorous, as exemplified by Senator Blair Moody of Michigan who shouted fervently that a vote to override would, in effect, be "striking a blow for Stalin." The result was close, the McCarran forces prevailing by a margin of only one, the Senate voting 57 to 26 to override Truman's veto.[26] The president had lost what was to be his last major battle with Congress. Some months before his veto of the McCarran-Walter Act, Truman had announced that he would not be a candidate for the presidency in 1952.

There had been considerable speculation in the early months of 1952 as to whether Truman would again seek his party's nomination. The general consensus seemed to be that the president ought not to seek a second full term. Such a view was stated quite firmly in the *New Republic*: "Harry Truman is a spent force politically."[27]

Truman ended all speculation in an address delivered on March 29 at the Jefferson-Jackson Day dinner. The speech was alive with typical Truman rhetoric, using especially the "give 'em hell" approach against the opposition party. In particular, the president went to considerable length to defend his anti-

Communist record against the oft-repeated charge that the Democratic administration was soft on communism.

> That's the record, and how do the Republicans propose to get around it? Here's what they will try to do. They will go to the voters and say, 'Did you know the Government was full of Communists?' And then the Republicans explain that somebody named Joe Doakes works for the Government, and he has a cousin who sells shoelaces, or a ribbon clerk in a department store, and this cousin has a wife who wrote an article, before Joe married her, that was printed in a magazine that also printed an article in favor of Chinese Communists—and they will continue that ad lib.

Truman concluded with a short concise statement of withdrawal. "I shall not be a candidate for reelection. I have served the country long, and I think efficiently and honestly. I shall not accept a renomination."[28]

The press was gentle but generally concluded that the president's decision to withdraw was a wise one. Truman's political stock was at low tide and, as many noted, it was doubtful whether he could have won even if nominated. It was pointed out in the *Washington Star* that one of the primary grievances that voters held against the president concerned "the charges of socialism and communist sympathies that have been lodged against his administration. . . ."[29]

On the other side of the coin, there were many who viewed Truman as the perpetrator of fear and suspicion, of overreaction in the face of possible Communist subversion. As the editor of the *New Republic* stated: "The angry dark clouds of Harry S. Truman's loyalty inquisition are beginning to mount in intensity." It was concluded that "the responsibility of this loyalty phobia must fall squarely in the lap of President Truman," who, it was said, had laid the foundation for McCarthyism.[30]

Such accusations were completely unsound, and destitute of reason. The Truman loyalty program, initiated in 1947, was a realistic response to the development of a long and persistent list of charges that Communists had infiltrated high places in the government. Assuredly one of the prime reasons for Executive Order 9835 was to take the initiative from a Congress running scared in the face of such charges, and to attempt to check the trend toward more repressive legislation. Truman consistently maintained, both then and later, that the threat from internal subversion was minor—that the great majority of government employees were loyal citizens. Certainly the statistical report on the operation of the loyalty program through 1952 strongly indicates that the president was altogether correct. It showed, after the perusal of 4,300,000 loyalty forms of new and incumbent employees, that only 414 had been removed or otherwise denied employment on loyalty grounds.[31]

Even Tom Clark, more prone to take a hard line than Truman, later decided that in 1947 the danger was more imaginary than real. Clark concluded, however, that the loyalty program did help restrain the Congress and this, it would seem, was the primary motive.[32]

Truman promised from the first that there would be no witch-hunt. So far as humanly possible, the president kept this promise. It is true that the program was too broad to make effective control possible; it could and should have been more limited in scope. Also, the violations of individual rights were too numerous to overlook, but they appear to have been exceptions. Overall, the loyalty program was administered with moderation. There is no reason to doubt Truman's commitment to individual rights. One of the most articulate expressions of that devotion appeared in the president's last State of the Union message in which he warned against an unreasoned fear of communism.

> Already the danger signals have gone up. Already the corrosive process has begun. And every diminution of our tolerance, each new act of enforced conformity, each idle

> accusation, each demonstration of hysteria—each new restrictive law—is one more sign that we can lose the battle against fear. The Communists cannot deprive us of our liberties—fear can. . . . To beat back fear, we must take our stand on the Bill of Rights. The inquisition, the star chamber, have no place in a free society.[33]

Still another expression of Truman's personal regard for human rights can be heard in his earlier address, December 15, 1952, at the National Archives.

> In my opinion, the Bill of Rights is the most important part of the Constitution. . . . The idea of freedom is in danger from others as well as the communists. There are some who hate communism, but, who, at the same time, are unwilling to acknowledge the ideals of the Constitution as the supreme law of the land. They are people who believe it is too dangerous to proclaim liberty throughout all the land to all the inhabitants. What these people really believe is that the Preamble ought to be changed from 'we, the people', to read, 'some of us—some of the people of the United States, but not including those we disapprove of or disagree with—do ordain and establish this Constitution.'[34]

What remains open to criticism, if not the president's concern for individual rights, is Truman's failure throughout 1949 and most of 1950 to lead the nation positively on the loyalty issue. The Congress reclaimed the initiative in the summer of 1948 and held it, except for a brief period after the election of 1948, until Truman left the presidency. The struggle that ensued drained the life from the administration. Truman, although he fought the good fight, must share the blame for the final result. The Catholic weekly *America*, noted after the president's announcement that he would not seek reelection:

> Though deeply anti-Communist and personally honest, Mr. Truman has allowed himself to be outmaneuvered by political opponents on two major issues; Communism and corrupt officials in his administration.[35]

From 1948 through July 1950, there were numerous suggestions offered, by staff members and others, for some positive action to improve the administration's loyalty program and to counter congressional demands for more repressive legislation. Truman made no affirmative move on any of the proposals until he appointed the Nimitz Commission in January 1951—four months after the passage of the McCarran Internal Security Act. There is no assurance that some earlier response would have altered the situation, but in view of the eventual fate of the administration, it would have been worth an effort.

When involved almost exclusively with a president's actions in one particular area, it is all too easy to forget the myriad other pressures that any president is constantly under. Truman's problems were many and complex, and to find satisfactory solutions to any of them would have taxed the combined wisdom of Washington, Jefferson, and Lincoln. Yet there is undoubtedly sufficient evidence to warrant a charge of inaction and procrastination in the area of loyalty and security.

The explanation of such a lack of administrative action may be found in Truman's very consistency. Through the entire contest he insisted that the country was in no grave danger from internal subversion, that the best way to oppose communism was to improve the quality of American life, and that Congress had turned the problem of security into a political issue for partisan advantage. On that basis the president stands vindicated. It was Congress who pushed the matter—beyond the bounds of necessity or reason—to the point of national hysteria. Truman's sin was at worst one of omission.

Dean Acheson, in comparing presidents, stated that "Mr. Truman will stand with the few who in the midst of great difficulty managed their offices with eminent benefit to the public interest."[36] There have indeed been few other presidents who exhibited more integrity than Harry Truman, or tried harder to perform the duties of the presidency in an exemplary manner. "In the last analysis," Acheson concluded, "Mr. Truman's methods reflected the basic integrity of his own character. He could have said of them what Mr. Lincoln said of his: 'I desire to so conduct the affairs of this administration that if, at the end . . . I have lost every other friend on earth, I shall have at least one friend left, and that friend shall be down inside of me.' "[37] Of all the qualities that people demand in a president, the one of personal honesty is perhaps the most desirable.

NOTES

1. State of the Union Message, January 9, 1952, Nash Papers, Truman Library.
2. *Newsweek*, January 14, 1952, p. 24.
3. Earl Latham, *The Communist Controversy in Washington: From the New Deal to McCarthy* (New York: Atheneum, 1969), pp. 296-316.
4. *Newsweek*, March 10, 1952, p. 29.
5. U.S., *Congressional Record*, 82nd Congress, 2d sess., 1952, pt. 1, p. 58.
6. *Newsweek*, February 11, 1952, p. 23.
7. U.S., *Congressional Record*, 82d Congress, 2d sess., 1952, 98 pt. 1, p. 820.
8. Presidential address to Congress on the matter of displaced persons, March 24, 1952, Nash Papers, Truman Library.
9. U.S., *Congressional Record*, 82d Congress, 2d sess., 1952, 98, pt. 12, pp. 5093-94.
10. Ibid., pt. 2, pp. 2140-41.
11. Ibid., pt. 12, p. 5102.
12. Ibid., p. 5111.
13. Ibid., p. 5154.
14. Memorandum, To Lloyd from R. W. Jones, February 18, 1952, Neustadt Papers, Truman Library.
15. U.S., *Congressional Record*, 82d Congress, 2d sess., 1952, 98, pt. 5, p. 5630.
16. Ibid., p. 5803.
17. Ibid., p. 6991.
18. Ibid., pt. 6, p. 7018.
19. Donald Nelson to Truman, June 20, 1952, OF 133, Truman Papers, Truman Library.
20. Mrs. James Patton to Truman, May 23, 1952, OF 133, Truman Papers, Truman Library.
21. Arthur G. Klein to Truman, June 5, 1952, OF 133, Truman Papers, Truman Library.

22. Murphy to Aaron Lewittes, June 12, 1952, Murphy Papers, Truman Library.

23. *Newsweek*, June 23, 1952, p. 25.

24. Interview with Stephen J. Spingarn, Washington, D.C., August 9, 1971.

25. Truman's veto of the McCarran-Walter Immigration Act, June 25, 1952, Nash Papers, Truman Library.

26. *Newsweek*, July 7, 1952, p. 25.

27. *New Republic*, February 4, 1952, p. 5.

28. Truman's address at Jefferson-Jackson Day dinner, Washington, D.C., March 29, 1952, Democratic National Committee Clipping File, Truman Library.

29. Article, *Washington Star*, March 31, 1952, Democratic National Committee Clipping File, Truman Library.

30. *New Republic*, April 14, 1952, p. 5.

31. Harold Chase, *Security and Liberty: The Problem of Native Communism, 1947—1955* (Garden City, N.Y.: Doubleday, 1955), p. 44.

32. Interview with Justice Thomas C. Clark, Washington D. C., August 22, 1969.

33. State of the Union Message, January 7, 1953, Neustadt Papers, Truman Library.

34. Truman's address at the National Archives, dedicating new shrine for the Declaration of Independence, Constitution, and the Bill of Rights, December 15, 1952, Lloyd Papers, Truman Library.

35. U.S., *Congressional Record*, 82d Congress, 2d sess., 98, pt. 9, p. A2174.

36. Dean Acheson, *Present at the Creation: My Years in the State Department* (N.Y.: Norton, 1969), p. 729.

37. Ibid., p. 734.

APPENDIXES

APPENDIX A: THE REPORT OF THE PRESIDENT'S TEMPORARY COMMISSION ON EMPLOYEE LOYALTY:* PART VI—RECOMMENDATIONS

Based on the foregoing general and specific conclusions of the Commission, the following recommendations are respectfully submitted:

Under Paragraph 3c of Executive Order No. 9806, it is recommended as Follows:

a. Each department and agency shall be responsible for prescribing and supervising its own loyalty procedures, in accordance with generally applicable minimum requirements hereinafter recommended.
b. A central master card index shall be maintained in the Civil Service Commission covering all persons on whom loyalty investigations have been made by any department or agency since September 1, 1939. The master file shall contain the name, adequate identifying information and an indication that a report can be found in the appropriate department or agency. The investigative report in each case shall remain in the investigating agency.
c. (1) At the request of the head of any department or agency an investigative agency shall make available to such head, personally, all investigative material and information collected

*OF 2521, Truman Papers, Truman Library.

by the investigative agency on any employee or prospective employee of the requesting department or agency, or shall make such material and information available to any officer or officers designated by such head and approved by the investigating agency.

(2) Notwithstanding the foregoing requirement, however, the investigative agency may refuse to disclose the names of confidential informants, provided it furnishes sufficient information about such informants on the basis of which the requesting department or agency can make an adequate evaluation of the information furnished by them, and provided it advises the requesting department or agency in writing that it is essential to the protection of the informants or to the investigation of other cases that the identity of the informants not be revealed. It is not intended that investigative agencies should use this discretion to decline to reveal sources of information where such action is not essential.

d. The attorney General shall currently furnish information to the Civil Service Commission on all organizations designated by him in accordance with the criterion established in subparagraph vi of the recommendations under Paragraph 3d of Executive Order 9806. The Civil Service Commission shall disseminate this information to all departments and agencies together with any other current information on related loyalty problems. It shall be the responsibility of the Loyalty Board, hereinafter provided, upon request, to advise any department or agency on loyalty matters.

e. The Loyalty Boards of the various departments and agencies, hereinafter provided, may be called upon by the Civil Service Commission or the Loyalty Review Board for reports to indicate the number of loyalty cases on which a determination has been made during a given period.

f. Each department or agency shall be responsible for the loyalty investigation of any of its employees whenever it is deemed necessary. Those departments and agencies not having investigative organizations will use the investigative facilities of the Civil Service Commission.

g. (1) There shall be a loyalty investigation of all persons entering the employ of any department or agency. All investigations of persons entering the competitive service shall be conducted by the Civil Service Commission, except in such cases as are covered by a special agreement between the Commission and any given department or agency. The investigation of all persons entering the employ of any department or agency, other than those entering the competitive service, shall be the responsibility of the employing department or agency.

(2) The investigation shall be conducted either before or after a person goes on the payroll. In the case of a person entering the competitive service, if the investigation continues after the date he goes on the payroll and is not completed within 18 months from that date, the condition that his employment is subject to investigation shall expire except in a case where the Civil Service Commission has made an adjudication of disloyalty and the case continues to be active by reason of appeal.

(3) A full field investigation shall be conducted of those applicants designated by the head of the employing department or agency, such designation to be based on what he considers to be in the best interest of national security.

(4) An investigation short of a full field investigation shall be made on all other applicants at all available pertinent sources of information, such as:

i. Federal Bureau of Investigation files;
ii. Civil Service Commission files;
iii. Military and naval intelligence files and the files of any other pertinent intelligence or governmental investigative agency not previously referred to;
iv. House Committee on Un-American Activities files;
v. Local law enforcement files at the place of residence or employment, such as municipal, county and state;
vi. School and college;
vii. Former employer or employers;
viii. References;
ix. Any other similar checks as may be appropriate.

If any of these sources reveal derogatory information, there shall then be a full field investigation.

h. Each department and agency to the extent that it has not already done so, or the Civil Service Commission, shall submit lists of the names of all of its incumbent employees (and such other necessary identifying material as the Federal Bureau of Investigation may require) to the Department of Justice, which shall check such lists against its records of persons concerning whom there is substantial evidence of being within the purview of paragraphs (i) to (vi) of the recommendations herein made under paragraph 3d of Executive Order 9806. After such check is made each department and agency shall make, or cause to be made by the Civil Service Commission, such other investigation of its employees as the head of the department or agency shall deem advisable, as indicated by the aforesaid check.

i. That the President direct the Security Advisory Board of the State-War-Navy Coordinating Committee to draft uniform minimum rules applicable to the handling or transmission of all confidential documents, or other documents or information which should not be publicly disclosed, and upon approval by the President, such rules shall apply to all departments and agencies of the Executive Branch of the Government.

Under Paragraph 3d of Executive Order No. 9806, it is recommended as follows:

a. The responsibility for acting upon investigative reports shall be left to the respective departments and agencies and not to a central agency or committee.

b. The head of each department and agency shall appoint a Loyalty Board or Boards of not less than three members each for the purpose of hearing loyalty cases.

c. There shall be established in the Civil Service Commission a Loyalty Review Board with power:

    i. to advise all departments and agencies on all problems related to employee loyalty;
    ii. to disseminate all information pertinent thereto;
    iii. to coordinate the employee loyalty policies and procedures of the various departments and agencies;
    iv. to make any rules and regulations deemed necessary to implement applicable statutes and Executive Orders;
    v. to make reports and submit recommendations to the President from time to time whenever such actions are

deemed necessary to the maintenance of the employee loyalty program;

vi. Except in cases arising in a department or agency which is authorized to remove an employee summarily for security reasons (as now provided for in Public Law No. 808 and under the McCarran Rider), the Loyalty Review Board shall have power to review cases involving subversive or disloyal persons and to make advisory recommendations thereon to the head of the employing department or agency. Cases which are subject to review may be referred to this Board for advisory recommendations *either by* an employing agency or department *or by* an employee in the Executive Branch of the Government who has been adjudged to be disloyal or subversive.

Under Paragraph 3c of Executive Order No. 9806, it is recommended as follows:

a. An employee who is charged with being disloyal shall have a right to an administrative hearing before a Loyalty Board in the employing department or agency. He may appear personally, accompanied by counsel or representative of his own choice, with witnesses, and present any evidence, including affidavits, in his behalf. Each department or agency shall prescribe regulations for the conduct of these hearings.

b. The employee shall have the right to reply in writing to the charges so made and each agency shall serve a written notice on such employee containing:

   i. a statement of the charges preferred against him, the specification of such charges to be as complete as security considerations permit;

   ii. a statement that he has a right to reply to the charges in writing within a reasonable period of time, to be specified;

   iii. a statement as to his right of hearing, if he so desires, at which he may personally appear with counsel or representative of his own choice, and witnesses, and present evidence, including affidavits, in his own behalf.

c. When a Loyalty Board recommends removal there shall be, prior to removal, a right of appeal under provisions prescribed by the head of each department or agency.

d. The rights of hearing, notice and appeal shall be accorded to all employees, irrespective of tenure or manner, method or nature of appointment.

Under Paragraph 3d of Executive Order No. 9806, it is recommended as follows:

The underlying standard for either the refusal of employment or removal from employment in loyalty cases shall be that, on all evidence, reasonable grounds exist for believing that the person involved is disloyal to the Government of the United States. Individual employee activities and associations which may be considered in this connection include one or more of the following:

i. Sabotage, espionage, or attempts or preparations therefore, or knowingly associating with spies or saboteurs;

ii. Treason or sedition or advocacy thereof;

iii. Advocacy of revolution or force or violence to alter our constitutional form of government;

iv. Intentional, unauthorized disclosure to any person of documents or information of a confidential or non-public character obtained by the person making the disclosure as a result of his employment by the Government of the United States;

v. Performing or attempting to perform his duties or otherwise acting, so as to serve the interests of another government in preference to the interests of the United States;

vi. Membership in, affiliation with or sympathetic association with any foreign or domestic organization, association, movement, group or combination of persons, designated by the Attorney General as totalitarian, fascist, communist, or subversive, or as having adopted a policy of advocating or approving the commission of acts of force or violence to deny others their constitutional rights, or as one which seeks to alter our form of government by unconstitutional means.

Under Paragraph 3e of Executive Order No. 9806, it is recommended as follows:

a. That the temporary legislation by which the Secretaries of the War, Navy and State Departments can presently remove any employee summarily for security reasons, be made permanent because of the sensitive nature of the operations of these three departments, and that permanent legislation of the same character be enacted to grant similar power to the Atomic Energy Commission.
b. That all of the recommendations contained in this report be effectuated by the promulgation of an Executive Order which will simultaneously provide for the abrogation of Executive Order No. 9300, dated February 5, 1943.

In conclusion, the Commission recommends that this report, together with any Executive Order which the President may issue, be submitted to Congress for consideration.

A. Devitt Vanech
Chairman
John E. Peurifoy
Edward H. Foley, Jr.
Kenneth C. Royall
John L. Sullivan
Harry B. Mitchell

APPENDIX B: EXECUTIVE ORDER 9835*

PRESCRIBING PROCEDURES FOR THE ADMINISTRATION OF AN EMPLOYEES LOYALTY PROGRAM IN THE EXECUTIVE BRANCH OF THE GOVERNMENT

WHEREAS each employee of the Government of the United States is endowed with a measure of trusteeship over the democratic processes which are the heart and sinew of the United States; and

WHEREAS it is of vital importance that persons employed in the Federal service be of complete and unswerving loyalty to the United States; and

WHEREAS, although the loyalty of by far the overwhelming majority of all Government employees is beyond question, the presence within the Government service of any disloyal or subversive person constitutes a threat to our democratic processes; and

WHEREAS maximum protection must be afforded the United States against infiltration of disloyal persons into the ranks of its employees, and equal protection from unfounded accusations of disloyalty must be afforded the loyal employees of the Government:

NOW, THEREFORE, by virtue of the authority vested in me by the Constitution and statutes of the United States, including the

*U.S., National Archives and Records Service, Federal Register Division, *Code of Federal Regulations*, 1943-48, Compilation, Executive Orders, pp. 627-31.

Civil Service Act of 1883 (22 Stat. 403), as amended, and section 9-A of the act approved August 2, 1939 (18 U.S.C. 61 i), and as President and Chief Executive of the United States, it is hereby, in the interest of the internal management of the Government, ordered as follows:

PART I—INVESTIGATION OF APPLICANTS

1. There shall be a loyalty investigation of every person entering the civilian employment of any department or agency of the executive branch of the Federal Government.
   a. Investigations of persons entering the competitive service shall be conducted by the Civil Service Commission, except in such cases as are covered by a special agreement between the Commission and any given department or agency.
   b. Investigations of persons other than those entering the competitive service shall be conducted by the employing department or agency. Departments and agencies without investigative organizations shall utilize the investigative facilities of the Civil Service Commission.
2. The investigations of persons entering the employ of the executive branch may be conducted after any such person enters upon actual employment therein, but in any such case the appointment of such person shall be conditioned upon a favorable determination with respect to his loyalty.
   a. Investigations of persons entering the competitive service shall be conducted as expeditiously as possible; provided, however, that if any such investigation is not completed within 18 months from the date on which a person enters actual employment, the condition that his employment is subject to investigation shall expire, except in a case in which the Civil Service Commission has made an initial adjudication of disloyalty and the case continues to be active by reason of an appeal, and it shall then be the responsibility of the employing department or agency to

conclude such investigation and make a final determination concerning the loyalty of such person.

3. An investigation shall be made of all applicants at all available pertinent sources of information and shall include reference to:
   a. Federal Bureau of Investigation files.
   b. Civil Service Commission files.
   c. Military and naval intelligence files.
   d. The files of any other appropriate government investigative or intelligence agency.
   e. House Committee on un-American Activities files.
   f. Local law-enforcement files at the place of residence and employment of the applicant, including municipal, county, and State law enforcement files.
   g. Schools and colleges attended by applicant.
   h. Former employers of applicant.
   i. References given by applicant.
   j. Any other appropriate source.

PART II—INVESTIGATION OF EMPLOYEES

1. The head of each department and agency in the executive branch of the Government shall be personally responsible for an effective program to assure that disloyal civilian officers or employees are not retained in employment in his department or agency.
   a. He shall be responsible for prescribing and supervising the loyalty determination procedures of his department or agency, in accordance with the provisions of this order, which shall be considered as providing minimum requirements.
   b. The head of a department or agency which does not have an investigative organization shall utilize the investigative facilities of the Civil Service Commission.
2. The head of each department and agency shall appoint one or more loyalty boards, each composed of not less than three

representatives of the department or agency concerned, for the purpose of hearing loyalty cases arising within such department or agency and making recommendations with respect to the removal of any officer or employee of such department or agency on grounds relating to loyalty, and he shall prescribe regulations for the conduct of the proceedings before such boards.

a. An officer or employee who is charged with being disloyal shall have a right to an administrative hearing before a loyalty board in the employing department or agency. He may appear before such board personally, accompanied by counsel or representative of his own choosing, and present evidence on his own behalf, through witnesses or by affidavit.

b. The officer or employee shall be served with a written notice of such hearing in sufficient time, and shall be informed therein of the nature of the charges against him in sufficient detail, so that he will be enabled to prepare his defense. The charges shall be stated as specifically and completely as, in the discretion of the employing department or agency, security considerations permit, and the officer or employee shall be informed in the notice (1) of his right to reply to such charges in writing within a specified reasonable period of time, (2) of his right to an administrative hearing on such charges before a loyalty board, and (3) of his right to appear before such board personally, to be accompanied by counsel or representative of his own choosing, and to present evidence on his behalf, through witnesses or by affidavit.

3. A recommendation of removal by a loyalty board shall be subject to appeal by the officer or employee affected, prior to his removal, to the head of the employing department or agency or to such person or persons as may be designated by such head, under such regulations as may be prescribed by him, and the decision of the department or agency concerned shall be subject to appeal to the Civil Service Commission's Loyalty Review Board, hereinafter provided for, for an advisory recommendation.

4. The rights of hearing, notice thereof, and appeal therefrom

shall be accorded to every officer or employee prior to his removal on grounds of disloyalty, irrespective of tenure, or of manner, method, or nature of appointment, but the head of the employing department or agency may suspend any officer or employee at any time pending a determination with respect to loyalty.

5. The loyalty boards of the various departments and agencies shall furnish to the Loyalty Review Board, hereinafter provided for, such reports as may be requested concerning the operation of the loyalty program in any such department or agency.

PART III—RESPONSIBILITIES OF CIVIL SERVICE COMMISSION

1. There shall be established in the Civil Service Commission a Loyalty Review Board of not less than three impartial persons, the members of which shall be officers or employees of the Commission.
   a. The board shall have authority to review cases involving persons recommended for dismissal on grounds relating to loyalty by the loyalty board of any department or agency and to make advisory recommendations thereon to the head of the employing department or agency. Such cases may be referred to the Board either by the employing department or agency, or by the officer or employee concerned.
   b. The Board shall make rules and regulations, not inconsistent with the provisions of this order, deemed necessary to implement statutes and Executive orders relating to employee loyalty.
   c. The Loyalty Review Board shall also:
      i. Advise all departments and agencies on all problems relating to employee loyalty.
      ii. Disseminate information pertinent to employee loyalty programs.
      iii. Coordinate the employee loyalty policies and procedures of the several departments and agencies.

iv. Make reports and submit recommendations to the Civil Service Commission for transmission to the President from time to time as may be necessary to the maintenance of the employee loyalty program.

2. There shall also be established and maintained in the Civil Service Commission a central master index covering all persons on whom loyalty investigations have been made by any department or agency since September 1, 1939. Such master index shall contain the name of each person investigated, adequate identifying information concerning each such person, and a reference to each department and agency which has conducted a loyalty investigation concerning the person involved.
   a. All executive departments and agencies are directed to furnish to the Civil Service Commission all information appropriate for the establishment and maintenance of the central master index.
   b. The reports and other investigative material and information developed by the investigating department or agency shall be retained by such department or agency in each case.
3. The Loyalty Review Board shall currently be furnished by the Department of Justice the name of each foreign or domestic organization, association, movement, group or combination of persons which the Attorney General, after appropriate investigation and determination, designates as totalitarian, fascist, communist or subversive, or as having adopted a policy of advocating or approving the commission of acts of force or violence to deny others their rights under the Constitution of the United States, or as seeking to alter the form of government of the United States by unconstitutional means.
   a. The Loyalty Review Board shall disseminate such information to all departments and agencies.

PART IV—SECURITY MEASURES IN INVESTIGATIONS

1. At the request of the head of any department or agency of the

executive branch an investigative agency shall make available to such head, personally, all investigative material and information collected by the investigvative agency concerning any employee or prospective employee of the requesting department or agency, or shall make such material and information available to any officer or officers designated by such head and approved by the investigative agency.

2. Notwithstanding the foregoing requirement, however, the investigative agency may refuse to disclose the names of confidential informants, provided it furnishes sufficient information about such informants on the basis of which the requesting department or agency can make an adequate evaluation of the information furnished by them, and provided it advises the requesting department or agency in writing that it is essential to the protection of the informants or to the investigation of other cases that the identity of the informants not be revealed. Investigative agencies shall not use this discretion to decline to reveal sources of information where such action is not essential.
3. Each department and agency of the executive branch should develop and maintain, for the collection and analysis of information relating to loyalty of its employees and prospective employees, a staff specially trained in security techniques, and an effective security control system for protecting such information generally and for protecting confidential sources of such information particularly.

PART V—STANDARDS

1. The standard for the refusal of employment or the removal from employment in an executive department or agency on grounds relating to loyalty shall be that, on all the evidence, reasonable grounds exist for belief that the person involved is disloyal to the Government of the United States.
2. Activities and associations of an applicant or employee which may be considered in connection with the determination of disloyalty may include one or more of the following:

a. Sabotage, espionage, or attempts or preparations therefor, or knowingly associating with spies or saboteurs;
b. Treason or sedition or advocacy thereof;
c. Advocacy of revolution or force or violence to alter the constitutional form of government of the United States.
d. Intentional, unauthorized disclosure to any person, under circumstances which may indicate disloyalty of a confidential or non-public character obtained by the person making the disclosure as a result of his employment by the Government of the United States;
e. Performing or attempting to perform his duties, or otherwise acting, so as to serve the interests of another government in preference to the interests of the United States.
f. Membership in, affiliation with or sympathetic association with any foreign or domestic organization, association, movement, group or combination of persons, designated by the Attorney General as totalitarian, fascist, communist, or subversive, or as having adopted a policy of advocating or approving the commission of acts of force or violence to deny other persons their rights under the Constitution of the United States, or as seeking to alter the form of government of the United States by unconstitutional means.

PART VI—MISCELLANEOUS

1. Each department and agency of the executive branch, to the extent that it has not already done so, shall submit, to the Federal Bureau of Investigation of the Department of Justice, either directly or through the Civil Service Commission, the names (and such other necessary identifying material as the Federal Bureau of Investigation may require) of all of its incumbent employees.
   a. The Federal Bureau of Investigation shall check such names against its records of persons concerning whom there is substantial evidence of being within the purview of paragraph

2 of Part V hereof, and shall notify each department and agency of such information.

b. Upon receipt of the above-mentioned information from the Federal Bureau of Investigation, each department and agency shall make, or cause to be made by the Civil Service Commission, such investigation of those employees as the head of the department or agency shall deem advisable.

2. The Security Advisory Board of the State-War-Navy Coordinating Committee shall draft rules applicable to the handling and transmission of confidential documents and other documents and information which should not be publicly disclosed, and upon approval by the President such rules shall constitute the minimum standards for the handling and transmission of such documents and information, and shall be applicable to all departments and agencies of the executive branch.

3. The provisions of this order shall not be applicable to persons summarily removed under the provisions of section 3 of the act of December 17, 1942, 56 Stat. 1053, of the act of July 5, 1946, 60 Stat. or of any other statute conferring the power of summary removal.

4. The Secretary of War and the Secretary of the Navy, and the Secretary of the Treasury with respect to the Coast Guard, are hereby directed to continue to enforce and maintain the highest standards of loyalty within the armed services, pursuant to the applicable statutes, the Articles of War, and the Articles for the Government of the Navy.

5. This order shall be effective immediately, but compliance with such of its provisions as require the expenditure of funds shall be deferred pending the appropriation of such funds.

6. Executive Order No. 9300 of February 5, 1943, is hereby revoked.

HARRY S. TRUMAN

THE WHITE HOUSE
March 21, 1947

APPENDIX C: CRITERIA FOR DESIGNATING ORGANIZATIONS UNDER EXECUTIVE ORDER NO. 9835*

July 24, 1947

Douglas W. McGregor, Assistant to the Attorney General

David N. Edelstein and Joseph C. Duggan

The specific criteria to be considered in determining whether any foreign or domestic organization should be designated by the Attorney General as within the purview of the standard defined in Paragraph 2f of Part 7 of Executive Order No. 9835 are as follows:

1. a "totalitarian" organization is one which subscribes to the principles of, advocates the policies of, or favors or advances the methods of the unitary state characterized by a highly centralized government under the control of a political caste which allows no recognition of or representation to opposition parties or minority groups. Such a state is best exemplified by that which existed in Nazi Germany or Fascist Italy; and for practical purposes, a "totalitarian organization" is one which advocates the replacement of the American democratic form of government by the creation, establishment and perpetuation of such a state in the United States;

*Vanech Papers, Loyalty Folder, Truman Library.

2. in form, the totalitarian political and economic state may be either Fascist or Communist. In both instances it is monolithic and makes no provision for representative government. Hence, any organization which actually advocates the political, economic or social philosophy of either form may be aptly designated as "totalitarian";
3. a "fascist" organization is one which advocates the principles, policies or methods of Fascism or Nazism as expressed through a highly centralized state, totalitarian in form, authoritarian an absolute in substance, and which is the negation of representative democratic government in that it brooks no opposition to the ruling party, supresses minorities, denies civil rights, and makes of the citizen a creature and chattel of the state;
4. a "communist" organization is one which advocates the principles, policies and methods of the Communist Party (based upon the political and economic theories of Karl Marx, Friedrich Engels and Nicolai Lenin) as expressed through a highly centralized state, totalitarian in form, authoritarian and absolute in substance, and in which representative, democratic government is replaced by the form of political organization known as the "dictatorship of the proletariat."
5. In addition to the Communist Party itself, other organizations may be properly designated "communist" if they
   a. consistently follow the "Communist Party line" through one or more changes particularly where such change is in accord with the governmental policy of Soviet Russia and opposed to that of the United States;
   b. advocate revolution or the use of force, if necessary, in order to bring about political or economic changes;
   c. advocate Communist Party policies and objectives while subscribing to democratic forms and principles and generally through utilization of deceptive "fronts";
   d. consistently adhere to, approve and advocate Communist Party "causes" and the political and economic policies and programs of the government of Soviet Russia and its satellite nations in opposition to those of the government of the United States.

6. While "fascist" and "communist" organizations are both "totalitarian" in essence, they violently disagree in technique and methodology. Each type of organization, therefore, has adopted a policy of condemning the other by publicly opposing its principles and castigating it by name-calling and opprobrious epithets. Hence, a totalitarian organization which consistently castigates and condemns any opposition as "Fascist" may properly be designated as "Communist," and, conversely, any totalitarian organization which consistently castigates and condemns any organization as "Communist" may properly be designated as "Fascist."
7. A "Subversive" organization is one which seeks to undermine confidence in, pervert or corrupt the integrity of the operations of, overthrow, ruin, betray, cause the downfall of, change by revolution or force, or subordinate to a foreign power the government of the United States. Advocacy of any such purposes categorizes an organization as subversive regardless of the means or methods adopted to effectuate such purposes.

The foregoing criteria have been formulated on the assumption that their use will be restricted to the Attorney General or his subordinates and that they are not for publication.

DAVID N. EDELSTEIN,
Special Assistant to the
Attorney General

JOSEPH C. DUGGAN,
Special Assistant to the
Attorney General

APPENDIX D: MEMORANDUM TO ALL OFFICERS AND EMPLOYEES IN THE EXECUTIVE BRANCH OF THE GOVERNMENT*

The efficient and just administration of the Employee Loyalty Program, under Executive Order No. 9835 of March 21, 1947, requires that reports, records, and files relative to the program be preserved in strict confidence. This is necessary in the interest of our national security and welfare, to preserve the confidential character and sources of information furnished, and to protect Government personnel against the dissemination of unfounded or disproved allegations. It is necessary also in order to insure the fair and just disposition of loyalty cases.

For these reasons, and in accordance with the long-established policy that reports rendered by the Federal Bureau of Investigation and other investigative agencies of the executive branch are to be regarded as confidential, all reports, records, and files relative to the loyalty of employees or prospective employees (including reports of such investigative agencies), shall be maintained in confidence, and shall not be transmitted or disclosed except as required in the efficient conduct of business.

Any subpena [*sic*] or demand or request for information, reports, or files of the nature described, received from sources other than those persons in the executive branch of the Government who are entitled thereto by reason of their official duties, shall be respectfully declined, on the basis of this directive, and the subpena [*sic*] or de-

*Elsey Papers, Internal Security Folder, Truman Library.

mand or other request shall be referred to the Office of the President for such response as the President may determine to be in the public interest in the particular case. There shall be no relaxation of the provisions of this directive except with my express authority.

This directive shall be published in the Federal Register.

HARRY S. TRUMAN

THE WHITE HOUSE
March 31, 1948

APPENDIX E: INTERNAL SECURITY ACT, 1950—VETO MESSAGE FROM THE PRESIDENT OF THE UNITED STATES*

The Speaker laid before the House the following veto message from the President of the United States: *To the House of Representatives*:

I return herewith, without my approval, H.R. 9490, the proposed "Internal Security Act of 1950."

I am taking this action only after the most serious study and reflection and after consultation with the security and intelligence agencies of the Government. The Department of Justice, the Department of Defense, the Central Intelligence Agency, and the Department of State have all advised me that the bill would seriously damage the security and intelligence operations for which they are responsible. They have strongly expressed the hope that the bill would not become law.

This is an omnibus bill containing many different legislative proposals with only one thing in common: they are all represented to be "anticommunist." But when the many complicated pieces of the bill are analyzed in detail, a startling result appears.

H.R. 9490 would not hurt the Communists. Instead, it would help them.

It has been claimed over and over again that this is an "anticommunist" bill—a "Communist control" bill. But in actual operation the bill would have results exactly the opposite of those intended.

*U.S., *Congressional Record*, 81st Congress, 2d sess., 1950, 96, pt. 11, pp. 15629-32.

It would actually weaken our existing internal security measures and would seriously hamper the Federal Bureau of Investigation and our other security agencies.

It would help the Communists in their efforts to create dissension and confusion within our borders.

It would help the Communist propagandists throughout the world who are trying to undermine freedom by discrediting as hypocrisy the efforts of the United States on behalf of freedom.

Specifically, some of the principal objections to the bill are as follows:

1. It would aid potential enemies by requiring the publication of a complete list of vital defense plants, laboratories, and other installations.

2. It would require the Department of Justice and its Federal Bureau of Investigation to waste immense amounts of time and energy attempting to carry out its unworkable registration provisions.

3. It would deprive us of the great assistance of many aliens in intelligence matters.

4. It would antagonize friendly governments.

5. It would put the Government of the United States in the thought-control business.

6. It would make it easier for subversive aliens to become naturalized as United States citizens.

7. It would give Government officials vast powers to harass all of our citizens in the exercise of their right of free speech.

Legislation with these consequences is not necessary to meet the real dangers which communism presents to our free society. Those dangers are serious and must be met. But this bill would hinder us, not help us, in meeting them. Fortunately, we already have on the books strong laws which give us most of the protection we need from the real dangers of treason, espionage, sabotage, and actions looking to the overthrow of our Government by force and violence. Most of the provisions of this bill have no relation to these real dangers.

One provision alone of this bill is enough to demonstrate how far it misses the real target. Section 5 would require the Secretary of Defense to "proclaim" and "have published in the Federal Register" a public catalogue of defense plants, laboratories, and all other facilities vital to our national defense—no matter how secret. I cannot imagine any document a hostile foreign government would desire more. Spies and saboteurs would willingly spend years of effort seeking to find out the information that this bill would require the Government to hand them on a silver platter. There are many provisions of this bill which impel me to return it without my approval, but this one would be enough by itself. It is inconceivable to me that a majority of the Congress could expect the Commander in Chief of the Armed Forces of the United States to approve such a flagrant violation of proper security safeguards.

This is only one example of many provisions in the bill which would in actual practice work to the detriment of our national security.

I know that the Congress had no intention of achieving such results when it passed this bill. I know that the vast majority of the Members of Congress who voted for the bill sincerely intended to strike a blow at the Communists.

It is true that certain provisions of this bill would improve the laws protecting us against espionage and sabotage. But these provisions are greatly outweighed by others which would actually impair our security.

I repeat, the net results of this bill would be to help the Communists, not to hurt them.

I therefore most earnestly request the Congress to reconsider its action. I am confident that on more careful analysis most Members of Congress will recognize that this bill is contrary to the best interests of our country at this critical time.

H.R. 9490 is made up of a number of different parts. In summary, their purposes and probable effects may be described as follows:

Sections 1 through 17 are designed for two purposes. First, they are intended to force Communist organizations to register and to divulge certain information about themselves—information on their officers, their finances, and, in some cases, their membership. These provisions would in practice be ineffective, and would result in obtaining no information about Communists that the FBI and our other security agencies do not already have. But in trying to enforce these sections, we would have to spend a great deal of time, effort, and money—all to no good purpose.

Second, these provisions are intended to impose various penalties on Communists and others covered by the terms of the bill. So far as Communists are concerned, all these penalties which can be practicably enforced are already in effect under existing laws and procedures. But the language of the bill is so broad and vague that it might well result in penalizing the legitimate activities of people who are not Communists at all, but loyal citizens.

Thus, the net result of these sections of the bill would be: no serious damage to the Communists, most damage to the rest of us. Only the Communist movement would gain from such an outcome.

Sections 18 through 21 and section 23 of this bill constitute, in large measure, the improvements in our internal security laws which I recommended some time ago. Although the language of these sections is in some respects weaker than is desirable, I should be glad to approve these provisions if they were enacted separately, since they are improvements developed by the FBI and other Government security agencies to meet certain clear deficiencies of the present law. But even though these improvements are needed, other provisions of the bill would weaken our security far more than these would strengthen it. We have better protection for our internal security under existing law than we would have with the amendments and additions made by H.R. 9490.

Sections 22 and 25 of this bill would make sweeping changes in our law governing the admission of aliens to the United States and their naturalization as citizens.

The ostensible purpose of these provisions is to prevent persons who would be dangerous to our national security from entering the country or becoming citizens. In fact, present law already achieves that objective.

What these provisions would actually do is to prevent us from admitting to our country, or to citizenship, many people who could make real contributions to our national strength. The bill would deprive our Government and our intelligence agencies of the valuable services of aliens in security operations. It would require us to exclude and to deport the citizens of some friendly non-Communist countries. Furthermore, it would actually make it easier for subversive aliens to become United States citizens. Only the Communist movement would gain from such actions.

Section 24 and sections 26 through 30 of this bill make a number of minor changes in the naturalization laws. None of them is of great significance—nor are they particularly relevant to the problem of internal security. These provisions, for the most part, have received little or no attention in the legislative process. I believe that several of them would not be approved by the Congress if they were considered on their merits, rather than as parts of an omnibus bill.

Section 31 of this bill makes it a crime to attempt to influence a judge or jury by public demonstration, such as picketing. While the courts already have considerable power to punish such actions under existing law, I have no objection to this section.

Sections 100 through 117 of this bill (title II) are intended to give the Government power, in the event of invasion, war, or insurrection in the United States in aid of a foreign enemy, to seize and hold persons who could be expected to attempt acts of espionage or sabotage; even though they had as yet committed no crime. It may be that legislation of this type should be on the statute books. But the provisions in H.R. 9490 would very probably prove ineffective to achieve the objective sought, since they would not suspend the writ of habeas corpus, and under our legal system to detain a man not charged with a crime would raise serious constitutional questions unless the writ of habeas corpus were suspended. Furthermore, it may well be that other persons than those covered by these provisions would be more important to detain in the event of emergency. This whole problem, therefore, should clearly be studied more thoroughly before further legislative action along these lines is considered.

In brief, when all the provisions of H.R. 9490 are considered together, it is evident that the great bulk of them are not directed toward the real and present dangers that exist from communism. Instead of striking blows at communism, they would strike blows at our own liberties and at our position in the forefront of those working for freedom in the world. At a time when our young men are fighting for freedom in Korea, it would be tragic to advance the objectives of communism in this country, as this bill would do.

Because I feel so strongly that this legislation would be a terrible mistake, I want to discuss more fully its worse features—sections 1 through 17, and sections 22 and 25.

Most of the first 17 sections of H.R. 9490 are concerned with requiring registration and annual reports, by what the bill calls Communist-action organizations and Communist-front organizations, of names of officers, sources and uses of funds, and, in the case of Communist-action organizations, names of members.

The idea of requiring Communist organizations to divulge information about themselves is a simple and attractive one. But it is about as practical as requiring thieves to register with the sheriff. Obviously, no such organization as the Communist Party is likely to register voluntarily.

Under the provisions of the bill, if an organization which the Attorney General believes should register does not do so, he must request a five-man Subversive Activities Control Board to order the organization to register. The Attorney General would have to produce proof that the organization in question was in fact a Communist-action or a Communist-front organization. To do this he would have to offer evidence relating to every aspect of the organization's activities. The organization could present opposing evidence. Prolonged hearings would be required to allow both sides to present proof and to cross-examine opposing witnesses.

To estimate the duration of such a proceeding involving the Communist Party, we need only recall that on much narrower issues the trial of the 11 Communist leaders under the Smith Act consumed 9 months. In a hearing under this bill, the difficulties of proof would be much greater and would take a much longer time.

The bill lists a number of criteria for the Board to consider in deciding whether or not an organization is a Communist-action or Communist-front organization. Many of these deal with the attitudes or states of mind of the organization's leaders. It is frequently difficult in legal proceedings to establish whether or not a man has committed an overt act, such as theft or perjury. But under this bill, the Attorney General would have to attempt the immensely more difficult task of producing concrete legal evidence that men have particular ideas or opinions. This would inevitably require the disclosure of many of the FBI's confidential sources of information and thus would damage our national security.

If, eventually, the Attorney General should overcome these difficulties and get a favorable decision from the Board, the Board's decision could be appealed to the courts. The courts would review any questions of law involved, and whether the Board's findings of fact were supported by the preponderance of the evidence.

All these proceedings would require great effort and much time. It is almost certain that from 2 to 4 years would elapse between the Attorney General's decision to go before the Board with a case, and the final disposition of the matter by the courts.

And when all this time and effort had been spent, it is still most likely that no organization would actually register.

The simple fact is that when the courts at long last found that a particular organization was required to register, all the leaders of the organization would have to do to frustrate the law would be to dissolve the organization and establish a new one with a different name and a new roster of nominal officers. The Communist Party has done this again and again in countries throughout the world. And nothing could be done about it except to begin all over again the long dreary process of investigative, administrative, and judicial proceedings to require registration.

Thus the net result of the registration provision of this bill would probably be an endless chasing of one organization after another, with the Communists always able to frustrate the law enforcement agencies and prevent any final result from being achieved. It could only result in wasting the energies of the Department of Justice and in destroying the sources of information of its FBI. To impose these fruitless burdens upon the FBI would divert it from its vital security duties and thus give aid and comfort to the very Communists whom the bill is supposed to control.

Unfortunately, these provisions are not merely ineffective and unworkable. They represent a clear and present danger to our institutions.

Insofar as the bill would require registration by the Communist Party itself, it does not endanger our traditional liberties. However, the application of the registration requirements to so-called Communist-front organizations can be the greatest danger to freedom of speech, press, and assembly, since the Alien and Sedition Laws of 1798. This danger arises out of the criteria or standards to be applied in determining whether an organization is a Communist-front organization.

There would be no serious problem if the bill required proof that an organization was controlled and financed by the Communist Party before it could be classified as a Communist-front organization. However, recognizing the difficulty of proving those matters, the bill would permit such a determination to be based solely upon the extent to which the positions taken or advanced by it from time to time on matters of policy do not deviate from those of the Communist movement.

This provision could easily be used to classify as a Communist-front organization any organization which is advocating a single policy or objective which is also being urged by the Communist Party or by a Communist foreign government. In fact, this may be the intended result, since the bill defines "organization" to include "a group of persons permanently or temporarily associated together for joint action on any subject or subjects." Thus, an organization which advocates low-cost housing for sincere humanitarian reasons might be classified as a Comunist-front organization because the Communists regularly exploit slum conditions as one of their fifth-column techniques.

It is not enough to say that this probably would not be done. The mere fact that it could be done shows clearly how the bill would open a Pandora's box of opportunities for official condemnation of organizations and individuals for perfectly honest opinions which happen to be stated also by Communists.

The basic error of these sections is that they move in the direction of suppressing opinion and belief. This wold be a very dangeorus course to take, not because we have any sympathy for Communist opinions, but because any governmental stifling of the free expression of opinion is a long step toward totalitarianism.

There is no more fundmental axiom of American freedom than the familiar statement: In a free country, we punish men for the crimes they commit, but never the opinions they have. And the reason this is so fundamental to freedom is not, as many suppose, that it protects the few unorthodox from suppression by the majority. To permit freedom of expression is primarily for the benefit of the majority because it protects criticism, and criticism leads to progress.

We can and we will prevent espionage, sabotage, or other actions endangering our national security. But we would betray our finest traditions if we attempted, as this bill would attempt, to curb the simple expression of opinion. This we should never do, no matter how distasteful the opinion may be to the vast majority of our people. The course proposed by this bill would delight the Communists, for it would make a mockery of the Bill of Rights and of our claims to stand for freedom in the world.

And what kind of effect would these provisions have on the normal expression of political views? Obviously, if this law were on the statute books, the part of prudence would be to avoid saying anything that might be construed by someone as not deviating sufficiently from the current Communist propaganda line. And since no one could be sure in advance what views were safe to express, the inevitable tendency would be to express no views on controversial subjects.

The result could only be to reduce the vigor and strength of our political life—an outcome that the Communists would happily welcome, but that free men should abhor.

We need not fear the expression of ideas—we do need to fear their suppression.

Our position in the vanguard of freedom rests largely on our demonstration that the free expression of opinion, coupled with government by popular consent, leads to national strength and human advancement. Let us not, in cowering and foolish fear, throw away the ideals which are the fundamental basis of our free society.

Not only are the registration provisions of this bill unworkable and dangerous, they are also grossly misleading in that all but one of the objectives which are claimed for them are already being accomplished by other and superior methods—and the one objective which is not now being accomplished would not in fact be accomplished under this bill either.

It is claimed that the bill would provide information about the Communist Party and its members. The fact is, the FBI already possesses very complete sources of information concerning the Communist movement in this country. If the FBI must disclose its sources of information in public hearings to require registration under this bill, its present sources of information, and its ability to acquire new information, will be largely destroyed.

It is claimed that this bill would deny income-tax exemption to Communist organizations. The fact is that the Bureau of Internal

Revenue already denies income-tax exemption to such organizations.

It is claimed that this bill would deny passports to Communists. The fact is that the Government can and does deny passports to Communists under existing law.

It is claimed that this bill would prohibit the employment of Communists by the Federal Government. The fact is that the employment of Communists by the Federal Government is already prohibited and, at least in the executive branch, there is an effective program to see that they are not employed.

It is claimed that this bill would prohibit the employment of Communists in defense plants. The fact is that it would be years before this bill would have any effect of this nature—if it ever would. Fortunately, this objective is already being substantially achieved under the present procedures of the Department of Defense, and if the Congress would enact one of the provisions I have recommended—which it did not include in this bill—the situation would be entirely taken care of, promptly and effectively.

It is also claimed—and this is the one new objective of the registration provisions of this bill—that it would require Communist organizations to label all their publications and radio and television broadcasts as emanating from a Communist source. The fact is that this requirement, even if constitutional, could be easily and permanently evaded, simply by the continuous creation of new organizations to distribute Communist information.

Section 4 (a) of the bill, like its registration provisions, would be ineffective, would be subject to dangerous abuse, and would seek to accomplish an objective which is already better accomplished under existing law.

This provision would make unlawful any agreement to perform any act which would substantially contribute to the establishment within the United States of a foreign-controlled dictatorship. Of course, this provision would be unconstitutional if it infringed upon the fundamental right of the American people to establish for themselves by constitutional methods any form of government they choose. To avoid this, it is provided that this section shall not apply to the proposal of a constitutional amendment. If this language limits the prohibition of the section to the use of unlawful methods, then it adds nothing to the Smith Act, under which 11 Communist leaders have been convicted, and would be more difficult to enforce. Thus, it would accomplish nothing. Moreover, the bill does not even purport to define the phrase, unique in a criminal statute, "substantially contribute." A phrase so vague raises a serious constitutional question.

Sections 22 and 25 of this bill are directed toward the specific questions of who should be admitted to our country, and who should be permitted to become a United States citizen. I believe there is general agreement that the answers to these questions should be: We should admit to our country, within the available quotas, anyone with a legitimate purpose who would not endanger our security, and we should admit to citizenship any immigrant who will be a loyal and constructive member of the community. Those are essentially the standards set by existing law. Under present law, we do not admit to our country known Communists, because we believe they work to overthrow our Government, and we do not admit Communists to citizenship, because we believe they are not loyal to the United States.

The changes which would be made in the present law by sections 22 and 25 would not reinforce those sensible standards. Instead, they would add a number of new standards, which, for no good and sufficient reason, would interfere with our relations with other countries and seriously damage our national security.

Section 22 would, for example, exclude from our country anyone who advocates any form of totalitarian or one-party government. We, of course, believe in the democratic system of competing political parties, offering a choice of candidates and policies. But a number of countries with which we maintain friendly relations have a different form of government.

Until now, no one has suggested that we should abandon cultural and commercial relations with a country merely because it has a form of government different from ours. Yet section 22 would require that. As one instance it is clear that under the definitions of the bill the present Government of Spain, among others, would be classified as "totalitarian." As a result, the Attorney General would be required to exclude from the United States all Spanish businessmen, students, and other nonofficial travelers who support the present Government of their country. I cannot understand how the sponsors of this bill can think that such an action would contribute to our national security.

Moreover, the provisions of Section 22 of this bill would strike a serious blow to our national security by taking away from the Government the power to grant asylum in this country to foreign diplomats who repudiate Communist imperialism and wish to escape its reprisals. It must be obvious to anyone that it is in our national interest to persuade people to renounce communism, and to encourage their defection from Communist forces. Many of these people are extremely valuable to our intelligence operations. Yet under this bill the Government would lose the limited authority it now has to offer asylum in our country as the great incentive for such defection.

In addition, the provisions of section 22 would sharply limit the authority of the Government to admit foreign diplomatic representatives and their families on official business. Under existing law, we already have the authority to send out of the country any person who abuses diplomatic privileges by working against the interests of the United States. But under this bill a whole series of unnecessary restrictions would be placed on the admission of diplomatic personnel. This is not only ungenerous, for a country which eagerly sought and proudly holds the honor of being the seat of the United Nations, it is also very unwise, because it makes our country appear to be fearful of foreigners, when in fact we are working as hard as we know how to build mutual confidence and friendly relations among the nations of the world.

Section 22 is so contrary to our national interests that it would actually put the Government into the business of thought control by requiring the deportation of any alien who distributes or publishes, or who is affiliated with an organization which distributes or publishes, any written or printed matter advocating (or merely expressing belief in) the economic and governmental doctrines of any form of totalitarianism.

This provision does not require an evil intent or purpose on the part of the alien, as does a similar provision in the Smith Act. Thus, the Attorney General would be required to deport any alien operating or connected with a well-stocked bookshop containing books on economics or politics written by supporters of the present government of Spain, of Yugoslavia or any one of a number of other countries. Section 25 would make the same aliens ineligible for citizenship. There should be no room in our laws for such hysterical provisions. The next logical step would be to "burn the books."

This illustrates the fundamental error of these immigration and naturalization provisions. It is easy to see that they are hasty and ill-considered. But far more significant—and far more dangerous—is their apparent underlying purpose. Instead of trying to encourage the free movement of people, these provisions attempt to bar movement to anyone who is, or once was, associated with ideas we dislike, and in the process, they would succeed in barring many people whom it would be to our advantage to admit.

Such an action would be a serious blow to our work for world peace. We uphold—or have upheld until now, at any rate—the concept of freedom on an international scale. That is the root concept of our efforts to bring unity among the free nations and peace in the world.

The Communists, on the other hand, attempt to break down in every possible way the free interchange of persons and ideas. It will be to their advantage, and not ours, if we establish for ourselves an "iron curtain" against those who can help us in the fight for freedom.

Another provision of the bill which would greatly weaken our national security is section 25, which would make subversive aliens eligible for naturalization as soon as they withdraw from organizations required to register under this bill, whereas under existing law they must wait for a period of 10 years after such withdrawal before becoming eligible for citizenship. This proposal is clearly contrary to the national interest, and clearly gives to the Communists an advantage they do not have under existing law.

I have discussed the provisions of this bill at some length in order to explain why I am convinced that it would be harmful to our security and damaging to the individual rights of our people if it were enacted.

Earlier this month, we launched a great Crusade for Freedom designed, in the words of General Eisenhower, to fight the big lie with the big truth. I can think of no better way to make a mockery of that crusade and of the deep American belief in human freedom and dignity which underlie it than to put the provisions of H.R. 9490 on our statute books.

I do not undertake lightly the responsibility of differing with the majority in both Houses of Congress who have voted for this bill. We are all Americans; we all wish to safeguard and preserve our constitutional liberties against internal and external enemies. But I cannot approve this legislation, which instead of accomplishing its avowed purpose would actually interfere with our liberties and help the Communists against whom the bill was aimed.

This is a time when we must marshal all our resources and all the moral strength of our free system in self-defense against the threat of Communist aggression. We will fail in this, and we will destroy all that we seek to preserve, if we sacrifice the liberties of our citizens in a misguided attempt to achieve national security.

There is no reason why we should fail. Our country has been through dangerous times before, without losing our liberties to external attack or internal hysteria. Each of us, in Government and out, has a share in guarding our liberties. Each of us must search his own conscience to find whether he is doing all that can be done to preserve and strengthen them.

No considerations of expediency can justify the enactment of such a bill as this, a bill which would so greatly weaken our liberties and give aid and comfort to those who would destroy us. I have, therefore, no alternative but to return this bill without my approval, and I earnestly request the Congress to reconsider its action.

HARRY S. TRUMAN

THE WHITE HOUSE
September 22, 1950

BIBLIOGRAPHY

MATERIALS FROM THE HARRY S. TRUMAN LIBRARY, INDEPENDENCE, MISSOURI

Papers of Clark M. Clifford
Papers of George M. Elsey
Papers of David D. Lloyd
Papers of J. Howard McGrath
Papers of Charles S. Murphy
Papers of Philleo Nash
Papers of Richard E. Neustadt
Papers of Stephen J. Spingarn
Papers of Harry S. Truman
Papers of A. Devitt Vanech
- Bill File
- Files of Clark M. Clifford
- Democratic National Committee Clipping Files
- Files of Philleo Nash
- Files of Richard E. Neustadt
- Official Files
- President's Personal Files
- Records of the President's Commission on Internal Security and Individual Rights

MATERIAL FROM THE LIBRARY OF CONGRESS, WASHINGTON, D. C.

Papers of Theodore F. Green

PERSONAL INTERVIEWS

Justice Thomas C. Clark, August 22, 1969, Washington, D. C.

Stephen J. Spingarn, August 9, 1971, Washington, D. C.

PUBLIC DOCUMENTS

U.S., *Congressional Record*. vols. 92-98.

U.S., National Archives and Records Service, Federal Register Division. *Code of Federal Regulations: 1943-1958 Compilation*.

UNPUBLISHED MATERIAL

Harper, Alan, "The Free Speech Issue in Post-World War II Reconstruction." Copy of manuscript in Truman Library.

Street, Kenneth W., "Harry S. Truman: His Role as a Legislative Leader, 1945-1948." Ph.D. dissertation, University of Texas, 1963.

Tanner, William R., "The Passage of The Internal Security Act of 1950." Ph.D. dissertation, University of Kansas, 1971.

Theoharis, Athan G., "The Rhetoric of Politics: Foreign Policy, Internal Security and Domestic Politics in the Truman Era, 1945-1950." Copy of manuscript in Truman Library.

ARTICLES

Abbott, Roger S. "Federal Loyalty Program: Background and Problems," *American Political Science Review*, 42 (June 1948): 486-99.

Commager, Henry S. "Red Baiting in the Colleges," *New Republic* 121 (July 25, 1949): 10-13.

Levitan, David M. "The Responsibility of Administrative Officials in a Democratic Society," *Political Science Quarterly* 62 (December 1946): 562-98.

Rovere, Richard. "President Harry," *Harpers Magazine* 197 (July 1948): 27-35.

Sutherland, Arthur. "Freedom and Internal Security," *Harvard Law Review* 64 (January 1951): 383-416.

Wechsler, James, "How to Rid the Government of Communists," *Harpers Magazine* 195 (November 1947): 438-43.

PERIODICALS

Business Week.

Christian Century.

Nation.

Newsweek.

New Republic.

Time.

U. S. News and World Report.

NEWSPAPERS

New York Times, 1946-1952.

Washington Post, 1946-1952.

BOOKS

Acheson, Dean. *Present at the Creation: My Years in the State Department*. New York: W. W. Norton, 1961.

Allen, Robert S., and Shannon, William V. *The Truman Merry-Go-Round*. New York: Vanguard Press, 1950.

Andrews, Bert. *Washington Witch Hunt*. New York: Random House, 1948.

Barth, Alan. *The Loyalty of Free Men*. New York: Viking Press, 1951.

——— *Government by Investigation*. New York: Viking Press, 1955.

Bentley, Eric, ed. *Thirty Years of Treason: Excerpts from Hearings before the House Committee on Un-American Activities*. New York: Viking Press, 1971.

———, ed. *Are You Now or Have You Ever Been: The Investigations of Show Business by the Un-American Activities Committee, 1947-1958*. New York: Harper ¿ Row, 1972.

Bernstein, Barton J., and Matusow, Allen J., eds. *The Truman Administration: A Documentary History*. New York: Harper & Row, 1966.

Biddle, Francis. *The Fear of Freedom*. Garden City, N.Y. Doubleday, 1952.

Bontecou, Eleanor. *The Federal Loyalty-Security Program*. Ithaca, N.Y.: Cornell University Press, 1953.

Brown, Ralph S., Jr. *Loyalty and Security: Employment Tests in the United States*. New Haven, Conn.: Yale University Press, 1958.

Carleton, William G. *The Revolution in American Foreign Policy: Its Global Range*. 2d ed. New York: Random House, 1967.

Carr, Robert K. *The House Committee on Un-American Activities: 1945-1950*. Ithaca, N.Y.: Cornell University Press, 1952.

Caughey, John W. *In Clear and Present Danger: The Crucial State of Our Freedoms*. Chicago: University of Chicago Press, 1958.

Chafee, Zechariah, Jr. *Free Speech in the United States*. Cambridge: Harvard University Press, 1946.

———. *The Blessings of Liberty*. New York: J. B. Lippincott, 1956.

Chase, Harold W. *Security and Liberty: The Problem of Native Communism, 1947-1955*. Garden City, N.Y.: Doubleday, 1955.

Cochran, Bert. *Harry Truman and the Crisis Presidency*. New York: Funk and Wagnalls, 1973.

Commager, Henry S. et al. *Civil Liberties Under Attack*. Philadelphia: University of Pennsylvania Press, 1951.

Commager, Henry S. *Freedom, Loyalty and Dissent*. New York: Oxford University Press, 1954.

———, ed. *Documents of American History*, vol. 2, *Since 1898*. 8th ed. New York: Appleton-Century-Crofts, 1968.

Congressional Quarterly Service. *Congress and the Nation: 1945-1964*. Washington, D. C.: Congressional Quarterly Service, 1965.

Current, Richard N., and Garraty, John A., eds. *Words That Made American History: Colonial Times to the 1870's*. 2d ed. Boston: Little, Brown, 1965.

Cushman, Robert E. *Civil Liberties in The United States: A Guide to Current Probems and Experience*. Ithaca, N.Y.: Cornell University Press, 1956.

Daniels, Jonathan. *The Man from Independence*. Philadelphia: J. B. Lippincott, 1950.

Douglas, William O. *An Almanac of Liberty*. Garden City, N.Y.: Doubleday, 1954.

Druks, Herbert M. *Harry S. Truman and the Russians: 1945-1953*. New York: Robert Speller & Sons, 1966.

Fellman, David. *The Limits of Freedom*. New Brunswick, N.J.: Rutgers University Press, 1959.

Freeland, Richard M. *The Truman Doctrine and the Origins of*

McCarthyism: Foreign Policy, Domestic Politics, and Internal Security 1946-1948. New York: Alfred A. Knopf, 1972.

Gellhorn, Walter. *Security, Loyalty, and Science*. Ithaca, N.Y.: Cornell University Press, 1950.

———. *American Rights: The Constitution*. New York: Macmillan Co., 1960.

Goldman, Eric. *The Crucial Decade and After: America 1945-60*. New York: Knoft, 1966.

Griffith, Robert. *The Politics of Fear: Joseph R. McCarthy and the Senate*. Lexington: University Press of Kentucky, 1970.

Hamby, Alonzo L. *Beyond the New Deal: Harry S. Truman and American Liberalism*. New York: Columbia University Press, 1973.

Harper, Alan. *The Politics of Loyalty: The White House and the Communist Issue*. Westport, Conn.: Greenwood Publishing Co., 1969.

Hartmann, Susan. *Truman and the 80th Congress*. Columbia: University of Missouri Press, 1971.

Kanfer, Stefan. *A Journal of the Plague Years*. New York: Atheneum, 1973.

Kirkendall, Richard S., ed. *The Truman Period as a Research Field: A Reappraisal, 1972*. Columbia: University of Missouri Press, 1974.

Koenig, Louis W., ed. *The Truman Administration: Its Principles and Practices*. New York: New York University Press, 1956.

Lamont, Corliss. *Freedom Is as Freedom Does: Civil Liberties Today*. New York: Horizon Press, 1956.

Latham, Earl. *The Communist Controversy in Washington: From the New Deal to McCarthy*. New York: Atheneum, 1969.

Lilienthal, David. *The Journals of David Lilienthal*, vol. 2, *The Atomic Years, 1945-1950*. New York: Harper & Row, 1964.

Longaker, Richard P. *The Presidency and Individual Liberties*. Ithaca, N.Y.: Cornell University Press, 1961.

Lubell, Samuel. *The Future of American Politics*. 2d ed. Garden City, N.Y.: Doubleday, 1952.

McWilliams, Carey, *Witch Hunt: The Revival of Heresay*. Boston: Little, Brown, 1950.

Parenti, Michael. *The Anti-Communist Impulse*. New York: Random House, 1969.

Pfeffer, Leo. *The Liberties of an American: The Supreme Court Speaks*. 2d ed. Boston: Beacon Press, 1963.

Phillips, Cabell. *The Truman Presidency: The History of a Triumphant Succession*. New York: Macmillan Co., 1966.

Pritchett, Herman C. *Civil Liberties and the Vinson Court*. Chicago: University of Chicago Press, 1954.

Rice, Charles E. *Freedom of Association*. New York: New York University Press, 1962.

Ross Irwin. *The Loneliest Campaign: The Truman Victory of 1948*. New York: New American Library, 1968.

Rovere, Richard. *Senator Joe McCarthy*. New York: Meridian Books, 1960.

Seldes, George. *Witch Hunt: The Techniques and Profits of Red Baiting*. New York: Modern Age Books, 1940.

Sellin, Thorsten, ed. *Internal Security and Civil Rights*. Philadelphia: The American Academy of Political and Social Sciences, 1955.

Shannon, David A. *The Decline of American Communism*. New York: Harcourt, Brace & Co., 1959.

Steinberg, Alfred. *The Man from Missouri: The Life and Times of Harry S. Truman*. New York: G. P. Putnam's 1962.

Summers, Robert E., ed. *Federal Information Controls in Peace-Time*. New York: H. W. Wilson Co., 1949.

Theoharis, Athan. *Seeds of Repression: Harry S. Truman and the Origins of McCarthyism*. Chicago: Quadrangle Books, 1971.

Thomas, Norman. *The Test of Freedom*. New York: W. W. Norton, 1954.

Truman, Harry S. *Memoirs*. 2 vols. Garden City, N.Y.: Doubleday, 1954.

Truman, Margaret. *Harry S. Truman*. New York: William Morrow, 1973.

White, William S. *The Taft Story*. New York: Harper & Row, 1954.

INDEX